Human Resource Management

A Guide for Employers

Pat Sheridan

Published by
OAK TREE PRESS
19 Rutland Street, Cork, Ireland
www.oaktreepress.com
and
INSTITUTE OF CHARTERED ACCOUNTANTS IN IRELAND
CA House, Pembroke Road, Ballsbridge, Dublin 4, Ireland
www.icai.ie

A catalogue record of this book is
available from the British Library.

ISBN 978-1-904887-15-7 (Oak Tree Press)
ISBN 978-0-903854-27-6 (ICAI)

Printed in Ireland by ColourBooks.

CONTENTS

FIGURES

FOREWORD

It gives me great pleasure to welcome the arrival of this guide to the management of human resources, published by Oak Tree Press in association with the Institute of Chartered Accountants in Ireland.

Looking through the wide range of topics covered serves to remind the reader of the many demands made on those managing companies, especially in smaller enterprises which might not have a dedicated, professional human resources management function. In such circumstances, not only is the manager faced with attracting, rewarding and retaining good quality staff who will be crucial to the success of the enterprise, but he/she must also be aware of their obligations to comply with a large *corpus* of employment and health and safety legislation. Providing in a single volume all the relevant information that managers need to know certainly presents a challenge.

Much of the material covered in the area of human resource management reflects best practice as it has developed over the years, combined with a reminder of legal obligations. However, I am struck by the scope of the demands made on employers by the State through employment legislation and how this relates to attempts to lighten the regulatory burden generally. Here, it is important to remember that this large *corpus* of legislation did not appear overnight and was not imposed by any government solely to complicate the lives of employers and managers of enterprises. It has grown over time, frequently in response to problems encountered in the workplace and generally seeks to clarify and protect the rights of employees. It is widely recognised that a contented workforce is a major asset to any organisation or enterprise and appropriate employment legislation, properly enforced, can make a major contribution to a positive industrial relations climate and to flexible and competitive enterprises.

The development of employment law has been driven by developments at a wider EU level, as well as by the rapid changes taking place in the world of work in Ireland. Some of the more significant pieces of legislation put on the statute books in recent years were a response to the agreement at EU level of a number of new directives setting out the rights of various labour market participants such as part-time workers, fixed-term workers and workers posted to another Member State by their employer.

The process of updating our employment legislation in Ireland is also closely intertwined with our social partnership model and concerns in this area were central to the most recently negotiated partnership agreement, *Towards 2016*. For example, that agreement sets out the Government's legislative commitments in areas such as those involving collective redundancies and a new employment rights compliance model, including the establishment of a National Employment Rights Authority (NERA). It is important to note that these developments reflect agreement reached by the Government and the representatives of employers and employees.

The very rapid changes in the Irish labour market in recent years have meant that legislation enacted in an earlier period and in different circumstances may not be adequate to address emerging problems in a globalised economy. It is quite likely that the continuing process of integrating the international economy will lead to the emergence of new challenges in the context of a flexible labour market, responsive to competitive challenges, but which still ensures that agreed employment standards are guaranteed and enforced. Finding the right balance is never easy and this will change with circumstances. In essence, the process is dynamic and, at any given point, there is a challenge to achieve even better outcomes.

The present volume succeeds in making a large volume of complex information available in an easily accessible format. I hope that, by the time a second edition appears, the task will be easier, as I believe that the time is right for a consolidation of employment law to be undertaken, which should make this *corpus* of legislation more user-friendly as well as appropriate for the circumstances of a changing society.

Micheál Martin TD
Minister for Enterprise, Trade & Employment

INTRODUCTION

This book is primarily aimed at employers – owners, directors and managers – in companies that have no formal Human Resource (HR) or Personnel Department.

In organisations without an experienced HR Manager, there will usually be a person designated to take care of some HR-related activities, such as records, letters of appointment, holiday schedules, etc. This person may have no formal training and very little experience in Human Resource Management concepts or employment law. Very often, this basic approach to the HR function tends to fall into the lap of the company accountant, along with many other activities that have a legal implication.

In the smallest companies, which have neither a HR Manager nor an in-house accountant, these responsibilities fall to the owner/director, who unfortunately has a myriad of other activities to address to keep the business viable – and so basic Human Resource Management activities go on the 'back burner' until a problem arises.

This book aims to cover the main areas that an employer should, or, in most cases, must, attend to with regard to the employment and management of employees. It is suitable, therefore, for all managers, supervisors, team leaders and anyone else who has responsibility for the work of others. While it does not purport to be a HR educational textbook, it is also suitable for all management students – particularly, Human Resource Management students, who wish to have an overview of the main Human Resource Management areas and employment law in an easy-to-read format.

Proactive Human Resource Management

Employers have a multitude of responsibilities to their employees under Irish employment legislation, which gives rise to the implementation of a wide range of practices and procedures in companies that, in turn, impact on the working relationship between the employer and the employee.

Anything that affects this working relationship impacts on company performance – either positively or negatively. Since it is generally the employer who takes the initiative to develop a positive result for the business, it is prudent for him/her, through the company's managers, to adopt a structured and proactive approach to people management and development.

The title attached to this people management function has evolved over the years, from Welfare Officer to Personnel Manager, and now the more commonly used Human Resource Manager or Personnel Manager (either terminology will do, although the fashion-conscious currently prefer Human Resource Manager). The responsibility and complexity of this management function has advanced, just as the titles have evolved, and undoubtedly the range of responsibility and complexity will continue to expand.

Most medium to large-sized companies have a full-time manager in charge of all people-related matters in the company. The current 'best practice' approach taken by such HR professionals is to ensure compliance with employment legislation, while maintaining a good employer/employee relationship. They do this by developing policies, practices and procedures specifically related to their business requirements and, for the most part, in conjunction with their employees. This is a proactive approach to establishing and maintaining good working relations.

I know that the word 'proactive' is one of the most abused management buzzwords. It probably has already touched a raw nerve when you read it, right? However, it does have a genuine meaning and value if given the attention it deserves, so in this book it is assumed that the practitioner will adopt a genuine approach. By genuine, I mean giving time to thinking about and acting on the tried and proven HR practices outlined and promoted here. The objective is to develop a good working environment that positively contributes to high performance and, therefore, to the success of the enterprise.

On the other hand, companies that devote little time to such proactive policies are generally reactive in style, trying to resolve issues retrospectively and often in difficult circumstances, involving industrial relations conflict and its adverse affects in terms of cost, disruption and the long-term damage caused by confrontation.

Every supervisor, manager, owner, director or any person who has responsibility for the work of others, or who has responsibility for achieving results indirectly through others, can be considered to be a manager. That is, they plan what must be done within time and cost factors; they organise resources by whatever means to achieve such plans; they monitor and control all aspects of such processes during a given period of time to ensure they are fully aware of issues and deviations in time to take corrective action; and, finally, they motivate all those associated with achieving the plan to perform to the best of their abilities.

The manager's understanding of the knowledge and skill requirements of every category of employee is essential. Attitude is a critical aspect of motivation. A good and positive attitude towards work can often help make up for shortfalls in knowledge or skill. Nonetheless, achieving 'motivational nirvana' has been the holy grail of behavioural psychologists and progressive managers for over 100 years – and the search continues. Perfection is always aspirational and elusive. Effective motivation, leading to good co-operative teamwork and producing consistent high performance, is very difficult to achieve.

While high performance and motivation may appear to occur by accident, on occasion a closer look will reveal that the manager involved has a natural tendency to do all the right things, that motivate his/her people. However, the good manager will not want to leave the achievement of performance targets to chance and, instead, will follow a professional management approach.

While motivation is difficult, de-motivation is quite easy to achieve. Managers do it all the time, without even being aware of it. Perhaps that is the problem – a lack of awareness. A manager does not even have to be abusive to de-motivate an employee; it can be done as simply as accidentally ignoring them or treating them unequally.

The Human Resource Management approach recognises these behavioural facts and the legal compliance requirements, and endeavours to develop and install policies, practices and procedures that are most suitable for the company's business needs and which contribute to positive motivation.

Industrial Relations

No matter how well we prepare as an organisation to ensure best practice and the 'right' environment, inevitably things go wrong. There is often an urgent need to deal with an issue from an industrial relations viewpoint, requiring the application of internal procedures to enforce discipline or deal with grievances. Within the whole HR Management function, these confrontational issues burn most of our people-related management energy, as the potential risks and costs can be significant. I find that many clients only come for advice and assistance when they are already knee-deep in a complex problem and where the company's procedures are non-existent, not properly documented or have been applied inequitably. Whether the issue is related to poor performance, time-keeping and attendance, unacceptable behaviour towards others, breaches in codes of practice or operational procedures, or poor quality, it needs to be dealt with sooner rather than later, within the company, in a way that will not expose the company to additional 'knock-on' claims and which will not expose the company to a breakdown in the employee/ employer relationship with all other staff.

While industrial relations is often perceived as the reactive element of HR, there are many proactive aspects to dealing with such cases through the development and implementation of policies and procedures that will ensure a consistent and fair processing of all issues and in a way that will stand up to testing in a court of law. These include both internal policies and procedures and the external procedures, which are clearly defined within the services of the Labour Relations Commission, Rights Commissioner, Employment Appeals Tribunal and the Labour Court.

The Structure of the Book

Chapters 1 and **2** of this book reflect important best practice approaches that contribute to the development of a modern proactive employer/employee relationship.

Chapter 3 concentrates on the Industrial Relations processes and procedures in common use in Ireland, providing opportunities for employers and employees to resolve issues through investigation and negotiation procedures and involving external third party bodies, such as the services of the Labour Relations Commission, the Rights Commissioner, the Employment Appeals Tribunal and the Labour Court.

Chapter 4 explains the legal requirements for employers arising from the wide range of employment legislation.

Most people, managers included, find business books difficult to read from cover to cover. They tend to dip in and out of books, to find information related to a particular topic, as the need arises. Therefore, each section in this book is as 'stand-alone' as possible, providing sufficient issue resolution material to avoid, insofar as possible, referring the reader to other sections in the book to find a meaningful input or solution. Nonetheless, some navigation is required and there may be some repetition of key information.

The contents are not meant to be totally comprehensive, which would make it difficult to lift the book as well as to read! In fact, its volume has already been substantially reduced since its initial draft, in an attempt to make for easier usage.

In my work as a management consultant over the last 15 years, I have found that many managers who are not aware of the need for Human Resource Management, or who feel they can 'take it or leave it' as it does not really matter, often tend to make errors of judgement that work in opposition to basic business ethics and the requirement to respect the human dignity needs of others. This attitude inevitably results in a direct and/or indirect cost for the company, if not for the actual manager in question. The alternative – a much better alternative, in my experience – is the proactive approach to Human Resource Management, the basics of which are set out in this book.

For those who find the prospect of implementation daunting, I have created *1 Stop HR*, a support service ideally suited for small to medium enterprises or for those employers who wish to outsource the function.

Pat Sheridan
Cork
March 2007

ACKNOWLEDGEMENTS

The author wishes to thank his colleagues at 1stopHR for their support during the writing of this book, especially Lisa O'Callaghan for her dedication.

CHAPTER 1
HUMAN RESOURCES
POLICY, PRACTICE
& PROCEDURE

MANAGEMENT

Introduction

It is important for you, the reader, whether as a student or a manager, to try and 'fit' the information on Human Resource Management contained in this book into a general understanding and application of the management function. It will help you to adopt and to adapt the practices and procedures in this book so as to integrate them into who you are, what you do or what you want to achieve as a manager.

The real starting point is being clear about the broad management role first, before describing the HR management role and how it, in turn, should integrate professionally into all other management roles.

Regardless of whether the company has a HR function, the policies, principles, practices and procedures outlined in this book are valid and important in creating a professionally-operated organisation that is proactively engaged with people as a core business resource.

Describing the Management Role

When managers or supervisors are asked to summarise the concept of management, despite their practical experience, they often find it difficult to articulate. Eventually, they explain what they themselves do, through a list of duties interspersed with various responsibilities and in no particular order of merit. But, almost without exception, managers find it difficult to provide a concise view of the management concept. This is a fairly normal response, which you can test with your management colleagues. However, it is rather strange that a professional can tell you what they do, but without a clear context – after all, management is the nuts and bolts of their daily working life.

It is both interesting and rewarding to run a brief management training session that helps managers to integrate a practical definition of management into their daily lives. This helps the management and supervisory participants to become more professional, as they carry out their duties and responsibilities. It also helps them to integrate key HR Management attributes and values into other management activities.

Once managers see the logic, the sequence of activities and the people interaction aspects of management, they can alter their own behaviour. This process is enlightening, and creates a desire to learn more and to expand their newfound knowledge. Thus, learning becomes its own motivator, as the knowledge converts to skills and as human capacity integrates these incrementally into the person as a whole.

This learning process should be at the core of every manager's personal objective, if they are to develop themselves and grow. Any bad experience in a company leads to demotivation. This holds true, even for the very managers who are required to inject motivation into those under their care. If motivation is not inherent in a manager, or has been replaced by cynicism often arising from such demotivation, the desire to learn and develop will be curtailed. This is a frightening and unnatural position for any organisation that is dependent on its managers/leaders to create a successful environment.

Some educators use the acronym POCM (**P**lan, **O**rganise, **C**ontrol and **M**otivate) to describe management, others use POLCA (**P**lan, **O**rganise, **L**ead, **C**ontrol, **and Achieve**). However, they both mean the same thing.

Plan (P)
One can do practically nothing properly without a plan. It is like setting off on a journey with no destination in mind, no mode of transport and no idea what you intend doing when you arrive. It might be a waste of time; it might be exciting, but cost too much.

A plan requires investigation, analysis and decision-making, to ensure that the purpose is clear from the start, that the pros and cons are assessed and that important decisions are made before even commencing.

Organise (O)
Once the plan is clear, it is easy to organise the key elements required to achieve the plan. You contract with others inside and outside the company to do things within agreed time, cost and quality parameters to achieve the plan. In essence, you are assembling the resources to achieve the details of the plan.

Using the same journey analogy, it is like buying the petrol, figuring out the stops and monetary requirements for meals *en route*, booking the B&B in advance so that you are well-prepared and knowing where you are going to sleep.

Control (C)
Once the plan is underway, the manager regularly monitors and adjusts all the elements of the work, to ensure that the various targets are achieved as stated in the plan. There are generally unexpected (unplanned) occurrences that cause him/her to modify activities and the use of resources to achieve the plan.

For example, telephoning *en route* to make sure that you are expected, confirming at what time you will have the evening meal, and advising of any delays, if you have a puncture or other breakdown.

Motivate (M)

The three previous phases of planning, organisation and control all involve a skill-set input from people. It is important, therefore, if the work is to be done effectively and within a set of standards, that all involved are well-motivated – otherwise, the costs and other objectives will not be achieved and the plan will fail.

So management is simply the application of this POCM concept, especially in jobs that carry a responsibility for the work of others – for example, senior executives, heads of function managers, supervisors, team leaders and charge-hands.

Obviously, the level of complexity and responsibility for POCM varies throughout a business, but these four key management attributes are consistently present in any management occupation. In fact, it is impossible to ignore any aspect of POCM and maintain a successful operation in the long-term.

Being Aware

It is important that every manager knows, at any moment in time, whether they are in the planning, organising, controlling or motivational phase when engaged in any management activity. It makes it much easier to figure out what might be the most appropriate thing to do next if one has this level of awareness.

The Human Resource Management Contribution

The overlap between all managers and a Human Resource Manager in a company is in the motivation (M) piece of POCM. The motivation of all those involved in the business is a complex and difficult objective, which all managers have a responsibility for understanding and contributing to.

Unfortunately, many managers demotivate their staff and colleagues, more often by accident rather than by design, when, in fact, they are required to motivate so as to achieve co-operation from all and to achieve their department's objectives, in particular. This could be due to a lack of understanding of the concept or because the manager him/herself might not be as motivated as he/she should be.

The Human Resource Manager uses POCM but applies it to a different set of criteria than, say, the Production Manager. The latter has the primary objective of producing a product within standards of quality and costs and must pursue his or her own version of POCM to that end. The Human Resource Manager, on the other hand, is responsible for creating the policies, practices and procedures that must address the motivational aspects of POCM on a company-wide basis, reflecting the company's objectives as defined in the overall business plan.

The clear set of policies, practices, procedures and principles that arises from the Human Resource Management considerations is used as a guide for all other managers to help and support them in addressing their individual requirement of motivation within their particular, and very different, POCM responsibilities.

In companies that have no formal HR Management expertise, it is essential that all the managers, and in particular the Chief Executive, has some understanding of this management concept and also of the HR Management values that must be integrated.

FIGURE 1: MANAGEMENT – POCM

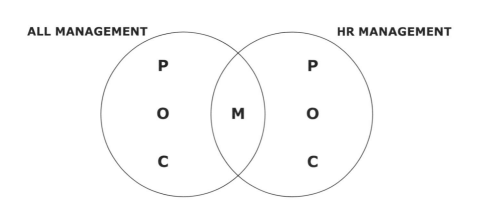

ALL MANAGEMENT

HR MANAGEMENT

P

O

C

M

P

O

C

A SYSTEMATIC CHANGE MANAGEMENT APPROACH

Introduction

Advancing your company into the modern Human Resource Management world is both necessary and desirable.

Necessary, because there are a multitude of employment laws that require companies to behave in a particular way and because failing to do so can be costly. Actually, it can be less costly to proactively install good HR practices than to leave the situation to chance and the courts. In addition, there is a wealth of established precedents arising from civil and industrial relations cases that clearly indicates that it is better to be aware, prepared and proactively people-focused. Many companies find that their cases collapse because they have been procedurally incorrect in dealing with people-related issues and, thus, recommendations, determinations and awards go against them.

It is desirable to install best practice, in order to create a high trust and high performance environment, where dependability and flexibility occurs as a way of life. The more effort management puts into creating a sound employee relations environment, the better the results.

If your company is not HR-orientated, then you should consider the areas within which your company could benefit from a professional approach to people management and the steps required to implement suitable policies and practices to address the company's needs.

This book outlines the main areas of HR Management and the key requirements for each aspect of this people-focused approach.

In this section, we look at the process of introducing the HR Management approach in typical change management phases, systematically considering what to do and why, then incrementally making the changes, and communicating each step to all concerned in a structured and timely manner before, and during, implementation.

What is Change?

Change is any shift from one state to another. It amounts, in human terms, to doing things differently. This can occur by accident, habit, evolution or it can be planned and deliberate.

In the context of this book, we are obviously looking at the last – a planned and deliberate approach. So, if it is planned and deliberate, it should have a purpose and clear objectives.

There are various motivators that cause us to want to change, or recognise the need for change. These motivators can be external or internal, arising either from threats to the business or from opportunities. Planned change should have an element of benefit, although there may also be negative aspects as a necessary part of the change requirements.

Changes in business are generally perceived as necessary and beneficial. Nonetheless, they do not always run smoothly and changes are not always pleasant for all *en route* to the required result.

If you try to develop and install changes on your own, without considering the attitudes, motivation and the feelings of others, and also the environment and history in which you are operating, the chances are that there will be problems. Good communications practices can greatly reduce the risk of failure. Good leadership generally ensures that all those who are to be affected by change are brought along incrementally with the process, and that they have an understanding of the concept and a genuine input to the content.

The Change Management Process

Step 1: Preliminary preparation

This step is all about getting enough information to aid your decision-making. Generally, the more information, you have the better the quality of the decision-making process.

Get a basic understanding of what HR Management is. This book is a good starting point. In doing any job, you require both knowledge and skill, so prepare yourself. The knowledge and skills must also be supported by a positive attitude. If you are in any way short on these three ingredients, you need to sort these out. How? Read, ask questions or seek professional help. Understand the background to the need for HR Management.

Understand motivation, particularly what motivates you and how you like to be treated by others. Reflect on what other companies do. Look at companies that have a positive employee relations environment.

Assess the areas in the company that are most exposed in terms of people. Start at the beginning of the people-related processes in the company – for example, recruitment practices, contracts of employment, induction, documentation and safety.

There are certain aspects of the HR change process that must be developed by management, if necessary with professional assistance, such as contracts, where there is a legal element to the content and where employees may not have the necessary skill-sets to make a contribution. Existing employees already have a contract of employment either in writing or inferred by custom and practice – this may need to change.

It is important to be aware of the customs and practices in operation in the company under each HR heading as you proceed. Ensure, if you are changing any of these, that employees are involved in the development of the changes, where applicable. Remember that, if you make a unilateral decision to change an existing procedure, it can be challenged through internal and/or external industrial relations procedures.

Existing practices represent the culture of the organisation, as perceived by managers and employees. Some of the traditions and customs embedded in your company may not be most suited to the changing nature of its work, may not be compliant with legislation and/or may represent barriers to business development. However, sometimes, these very practices are defended to the last, through manager/employee confrontation. This is obviously to be avoided. Discussion and participation in a joint effort to seek a mutually agreed solution is a preferable route.

Step 2: Communications - level one

Begin the first phase of communicating, testing the company's readiness to adapt and change. Some companies already have a change culture because of the nature of the business; others have not. So, understanding this cultural position is important.

Flag the needs and risks that you have uncovered in your preliminary investigations and your intentions to bring about broad changes and improvements in the HR Management area. Discuss the process, the needs and benefits with the board and/or with management colleagues, as appropriate. Get their views and, above all, ensure a full understanding of the issues. It is critical that you get full and genuine support and commitment from management colleagues to develop and install professional HR Management principles.

Obviously, the keystone for driving the change process and setting the main objectives is the chief executive. Unless he/she is fully committed to HR principles and their implementation, change is unlikely to succeed. So, if you are not the chief executive, ensure that he/she is your first target for those persuasive arguments.

Once the chief executive is fully on board, other managers will find it more difficult to reject the concepts. Your management colleagues may be your biggest barrier to your objectives. Some managers feel that HR is an unnecessary evil. They want to be able to do what they want, as they want, without policies and procedures getting in their way. Some managers may be bullies, apprehensive about their own inexperience or fearful of having to engage with employees in a new, different and more enlightened way. It is important that you discover all these potential barriers, if you are to progress. Each manager may need to be assessed, and even developed to a state of competence, where they are capable of supporting the intended change process and the ongoing HR culture, once established. Each manager must fully understand the new demands that the HR approach will make on them and be prepared to learn and support the stated processes.

Listen and record all suggestions, observations and concerns and incorporate these, as appropriate, into the development and implementation phases. Do not move forward until this step is complete, and you are satisfied that there is a majority support and commitment for the change process and its clearly-stated objectives.

Step 3: The initial outline plan

Once the level one discussions are reasonably well advanced, select a number of the HR elements that the core change management group have agreed to. These should be key issues that require change, which you consider to be most urgent. Prepare a brief plan to develop policy statements and procedures for these subjects.

Step 4: Communications - level two

Preparation is important. Summarise, in writing, your purpose and intentions regarding the change process and the benefits. Be brief and clear. This briefing document is your communications plan. You may wish to provide a copy to all employees. Your initial objective is to involve others and get buy-in to what all must see as a good idea. Avoid being too radical in the proposed changes. Sustained incremental changes, that are seen as beneficial and supported by the majority, should be considered as reasonable progress.

So, involve all employees in the process as far as practicable. Explain some of the key reasons or needs for change that the company must address.

Advise staff that the company wishes to make improvements to policies and procedures within the context of HR principles and that the management team have agreed on a preliminary list of items for change and improvement. Explain the list, and suggest that employees are welcome to comment or make their own suggestions as the company proceeds. Explain how such participation could take place – for example, through briefing meetings at which employees are invited to review the key changes and make comments.

Those involved in making these presentations and managing such meetings should be well-prepared and conscious of the need to listen and record all comments and suggestions for later consideration, response and inclusion, if appropriate. Avoid defending the proposals at this stage. Listening and recording is important. There may be very valid options proposed, which could be integrated into a revised model.

If there appears to be little understanding or support for the changes, it is better to resolve this first. Remember that change is often accompanied by fear, arising from lack of trust. Employees may understand that change is not always beneficial to all and sundry. Fears should be aired and reviewed and people's minds put at ease before proceeding. Usually, people perceive HR policies as being positive and developmental so this requirement should not be too difficult.

Step 5: Professional help and support

Difficulties will arise and it is important to get expert assistance and advice as needed, rather than make a mistake that could have long-reaching effects. Difficulties may emanate from individuals who have clear views, previous experience or something that they particularly want to preserve.

In all such cases, ensure that there is consistency. If there is a case for treating certain people or departments differently, from a procedural perspective, the background and reasoning should be aired as part of the communications process and employees should be convinced that the reasons given are logical, legitimate and legal.

You must be able and willing to detect resistance and you must seek to understand the basis of such resistance. Unless you get to the root cause and resolve it, moving forward will be difficult. Avoid sidelining an issue, deal with it as quickly as possible. Be straight and ask questions, get the opinions of others not directly associated with the issue. Consensus is ideal, but not always possible. Compromise is an option, but generally means that neither party is entirely satisfied. A solution that is perceived as a win/win is more acceptable, but generally requires a longer investment in discussion time. Nonetheless, one ideally needs to get agreement in preference to issuing a *diktat*.

Step 6: Final written copies of policies and procedures

As you proceed and policies are developed, including the practices and procedures required to implement the policies, it is important to ensure these are properly written and included in the company's HR manual or employee handbook. This handbook should be available to all employees in a central and easily-accessible location in the company. Some companies issue an individual copy to each employee, to ensure awareness and also to demonstrate the fact that the company considers the document to be a critical part of the employment contract.

Step 7: Support and maintenance

Once each phase of the HR plan is implemented, there will be an on-going requirement for support and maintenance. Flaws and issues will arise, and reconsideration, adaptation and communications will be important in the early stages following implementation, as employees become familiar with the reality of practices and procedures in operation. However, be clear and consistent. Modification and adaptation is fine, but needs careful consideration. Remember the long-term implications of all policies, practices and procedures, how hard it was to get to this stage and the recurring difficulties associated with further changes.

From time to time, changes to legislation and changes to HR best practice will arise that require you to add, subtract or adapt your policies, practices and procedures to ensure either compliance or further improvements. The person designated in the company to monitor such occurrences should have access to such information and also must be capable of assessing the impact on the company, preparing drafts of such change requirements and the correct process for inclusion.

FIGURE 2: HR CHANGE MANAGEMENT CHART

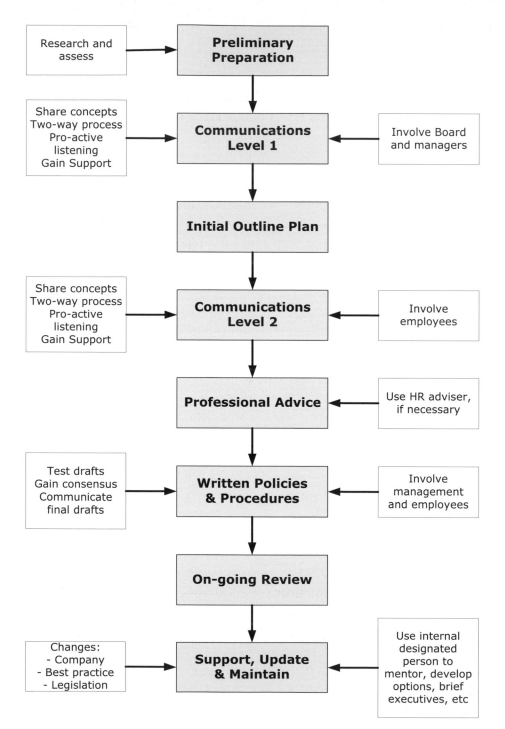

RECRUITMENT & SELECTION

Introduction

The employer/employee relationship begins the moment you decide that you need to recruit. Everything you do from this point on will impact on the working relationship that arises once the new person starts work with your company.

If carefully undertaken, the recruitment process can greatly reduce, or even eliminate, the selection of poor quality candidates. Careful recruitment practices can also help to reduce recruitment process costs and subsequent employee problems.

There are also legal requirements regarding recruitment and selection practices with which all companies must comply. This section takes you through all the necessary phases, policies, procedures and practices, which should be incorporated into your HR manual or employee handbook.

Knowledge, Skill & Attitude

All occupations require varying degrees of knowledge, skill and attitude (KSA) to accomplish the duties and responsibilities of an occupation. Knowledge means the specific information required to be able to perform tasks. Skill means the physical abilities, developed through experience, to apply the knowledge to achieve qualitative and quantitative objectives. Attitude refers to the most appropriate frame of mind of the individual doing the job to achieve the job requirements. For example:

- **Knowledge:** A general assembly worker responsible for assembling the electric element into a kettle requires very little job knowledge in terms of how the parts go together, the tools or jigs to use or how to recognise and resolve minor problems.

- **Skill:** The skill level for this job requires a degree of double-handed motion, hand/eye co-ordination and high-speed dexterity to achieve an experienced operator performance standard.

- **Attitude:** Attitude is a state of mind that alters how we think, feel and behave. If we want to do something, but are short on the knowledge or skill, a positive 'can do, will do' attitude will help us overcome the knowledge and skill shortfall reasonably quickly. However, if we do not wish to do something, our attitude being negative for whatever reason, our work rate will be poor, we may make more mistakes and we will become slow and even lethargic. This one factor therefore, for which we cannot provide training, can have a significant impact on a person's performance at work. How we treat people, as managers, will have an impact on their attitude. That is why the development of positive motivational approaches, policies and procedures is essential, responsibility for which rests with management.

It is important for each manager to understand that all the jobs within the company rely on different definitions and different standards of knowledge and skill. The application of these acquired attributes is, however, affected by the manager's own abilities, performance and attitude. If the motivation is positive, the knowledge and skill will be applied effectively and efficiently. Poor treatment of employees generally leads to demotivation and poor performance.

The Preparation Phase

Do not be put off by the amount of preparatory work suggested here. This is the 'ideal' professional recruitment process but you can make it as detailed or as simple as you wish. You can select and adapt the phases most suited to your company needs at any time.

Depending on the size of company, level of expertise required or job complexity, all of these recruitment phases can be carried out quickly. It really depends on the circumstances. The decision is yours as to which phases you give most attention to.

For example, if yours is a small engineering company and one of your best welders has resigned, you need a welder – and fast! You could write down the job description and personnel specification in five minutes (ideally this information will already be available to you in the company), focusing on the particular key welding skills needed for your company. From this, you can prepare a job advertisement and the process is underway.

As you wait for applications to arrive, you can visit the interview check sheets and adapt them as appropriate. These simple steps will structure your recruitment process, make it more effective and help you to avoid costly mistakes. The process can be reduced or expanded according to the volume of recruitment, the complexity of the jobs and the availability of candidates for each job category. However, when it comes to assessing the candidates, attention and accuracy is important.

Use the Recruitment & Selection Chart **(Figure 3)** to guide you through the process, as fairness and consistency are required.

FIGURE 3: RECRUITMENT & SELECTION CHART

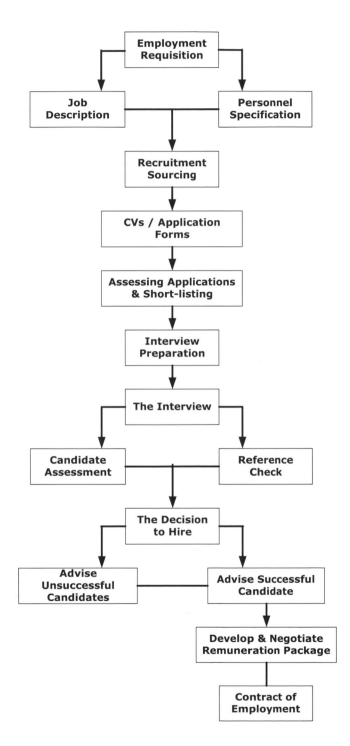

Employment requisitions

These are normally associated with the larger employer, where size makes it imperative to track costs and ensure management are in control of budgets. However, in a small business, the impact of poor recruitment and selection techniques can be equally disruptive. More positively, the right person in the job will have a beneficial impact on company results and on the atmosphere through the people to people relationships in the company.

Focus on the key aspects you wish to record in the employment requisition by asking yourself the following questions:

- Is it necessary to carry out this work? Is there still a need for the job? Have circumstances changed?
- Is there anyone already available in the company who has the time and ability to carry out these duties and responsibilities in addition to their own work and who satisfies the personnel specification?
- Is there anyone already available in the company who has the time and ability to carry out these duties and responsibilities in addition to their own work and who would satisfy the personnel specifications with some additional training?
- What salary/wage range is appropriate in relation to the desired skill-set?
- Would it be more economical and practical to sub-contract this work?

You may have other questions applicable to your circumstances that you can add to this list that will help your decision-making.

If you conclude that you must hire, then you must produce the necessary support information for hiring – job description, personnel specification and interview check-sheets. These practical documents will help you to identify clearly the critical aspects of the job and the best type of person required to satisfy the actual job demands. The requisition process often impacts one's thinking regarding the job or the skill-set requirements.

Job Description

Define the job in terms of duties and responsibilities. The approach to the development of a job description can be twofold:

- It can describe the job under the main duties and responsibilities required.
- It can describe the job down to individual tasks.

The second approach is generally required for training purposes only. If it is intended to employ an inexperienced person and to train them to do the job, then detailing all the tasks is essential for the application of professional systematic training techniques, which must include the safety training aspects of the job.

Figure 4 is an example of a job description for an Office Administrator. Each job description is specific to each company and developed with the existing, and future, requirements of the company in mind.

Always summarise a job in terms of the main purpose. If you have difficulty doing this, write down everything you feel needs to be done. First, state the individual areas and levels of responsibility, and then all the duties that the person must carry out to achieve the objectives under each responsibility. You may then find it easier to review these key points and to summarise the main purpose of the job.

Personnel Specification

Once the job description has been prepared and agreed by those who can make a useful input, it is possible to define the type of person you believe would be best suited to satisfy the job requirements defined under duties and responsibilities. This is called the personnel specification.

It quantifies the preferred level of education and expertise that you believe to be necessary to satisfy the job demands shortly after commencement, or after a little training, and which will suffice into the foreseeable future.

Defining the experience attributes requires you to ask a number of key questions:

- What must the person know, and be able to do, to achieve a particular result defined under the duties and responsibilities of the job description? To know, and to be able to do, generally refer to knowledge and skill, which are different. For example, knowing how to drive a car is different from having the skill or control to be able to do so safely. So, ensure you understand the difference when listing knowledge and skills.

- In what environment would candidates have gained the necessary experience previously? Is experience of any kind necessary? Will a few hours' basic training be sufficient? Are there risks and hazards involved that require a very experienced person? Consider induction and other training needs when determining the ideal employee.

There are many questions that could be asked, depending on the job complexity and safety implications. Define these for the various jobs in the company as you proceed.

FIGURE 4: JOB DESCRIPTION

Job Title	Office Administrator
Department	Office.
Company Description	Family-owned beauty clinic.
Products & Services	Beauty Treatment Products; Laser Treatment Services; Tanning; Hair Removal; Manicures; Facial Treatments.
Main Purpose of the Job	Take bookings, schedule treatment and collect fees.
Main Duties & Responsibilities	Check daily telephone and fax messages and relay to the appropriate person for action. Daily review all emails requesting information and respond as appropriate. Advise the appropriate member of staff of emails requiring special attention. Answer telephone queries. Order all office and clinic supplies. Meet customers and resolve any charge related queries. Responsible for office discipline and processing any office employee grievances. Take booking for treatments. Handle cash and credit card charges. Maintain schedules for all equipment and treatment bookings. Purchase and keep stocks of beauty treatment products. Ensure all office administration work is carried out accurately and on time.
Reporting To	Owner.
Authority Over	Junior staff and reception.
Location	Main Office at [insert location].
Created on	Day / Month / Year.
Modified on	Day / Month / Year.
Developed by	Owner.

FIGURE 5: PERSONNEL SPECIFICATION

Title	Office Administrator
Department	Office.
Company Description	Family-owned beauty clinic.
Education	Must have a Leaving Certificate, with good English and Maths results. Ideally, the person would also have some further qualification, such as an office administration diploma. Alternatively, it would be desirable if the person had a supervisory management diploma.
Experience	Minimum of three years' experience in a similar office environment. Supervision of staff. Running a small company payroll. Receptionist & Customer Care experience. Credit control. Ideally, the person will have experience of training other staff in all office administration work, including computer training – spreadsheets, payroll and invoicing.
Track Record	Very communicative, persuasive and outgoing, gets on well with people. Reasonably decisive and assertive but not aggressive or arrogant. Very steady, reliable, dependable and predictable. Compliant with important rules, regulations and systems. Care and attention to detail.
Personality & Other Factors	Friendly, outgoing, careful and reasonably firm.
Created on	Day / Month / Year.
Modified on	Day / Month / Year.
Developed by	Owner.

Figure 5 is an example of a personnel specification for an Office Administrator. Personnel specifications are specific to each occupation and developed with the requirements of the company in mind.

Recruitment Sourcing

Consider previous applications

You may already have received suitable applications either from job-seekers applying 'on spec', or from applicants for previous positions. Of course, you should always retain these on file. Since recruitment can be costly, particularly if you have to advertise or use a recruitment agency, applications on file could save you significantly if candidates are suitable and available. Even if these candidates are not available, they will be pleased and impressed that you checked back with them and they may suggest other colleagues or friends who they think might be interested. This type of networking is time-consuming, but is very cost-effective if you are successful.

Networking

Ask other employees who they know in the business. Existing employees are a great source of information. They know the company and some of their friends may have the necessary qualifications. You may identify a suitable person through existing staff quickly.

Of course, there is the risk of having to reject an employee's friend. Explain this possibility to any employees who wish to propose a friend.

Advertise internally

Advertising all jobs internally is good policy. It is positive and respectful to share information about the company with all employees. While you should know which employees might be suitable and which would not, you cannot assume this, as employees can take the initiative to develop themselves and may have gained qualifications and experience that you may not be aware of.

Not advertising jobs internally or, at least briefing staff about such opportunities, generally leads to demotivation. The difference between motivation and demotivation can be slight in terms of communications, but can be enormous in terms of behaviour, attitude and performance responses from staff.

Advertise externally

Advertising can be costly, depending on the level of job, the size of the advertisement and the advertising source. Remember you may not get the response you would like and you may end up having to go another route. So, use less costly recruitment source options initially, if possible. Consider which advertising route is most applicable for each recruitment campaign and determine the costs – for example, advertising via local or national newspapers, trade magazines, online recruitment websites, radio or TV, as appropriate.

Recruitment agencies

Usually, you can negotiate with a recruitment agency to source a panel of suitable candidates on a 'no hire, no fee' basis. In general, the agency will charge between 12.5% and 25% of the successful candidate's first year remuneration package, if you hire one of their candidates. The recruitment fees will be related to the seniority of the position and the candidates.

You may wish to place the candidate search with several recruitment companies on a no-hire-no-fee basis. However, it is probably better to check out a few recruitment agencies, identify someone you feel you can work with in one of those agencies and stick with this person if they are successful. If you feel the service is not satisfactory, then change agencies.

Remember that the agency's success will be related to the accuracy of your job description and personnel specification. In addition, you will need to provide a briefing sheet, which realistically and adequately describes your company, its products or services, the job, the wage or salary and any benefits. An organisational chart showing the position of the job within the company is also beneficial.

FÁS

FÁS has a database of various employment categories and also has access to all those undergoing specialised State-sponsored training programmes in a wide range of occupations. There is no cost for hiring through this source.

Job Applications

Curricula Vitae (CVs)

Regardless of which recruitment route you decide to take, you will end up (hopefully!) with candidates who must be interviewed, assessed and short-listed.

Candidates will normally send in a CV and a brief letter, stating that they wish to apply for the position. The CV lists the candidate's education and work experience. It can contain other information, which you may wish to consider if appropriate – for example, current studies, membership of professional bodies, participation in organisations and occasionally other interests that may be work-related and relevant or of no specific or immediate value.

You must rate the CVs so that you can differentiate between the various qualifications and experience levels and thus produce a list of those most suited for interview. Use the same shortlisting process for all and apply the process fairly. Keep a copy of the shortlist showing the criteria for candidates, in case you are challenged on the grounds of bias.

Finally, one must assume that candidates can, and do, take certain 'poetic licence' with the details in their CV, bending facts to make their application more attractive. However, sometimes, CVs may understate a candidate's ability or experience. The interview provides the opportunity to make such assessments and to uncover additional and important information that either adds or detracts from the candidate's profile.

Application forms

Some employers have a policy that all applicants must complete a standard company application form. There are pros and cons for this approach.

Candidates who have gone to the trouble to apply with a detailed CV may be discouraged, if they subsequently receive an application form, requesting mostly the same information that they have laid out in their CV. In some cases, application forms do little to acquire additional information of any value.

However, some employers believe that they get a better and more uniform perspective on applicants by standardising the information that they really want to review. An application form is also a record of certain key areas, which a company may wish to have on file in the event of a disciplinary matter arising at a later date. This is particularly important where a person has to list their qualifications, and where such qualifications are a prerequisite for a particular occupation. Due to the growing complexity of legislation and the increasing litigation culture, having a signed statement on the application form stating that the information is an accurate and complete reflection of the application's details may be of subsequent value. However, if you wish to use the candidate's CV only, without an application form, such a statement can be incorporated into an employment contract, which can refer to the specific CV and require verification that all the information contained therein is accurate.

Under equality legislation, it is unlawful to include any questions on an application form, where the information has no bearing on a person's ability to do the job – for example, gender, marital status, family status, sexual orientation, religion, age, disability, race or membership of the travelling community.

In designing an application form, ensure that it is user-friendly. Leave plenty of space for the candidates to enter a reasonable amount of information, without having to squeeze their writing into a small space.

Remember that you need as much relevant information as possible in a clear and readable format.

Assessing applications

It is easier if you have a systematic approach to assessing the key factors for each applicant, which allows you to demonstrate how you rate each applicant against the key requirements of the job. In this way, you can interview as many applicants as you feel appropriate and make detailed comparisons on each of the key requirements as set out in the personnel specification.

You will have to make the final choice as to who you hire: The one you like best? The one with the most qualifications? The one with the most hands-on experience? In the end, it will probably be a combination of all of these factors, and possibly some others too.

Under equality legislation, applicants may not be excluded from consideration for jobs, based on bias. Consequently, your check-sheets must only reflect the main criteria that you have determined as critical for success in the particular occupation. Rejection of applicants for other reasons could result in a claim against the company. It is important for you to retain selection documentation and criteria to enable you to prove that your approach was fair and equitable in the event of such a claim.

Use the application assessment check-sheet (**Figure 6**), for shortlisting candidates, based on the personnel specification, so that you are consistent in measuring the written applications against the key requirement or standards that you have set out. A similar form, using the same key factors for rating the written applications, can also be used to assess the candidates at interview (see **Figure 7**).

Use the application assessment check-sheet to rate the candidates into a shortlist of successful applicants as follows:

- Score each of the headings out of 10 for each applicant.
- You can also weight two or three key factors, using a multiplier. This will help to differentiate between the applicants based on key, job-related factors, which will change from job to job.
- Do not add up the scores for each applicant as you go.
- When interviews are complete, write down who you would choose without considering the scoring.
- Now complete the scoring totals.
- You can now cross-reference your 'gut' reaction with the check-sheet.
- It is great when the check-sheet confirms your 'gut' reaction – you can see at a glance the key high score areas for the successful applicants.

- On the other hand, if the check-sheet identifies a different applicant as being the most suitable, you can review the factors, establish why there is a difference and whether it is important. You should satisfy yourself that the rationale is correct and resolve any concerns before proceeding.

FIGURE 6: APPLICATION ASSESSMENT CHECK-SHEET

Assessor: _____ Date: _____

Job Title: _____

Headings	Applicant name	Applicant name	Applicant name	Applicant name	Applicant name	Applicant name
Qualifications						
Job knowledge						
Physical skills						
Social skills						
Years in similar work						
Enter specific skills						
Enter specific training						
Enter specific courses						
Enter other headings						
TOTAL SCORE						

Instructions

- Consider the key requirements set out in the personnel specification for the position.
- Rate each applicant's application form, CV, letter, etc against the criteria and award points. Maximum 10 points for having the particular requirement under each heading and lesser points in relation to how you measure their actual knowledge, skills, abilities, etc.
- You may need to add several additional rows to cater for some jobs which have multiple demands on talents, abilities, expertise, etc.
- The first reading of the applications may indicate some applicants who have little or none of the key criteria for the position. These applications can be set aside immediately and the candidates written to, advising them that they have not been successful (as suggested in the text).

Going through this process in a genuine way will mean that you have identified the best applicants to interview – and the check-sheets will serve a record of your fair procedures, if you are challenged later.

Then contact the shortlisted applicants to set up interviews and advise unsuccessful applicants.

Be professional. Unsuccessful applicants may not be suitable now, but they may be just right next time round. Thank them for their interest and explain briefly that they have not been shortlisted for interview on this occasion (as there were other candidates whose experience was particularly suited for this vacancy). State that you will maintain their details on file for future reference.

Interview Preparation

Communication

Ensure all relevant information is accurately conveyed to the interviewers and candidates, including the date and time for the interview. Ideally, this should be in writing (email is fine), and you should request confirmation of receipt.

Select a suitable and private office. If the company does not have a private office, or if you feel that the environment might not be conducive for a confidential interview, consider using a local hotel and take a private interview/conference room for whatever period you feel appropriate. Do not interview a candidate in a public place such as a hotel foyer – it is unreasonable and unprofessional.

Scheduling

Allow sufficient time for interviews. If you schedule an interview, and you have another interviewee to follow, be on time yourself to start the first interview, and allow enough time after the interview to complete the check-sheet properly, with a little time to spare.

Avoid interviewees meeting one another. Manage your time; you are responsible for sticking to the schedule. Even if you feel the interview is going well, this is no excuse to let it overrun. Remember that some candidates may be working to a tight travel schedule and depending on you to stick to the arranged time slot.

Interviews are an investment in the future of your company, so plan each step carefully.

Interviewers

Consider carefully who you select to participate in the interview process. For example, if you are hiring a technical person and you have limited hands-on experience yourself, you might wish to have a qualified person to deal solely with the key technical aspects of the job.

A second opinion on candidates is always of value. Ensure that the person or persons you select to participate in the interviewing process for each job are involved in the preparation and know what is expected of them.

Ensure that interviewers do not have any hidden agenda or bias regarding any candidate. Interviewers must be aware of the rights of the interviewee. Interviewers should avoid questions that are unreasonable or unlawful, as this could lead to litigation.

Paperwork

Ensure you have a copy of all relevant documentation available for the interviewers – for example, the individual's CV or application form, copies of the job description, personnel specification and company information briefing sheet and any other information you believe relevant. For example, if you were hiring an engineer, you may wish to have some relevant drawings available so that you can discuss technical points and test the individual's knowledge.

Interview assessment form

Prepare an interview check sheet (see **Figure 7**), which can be used to rate candidates systematically. Prior to an interview, you should decide on the key requirements necessary, based on the personnel specification.

Separate and list the most important qualification or experience items that will contribute most to the successful performance of the job. The scoring of these factors against each candidate will provide a valuable tool for the identification of the most suitable candidate.

There may be 10 or more items for your checklist. Rate the most important of the factors, and give them a multiplier – for example, if you have rated the candidate 8 out of 10 because they have most of the specific hands-on experience you require, and you have selected this factor as one of the key factors, a multiplier of 2 will score the candidate 16 points for that factor.

This scoring method will help to further differentiate the candidates in relation to those factors that are most important for the successful execution of the job. This multiplier or weighting approach will help to make the right candidate stand out from the rest – and for the right reasons.

FIGURE 7: INTERVIEW ASSESSMENT FORM

Job Title: _____   Date: _____

Interviewer: _____

Headings:	Key Weighting	Candidate Name	Candidate Name	Candidate Name	Candidate Name
General Education					
Relevant Qualifications					
Relevant Experience					
Technical Expertise					
Communication Skills					
Personality Fit					
Specific Skills					
Management Experience					
Enter other headings					
Enter other headings					
TOTAL SCORE					
Tick Candidate Selected					

Additional Comments

_____

_____

_____

_____

_____

[See over for Instructions]

Instructions

- Interviews should only be undertaken if the job description and personnel specification are completed and available. These documents should be available at the interview for briefing purposes, to help guide the interviewers and to answer any queries. They can be shared with each candidate, so they can refer to the job requirements in direct relation to their experience.
- The headings in the left-hand column should be modified to represent the key job requirements or factors.
- The scoring of these factors against each candidate will provide a valuable tool for the identification of the most suitable candidate.
- Do not use any headings that could be construed as biased or which provide an unreasonable and unrelated scoring assessment.
- You may have to use several forms to cover all the candidates.

Scoring

- Score each factor out of 10 points.
- Select the three most important factors for the job and apply a weighting multiplier. For example, if experience is one of the three key factors, and the candidate scores 8 points out of a possible 10 for this factor, by applying a weighting multiplier of 2, the candidate receives a score of 16 (8 x 2) for the experience factor.
- Each interviewer selects their preferred candidate and then checks this choice against the total assessment scores.
- If the results are different, then the reasons can be discussed and re-aligned as per the personnel specification and the scoring standard.

Meeting the interviewee for the first time

The first impression is a two-way reaction. The candidate will be judging the interviewer's professional conduct, as much as the interviewer is judging the candidate.

The interviewer should welcome the candidate, thank him/her for attending the interview and ensure the atmosphere and environment places them at ease. Since the purpose of the interview is to get as much relevant information as possible in the time that has been allocated, establishing the right atmosphere will aid this process. The interviewer can help by leading off and discussing the company's current status and any new developments.

The interviewer can explain whether the position is new or the company is replacing someone who is leaving or has left the company.

The interviewer should be honest at all times. The candidate may have carried out their own research. The candidate may even know the outgoing person and have been given a detailed briefing, which may not be as 'rosy' as the interviewer's presentation.

When the interviewer believes that the candidate is at ease, he/she should proceed with the main interview. Avoid spending too long on supplying information about the company. It is more important to learn as much as possible about the candidate, otherwise decision-making will be ambiguous, if not reckless.

Main interview structure

For various reasons, interviewers sometimes suggest to the interviewee that they talk about their career to date. This is sometimes a cop-out, because they have not prepared their questions or structured their interview in advance.

Other interviewers take this approach more deliberately, because they wish to hear the candidate tell their story without prompting, so that they can get a sense of the person's ability to communicate and also their ability to edit their career story to suit the position that they have applied for. The interviewer then interjects at appropriate times on points of clarification or where a particular experience is of special or relevant interest. Experienced interviewers will be capable of managing the acquisition of the relevant information and the interview times simultaneously. Inexperienced interviewers should stick to the more structured approach.

The interviewer may also have a list of questions to ask, regardless of the interviewee's presentation of their work history.

Alternatively, the structure might be planned around the contents of the candidate's CV, with the interviewer only focusing questions on those key experience requirements defined in the personnel specification.

It is important that the interviewer prepares in advance and knows which approach he/she is going to use and why. Each candidate should be subjected to the same interview structure to ensure fairness and equality.

It is useful to prepare your questions in advance and, in the main, these should focus on the candidate's perception of their suitability for the position, in relation to their various work experience(s) in their current and previous employment. Ask for examples of what they did in various situations. These questions should be determined before the interview and should directly reflect the key aspects of the occupation.

Questions from the interviewee

When the main investigative aspects of the interview are complete, the interviewer should allow some time for the interviewee to ask questions about the job or about the company and should be in a position to deal with these immediately.

Remember that the final candidate will also have to make a judgement about the interview and the company, so interviewers should consider the following factors carefully before they meet candidates:

- Remuneration package (salary, bonus or commissions and benefits, such as pension, health insurance, etc).
- Holidays.
- The working environment.
- Internal work relationships.
- Educational opportunities and career development.
- Training.
- Responsibility and authority.
- Promotional opportunities.
- The state of the company in terms of stability and growth.

Concluding the interview

Once the interviewer is satisfied that he/she has obtained the key information concerning the candidate's education and experience, vis-à-vis the job requirements, and that he/she has provided the appropriate briefing about the company and the job, he/she may terminate the interview by thanking the interviewee and explaining the next stages in the process and their likely timing.

Candidate Assessment

Candidate tests

A wide range of tests are available for various applications. Tests can be applied after the main interview, when the candidate is more relaxed.

If any tests are to be applied, they should be properly administered by a competent person and their relevance of the tests should be specific to the job. Candidates should be appropriately advised.

Psychometric tests

Psychometric tests are useful and very quickly assess the key characteristics of the candidate's probable behaviour in relation to the demands placed on them in a given occupation.

There are a number of methods of applying these psychometric tests:

- The interviewer can learn how to apply the test but can either fax or email the questionnaires to the test company for interpretation. A written report is normally available quite quickly by email.

- The interviewer can have the candidate complete the test on a computer, on or offline, and will get an immediate feedback, which may be discussed with the candidate, there and then if appropriate.

- The interviewer may have decided, at the interview planning stage, to have only two or three of the finalists complete such tests. In such a situation, the finalist candidates could be tested prior to the final interview and the test results could form part of the final interview process.

In general, interviewers do not use psychometric tests as a key decider but rather as a support tool. The decision to hire, therefore, is a combination of factors, including the interview interaction, the candidate's communications abilities and style, their knowledge, their track record, their skills, their attitude, the results of the tests (if any are applied) and the standard of reference received.

Reference checks
Candidates, for the most part, are on their best behaviour at interviews and naturally wish to persuade you that they are the best person for the job. Some stretch the facts regarding their qualifications, abilities and work experience; some even may lie profusely. Of course, those who seriously bend the facts and are later hired will generally be discovered in their shortfalls quite quickly and can be dismissed, but the costs and loss of valuable time for the company can be significant. So, the more important the job, the more important the vetting.

Some considerations when checking references:

- Advise the candidate of the requirement to check references.

- Get his/her approval to contact previous employers to verify key factors.

- Remember that most candidates would prefer that you did not contact their current employer, which is understandable and should be honoured.

- In addition to verifying their skills and knowledge, experience, attitude, co-operation and performance are equally important.

- The reference check should be in relation to the key requirements set out in the personnel specification.

There is no requirement for an employer to provide any guarantee to you regarding the accuracy or otherwise of the reference details supplied to you. In fact, there is no onus on an employer to provide a reference at all – so, when a reference is supplied, it is normally done in good faith.

Remember that a referee is giving an opinion based on personal experience with the candidate, which could be positively or negatively biased. You need to get some feel for this during the reference conversation.

Be consistent in your questioning of all referees in relation to each candidate and ensure you record and retain the reference information. Note that copies of any information so obtained and recorded by you may be requested by the candidate (under freedom of information rights).

You may need to be specific in your questioning about important technical or professional abilities or about behavioural issues or trustworthiness, if this is an important job requirement.

Develop a reference check-sheet, which should be adapted to suit the particular job you wish to fill. List the key factors you wish to verify, in addition to the general reference details – for example:

- The HR Manager, Department Manager or other person you wish to contact.

- The candidate's length of service.

- Did the company issue a written reference to the candidate?

- Specific technical abilities.

- The candidate's level of assertiveness, dependability, flexibility, accuracy and performance.

The decision to hire

If it is your job to make the final decision, you should try and make a decision in a reasonable period of time. If you delay too long, the best candidates will have doubts about you and the company and will go elsewhere or, at least, they will become disinterested or concerned about you and/or the company. Planning the recruitment process will assist the decision-making phase.

There are occasions when you may not find a suitable candidate from the applications. This means that you were either unlucky with the applications received or that your planning and organisation was at fault. Before repeating the recruitment process, you need to assess what went wrong and modify your approach to ensure a more successful outcome. It is a systematic step-by-step approach and it should be easy to analyse each step to identify what (if anything) went wrong.

Advise unsuccessful candidates

Following on from your recruitment planning, shortlisting, interviewing, reference checking and final choice, you must also ensure that all the unsuccessful candidates are advised that the position has been filled.

Once the job has been accepted by your chosen candidate, this information may quickly reach 'the grapevine'. It is important, therefore, that the other candidates are advised simultaneously that they have not been successful on this occasion, while thanking them for their interest in the position and in the company. This should be done as soon as possible. Advise candidates that you will keep their details on file, in case a suitable opportunity arises in the future. They are a good source for future reference and, presumably, they will be gaining additional experience in the meantime.

Developing the Remuneration Package

Let's assume at this stage that a suitable candidate has emerged and that you now wish to offer the job to this person. There are a number of considerations and decisions to be made regarding the remuneration package, including:

- The market value of the job.
- The value of the final candidate's current remuneration package.
- The candidate's expectations - are they reasonable?
- Whether the company can meet the candidate's expectations.
- The maximum package possible for the right candidate.
- Precedents already established for this job.
- What to do if the candidate turns the offer down.

Prior to the interview stage, you will have decided on the range within which the position fits in the company's wage or salary grading structure and having regard to local and other benchmark packages for similar occupations.

Additional considerations will arise from the finalist's package and expectations. You will need to find out about the candidate's current basic salary, bonus or commission, the details of their pension scheme and any other payments or benefits. If it is a management or sales representative position you are hiring for, you will know whether they have a fully- or partially-funded company car, the cost and the model. You will also have a good idea as to why the individual wishes to leave their current company – salary may not be the main criteria. Some or all of these factors may have an impact on the package needed to attract the individual to your company.

Develop a fair package, ensuring that you can explain how you arrived at it, and ensure that it does not create a dangerous precedent.

Employment Contracts

An employment contract is a written statement to employees setting out particulars of the employee's terms and conditions of employment. However, even if it is not written, it is implied by the terms and conditions applied, and the individual has a right to request the details in writing, which the employer is obliged to supply.

Under the Terms of Employment (Information) Acts 1994 & 2001, the letter (or contract) offering employment must include these minimum key headings:

- Name of employer.
- Address of employer.
- Place of work.
- Job title and description of the nature of the work.
- Commencement date. If the contract is temporary, the expected duration of employment or, if the contract is for a fixed term, the date on which the contract expires.
- Rate of remuneration, method of calculation, frequency of payment and method of payment.
- Hours of work, including overtime requirements.
- Statutory rest and break periods.
- Paid leave entitlements.
- Information on the terms or conditions relating to incapacity for work due to sickness or injury including, if applicable, payment during such leave – for example, sick pay schemes.
- Pensions.
- Notice periods.
- References to any collective agreements.

Contracts vary from company to company, job to job and by employment contract category – for example, full-time, fixed-term and part-time.

Use company headed paper, which states the registered company name and address and include the name and address of the new employee.

Non-statutory contract terms

In addition to the statutory requirements, many companies include some or all of the following in their contracts of employment. Review these headings and adjust them to suit your company's particular circumstances:

- **Personal Retirement Savings Accounts (PRSAs)**: Include the provider, scheme type, criteria, costs, etc.

- **Health insurance**: Detail any schemes operated by the company, eligibility requirements, costs, benefits, etc.

- **Health and safety:** Explain company and employee responsibilities under the Safety, Health & Welfare at Work Act 2005 and refer to the company's safety statement.

- **Probation**: Outline the duration of, and procedures related to, the probationary period, performance assessments and associated procedures.

- **Restrictive practices:** Outline restrictions on the employee working for other employers during the course of their employment with the company, procedures for receipt of gifts, appropriate security requirements and level of co-operation, competition and confidentiality policies, inducements, conflict of interest definitions, telephone and Internet usage.

- **Inventions and copyright**: Define clearly who has ownership of any soft or hard copy material produced by the employee for the employer during the contract period.

- **Grievance and disciplinary procedures:** Purpose, policy and procedures. Reference may be made to include the company employee handbook.

- **Termination**: Notice periods, reasons for termination of employment, and procedures.

- **HR manual or employee handbook**: Reference to all policies, practices and procedures contained elsewhere other than in the contract, which ideally will be amalgamated into the HR manual or employee handbook.

- **Contract acceptance:** Acceptance statement and provision for signature by the employer and the employee.

JOB ANALYSIS

Job analysis is a technique for designing or redesigning work by identifying all the parts that make up a job, the knowledge required to be able to do the job and the particular skills needed to be able to do the job to given standards of output, safety and quality. The purpose is to ensure that the best and most economic method for doing the job is identified and implemented.

Job analysis defines the relevant information about the job, for example, what must be done, and how, where and in what sequence the elements of the job must be done. As the term suggests, job analysis is about the job content and methods. It is not an analysis of the jobholder.

Applications of Job Analysis

There are different times and reasons for conducting a job analysis. One is when a job is being developed for the first time, at a 'green-field start up', when new equipment is being introduced, or when new methods and procedures are being developed. Alternatively, it could be in an established company, where changes in equipment, methods or practices and procedures are being introduced.

A job analysis is an important precursor to many Human Resource activities – for example:

- **Manpower planning:** It provides information to support manpower planning in the whole company or in individual departments.

- **Job design and evaluation:** A structured approach to understanding the content of a job, and the demands that it places on a jobholder, is imperative for the employer.

- **Job re-design and re-evaluation:** There are occasions when jobs need to be re-examined and be re-developed or made more efficient. This may lead to the amalgamation of different jobs, the eradication of jobs or the expansion of a job in terms of its range of activities and level of responsibility.

- **Recruitment and selection:** Being capable of matching candidates against the key requirements set out in the job and in the personnel specifications for that job is essential. Job analysis helps the interviewers to design appropriate questions that will help obtain the right information to aid the selection of the right person.

- **Training and development of new and existing staff:** Job analysis provides information regarding training needs.
- **Job evaluation:** It provides a logical step to job evaluation for remuneration packages.
- **Performance appraisals:** It provides crucial information to develop targets for performance appraisals.
- **Health and safety:** It highlights safety issues and helps to define safety training needs.

Who should be involved in a job analysis?

Senior managers will be responsible for the application of job analysis generally within their own department or area of expertise. However, there are others who can make useful contributions such as the job holder (if the position is not vacant), line managers, equipment suppliers and anyone else who can supply relevant information about the job or the identification of the skill-sets required.

Industrial engineers are required to carry out detailed analysis of jobs in terms of methods and work measurement to define maximum performance expectations and, if employed within the company, are an excellent source of information.

What aspects of a job are analysed?

Duties, responsibilities and tasks are the main details required on each job. The information required about the specific tasks and duties may include frequency, duration, physical and/or mental effort, skill, complexity, equipment and work standards, responsibility for quality.

Requirements

The objective is to identify the knowledge, skills, and other abilities required to perform the job. While the current jobholder may have higher levels of knowledge and skill than those required for the job, a job analysis typically states the minimum requirements to perform the job.

Jobs evolve; equipment changes and people modify their behaviour. Job analysis should be used to track such changes and modify standards accordingly. It is also used as a deliberate effort to improve productivity by redesigning the job to be more productive and/or effective.

Environment
This may have a significant impact on the physical requirements to be able to perform a job. Consider location, mobility, physical conditions, safety and social aspects of the job.

Tools and equipment
Some duties and tasks are performed using specific equipment and tools. These items need to be specified in a job analysis. For example, equipment complexity, tooling, jigs and fittings, safety considerations, protective clothing and equipment requirements, hazards identification and safety practices to be observed. Each element of the job is reviewed in terms of whether it is necessary and whether it could be done more effectively and/or efficiently.

Relationships
Examine the impact of all those who may come into contact with the jobholder in the course of the work. State the formal and informal relationships and the specific work interactions that bring value to the job – including relationships with management, colleagues, suppliers, quality inspectors, customers, visitors, etc. If there are aspects of such relationships that can have a negative impact, eliminate or reduce them.

What methods are used in conducting a job analysis?

Use a number of different methods of gathering information, if possible. Determine what these are in advance. For example:

- Existing records.
- Statistical summaries.
- Equipment suppliers.
- Jobholders.
- Work diaries.
- Observation / industrial engineering.
- Interviews.
- Questionnaires.
- Specialists.
- Product design engineers.
- Mechanical engineers.
- HR or safety specialists.

Job Analysis before Hiring Employees

Before hiring staff, it is important to ensure that you understand the nature of each job in terms of its content, its importance to the company and its value in terms of remuneration. This applies to all jobs in your company. Having suitably experienced and motivated staff, carrying out their work accurately and productively, is obviously very important. Employees are costly, so getting this right can make a significant difference to the bottom line.

If the company is setting up for the first time, it is essential that the jobs are well-constructed. There are obvious occupational categories that are easily identifiable, such as electricians, fitters, plumbers, plasterers and other craft workers. However, there might be slight variations between different companies in how the work is done, despite the general definition of the craft occupation. This trait might also apply to other occupations.

Using job analysis for new jobs

Prepare a job description (see **Figure 4**) that comprehensively describes all aspects of the job. This must include both regular and occasional activities.

Once you have listed the duties and responsibilities of the job, you need to establish the individual tasks required under each duty or responsibility. This is easier for operational jobs, as observation of a skilled person over several production cycles can easily provide the list of tasks, sequence and quality standards required. It is important that a critical analysis of these observed tasks is carried out from an industrial engineering perspective, to ensure that the most economic way of doing the job is ascertained and ultimately installed. It is difficult to apply this approach to management, supervisory, administrative or other non-repetitive occupations – these jobs have less repetition and there is a requirement for flexibility, so the duties and responsibilities are less rigid. Generally, there is a wider range of decision-making involved in these jobs, with certain intangible elements.

If one has access to experienced persons (even at a different location), it may be useful not only to observe and record how the job is done, but to video a reasonable number of job cycles for both job analysis and training purposes. Obviously, the person to be videoed should be a willing subject and the video should be made professionally and openly. Communication with the person demonstrating the methods, and their manager, is essential. All safety requirements should also be identified and highlighted as part of this process.

Language

The language used to describe a job must be absolutely clear, especially when there are important safety procedures in the job or when the job analysis will be used for training purposes. **Figure 8** shows how duties and responsibilities can be broken down and expanded into individual tasks.

FIGURE 8: JOB ANALYSIS – ASSEMBLY OPERATOR

The main *duties* and *responsibilities* for an engineering assembly job might be described as follows:

Level 1: Assemble main body components.

Level 2: Fit grommet and retaining nut to spindle and ensure it is tight enough to prevent leaks. Use compression test to verify the seal.

The Level 1 description would be adequate for a simple job description (a recruitment application, for example – although for a job advertisement, a simple definition of Assembly Operator would suffice).

In a training application, these broad descriptions would need to be broken down into tasks, for example:

◊ From supply container, using left hand, pick up the body component and place in bench jig.

◊ From the left bench component slide tray, pick up a grommet and place on spindle.

◊ From the right bench component slide tray, using right hand, pick up a retaining nut and fit to spindle.

◊ Acquire overhead compressed air screwdriver, using left or right hand as preferred, fit to retaining nut and drive the nut until screw driver automatically stops.

◊ Using left hand, remove the assembled component by the spindle end from the bench jig.

◊ Swivel seat 90 degrees to the test unit.

◊ While holding the assembled component by the spindle end, fit open ends between test pads.

◊ Depress left foot pedal to close the test pads onto the component.

◊ Depress right foot pedal to activate the compression test.

◊ If air escapes from the retaining nut, tighten the retaining screw further using a ten millimetre spanner, until leak stops.

◊ Depress foot pedals.

◊ Remove the assembled component by the spindle end.

◊ Place component into the finished container right hand side.

◊ Commence next cycle.
◊ If the leak failed to stop after final adjustment with the spanner, discontinue the test.
◊ Depress foot pedals.
◊ Remove the assembled component by the spindle end.
◊ Place component into the reject container tray on the right hand side of the test unit.
◊ Commence next cycle.

From this example, it is immediately clear why it is necessary to be so detailed if we are training new recruits into a new job that has lots of operations, simultaneous hand, eye and foot co-ordination, quality checks, bench tools, electrical, pneumatic, hydraulic or other hand tools.

You should build in any safety considerations into the task definitions. This example demonstrates how to incorporate a safe operating procedure for a particular hazard that could not be removed or guarded. The instruction, for example, to pick up the component by the spindle should be accompanied by a demonstration to show that doing it this particular way keeps the person's hands away from the action of the compression pads during the operation.

In summary, regardless of the job being analysed, there are simple descriptions that will suffice for one application and a complex description for another application. This is why it is essential to commence with the definition of the application. It will guide you to produce the appropriate job description in relation to the selected application.

Job Analysis Results

New jobs are designed, created and implemented. The objective is to design a job for a specific need. The job, to be legitimate, must be an absolute necessity in its own right or to service or satisfy another operation. either on a full-time or part-time basis.

Existing jobs can be:

• **Re-aligned with the original job definition**: This is where a job has drifted in its range of tasks to embrace other duties or responsibilities that the manager or other job specialist believes are unnecessary. The incumbents are required to revert to the original description and tasks that they were trained to do. Retraining might be necessary and communication, as always, is essential to elicit full co-operation.

- **Changed to a new definition:** Where the incumbents have developed the job operation to a more satisfactory performance standard, or where the employer requires the job to be done differently, because of developments in other areas such as quality standards, customer demands, etc. The job description is rewritten, the incumbents are retrained and, if necessary, the job is repositioned on the pay scale.

- **Made redundant:** If the job is no longer required, because it is to be done differently – for example, if a machine is to be used in place of a person or if the job is to be outsourced on contract with another employer, then the job is legitimately redundant. The person doing the job may be reallocated to other work or, where this is not available, the person might be made redundant. This requires certain procedures under redundancy legislation (see **Chapter 4**), in addition to established precedents through internal company custom and practice.

- **Amalgamated with other jobs:** Occasionally more than one job is discovered to have decreased in activity to the extent that it does not require full-time operation. These jobs may be operated on a part-time basis or amalgamated to make up one full-time occupation.

- **Improved, as training needs are identified:** Sometimes, when jobs are examined because the performance is not what it should be, the problem may lie with the incumbents. The jobholder may require retraining, until the standards are achieved on a regular basis.

- **Outsourced to other manufacturers or suppliers:** For economic or other reasons, a company may decide to outsource aspects of its work to other companies or subsidiary companies. In a manufacturing organisation, the employer may have the suppliers of components perform some additional work on the parts to produce sub-assembly of multiple parts. This might have the effect of making some jobs redundant, with the result that employees might be reallocated to other work or made redundant.

JOB EVALUATION

Job evaluation is a method of measuring the range of demands that a job makes on an individual. It is a logical process to determine job elements and their associated value.

Once a job, or range of jobs, has been clearly defined in terms of a job description, personnel specification (identifying the minimum requirements for a person to be able to do a job) or in a more detailed job analysis exercise, a systematic evaluation can be undertaken to differentiate the value of the jobs and how they fit within the company's pay scales. This can be done for wage or salaried positions. The process can also be used to set up pay scales in a new company start-up.

Using job evaluation helps management to ensure that different pay rates are directly related to the demands of the jobs, rather than any other historic, traditional or *ad hoc* criteria. Job evaluation is a logical and rational process and helps to avoid bias.

The criteria used for the evaluation carries weightings and point values for different aspects of work. This allows each job to be defined in terms of a numerical value, based on its content. The evaluation should be a fair and equitable process of determining job values in your company. It is always the job that is evaluated and not the current incumbent's specific qualifications or experience.

If all jobs in a company, or in a subsidiary of the same company, are subjected to the same evaluation process, the relative values can be established and integrated into pay scales based on the numerical differentials. This approach helps to ensure fair and equitable distribution of rates of pay. It also makes it easier to explain the differences and also to defend the rates, using the evaluation records, if necessary.

As stated in the job analysis section, jobs do evolve and can increase or decrease in value, as the duties and responsibilities change. It is important for companies to monitor and be aware of such drifts. Jobs can be brought back into line, or alternatively, the jobs can be made redundant or re-qualified and re-evaluated to see whether the drift warrants a shift in grade and pay. Some measurement system is certainly a lot better and easier to defend than a 'rule of thumb' positioning of pay rates.

The company is always responsible for setting its own pay scales. The job evaluation system is just a tool to help ensure a logical approach, which is consistent and fair.

Job Evaluation System

There are different job evaluation systems available and most will suffice, as the criteria involved, when applied to all the jobs, will be uniform. It is important that there are sufficient headings, and options within each heading, to allow the evaluators to have a reasonable choice, with minimum ambiguity, to aid decision-making.

The brief explanation below demonstrates how you can design your own evaluation system. It will require some careful reflection and many managers do not have the time or expertise to design such systems, so buying one off-the-shelf is usually a more practical option. You may find it more cost-effective to buy a generic system and modify it to suit your company's circumstances. Alternatively, use a HR consultant with job evaluation experience.

Participants

Ideally, the evaluators should be drawn from management, although some companies have policies that allow an employee representative to participate in the process, to further guarantee fair application of the system. An uneven number should be involved in the evaluation team to avoid a deadlock.

Key Evaluation Factors

There are four main elements to consider, each of which can be sub-divided further:

- Knowledge, skill and experience.
- Responsibility for equipment, materials, production, safety and the work of others.
- The environment and conditions.
- Physical, mental and/or visual demands, including exposure to unavoidable risk.

Figure 9 shows typical points values for the elements. These can be adjusted to reflect the key aspects of the work for any company. The logic behind the allocation of points is important and should be recorded in the evaluation handbook used by all evaluators.

FIGURE 9: JOB EVALUATION ELEMENTS

Element	Maximum Points
Formal education	40
Experience	100
Job complexity (machine) (see Note A1)	60
Job complexity (non-machine) (see Note A2)	60 - 108
Responsibility for actions and judgement	40
Physical demands of the job	50
Concentration and attention	30
Responsibility for fixed assets	20
Responsibility for materials and work in progress	25
Responsibility for continuity of workflow	50
Responsibility for supervision of staff (see Note B)	115 - 190
Responsibility for safety of others	25
Environment or working conditions	20
Unavoidable hazards of the job	40

Note A1

Job complexity should have two separate evaluation sheets:
1. Normal complexity of the job for machine-based jobs.
2. Normal complexity of the job for non-machine-based jobs.

Select the most appropriate for each job – whichever aspect takes up most of the incumbent's time.

Note A2

The second element, normal complexity for non machine operations, also has scope for further degrees (9 or 10) and an appropriate points spread. Over 60 points refers to jobs with any supervisory duties and responsibilities.

Note B

Element 11, responsibility for the work of others, is specifically for supervisory roles. This could have up to 10 degrees.

Note C

Each element must have several levels. For example, if 40 points is the maximum allowed for Education, there must be five (or more, if appropriate) levels of definition for this element, from which the evaluators can assess the value for a particular job.

Example

Only requires the ability to read and write	5 points
Primary education (read, write, add, subtract)	10 points
Secondary education	20 points
Vocational or technical qualification	30 points
University degree	40 points

Each of the elements described above will have such definitions and levels. The more information concerning the logic behind the definitions the better as it will assist the evaluators to focus in on the critical requirements for the job.

Benchmarking

It is important to use some clear and understandable benchmark positions for the pay scales, which correlate to a job evaluation process. For example, for a range of jobs, a company might have a mixture of craft/skilled, unskilled, supervisory, technical employees such as charge-hands, supervisors, fitters, electricians, welders, finishers, machine operators, assembly personnel, technicians, etc.

The rate for craft workers may be defined either by a trade union agreement or by local rates based on market value. So, how does that affect pay scales based on the job evaluation process?

The system should be able to define clearly the difference between the occupations involved. The market value will be known in some cases and this will help to determine certain rates on the scale. Some other occupations may also have an external comparator that provides useful information. These figures need to be married to the internal pay scale to see the relativities. These, in turn, should line up with the other jobs and the actual points spread.

As an example, suppose there are five distinct grades of staff in the company:

- Assembly operators.
- Machine operators.
- Production supervisors.
- Craft workers.
- Craft supervisors.

Suppose further that there are only these five grades. The craft rate is relatively predictable, because there is a consistency in the knowledge and skill-sets required and external pay rates are available, both nationally and locally for craft occupations. It is not necessary to evaluate the jobs to determine the required rate, it will be determined by the market. Nonetheless, it is necessary still to evaluate all the jobs, since the value relativity should be of interest to the company and the information will help to establish fair and equitable rates for other jobs that are not as easily determined by external market value.

Next, craft supervisors generally come from a craft background and, clearly, it is necessary to pay in excess of the basic craft rate for the additional duties and responsibilities of a supervisor, especially if the company wants to attract a high calibre person. So that rate will also be reasonably easy to identify – for example, a fixed percentage higher than the craft rate and related to the production supervisor rate in some way. The job evaluation process will help to determine what that relationship should be. This process will apply also to the production supervisor positions.

Some jobs come with 'ready-made' rates and others do not. But there is still a need to understand the relationship between the jobs that come with market rates and the rest of the jobs in the company. When the points values are scored, these can be applied in a logical way to reflect these differences. There will then be a logical balance that you can be reasonably confident is fair and equitable and even explainable, if the need arises.

The initial logic for putting actual pay rates against the occupations, and using the job evaluation points spread to determine the percentage shifts for jobs that are not related to external comparisons, is shown in **Figure 10**.

FIGURE 10: BENCHMARKING

Job Category	Comparators?	Rates
Assembly Operators	Possibly	X - % of Machine Operators
Machine Operators	Possibly	X - % of Craft
Production Supervisors	Possible local rate X + fixed %	Linked to Craft Supervisors
Craft	Local / union rate	X
Craft Supervisors	Local rate	X + fixed %

Every company will have its own benchmark jobs that help to determine the other job values. The job evaluation system will help to establish what the differences should be between all other jobs.

Summary

Many companies do not use job evaluation. You may even consider it unnecessary at the moment for your company. So, when is the right time to use it – if at all?

If there is dissatisfaction among your employees over pay rates, or between one group of employees and another, it will have demotivating impact on performance. The answer is not always to throw more money at the issue, in the hope that it will go away – it generally does not work that way. The best way to make any decision is to have as much information as possible about the differentials at your disposal, to allow you to make an informed decision. Job evaluation will provide that information. It may save you money in the end.

You may not wish to develop your own evaluation system. Shop around, there are plenty of systems to choose from. Pick one that requires little maintenance from external sources and that you find easy to understand and use. Get help, if in doubt. Staff are costly and decisions can have long-lasting implications. Getting pay rates right can save money and make staff easier to manage.

INDUCTION

The next logical phase after the recruitment and selection process is to integrate the new employees into the company. Induction simply means providing new employees with all the relevant information that they will need to begin work in the company and to integrate into the cultural norms.

The initial interaction, following such basics as where to put one's belongings and where the toilets are located, should ensure that the person understands their duties, responsibilities and practices regarding any personal interactions within the company or with clients and suppliers.

There are basic social interactions, as well as the actual training and performance of the work. This induction phase, to be successful, must be achieved in a logical sequence and within a reasonable time-frame. The value of a formal induction cannot be over-emphasised. If properly executed, it is motivating and displays the company's professionalism to the new starter. It also means that management are adjusting the individual's comfort level and integration formally, rather than allowing this to occur informally and less effectively.

The new employee's immediate manager should be responsible for the induction training programme and for presenting any additional information.

Sometimes, there are a number of new employees commencing at the same time and, as most of the information will probably be the same, one person can be designated to present the induction programme for all. Alternatively, several different people may be responsible for presenting various aspects of an induction training programme under different headings. If so, the most experienced person may be the best person to develop and present an aspect of the induction training programme, such as a safety officer or quality manager.

The induction training programme content and duration, including any breaks, should be planned in advance and should be in writing.

Considerations for induction:
- The size of your company.
- The number of employees.
- The complexity of the work.

- Safety implications – the level of risk and hazards associated with the work and the environment from a safety, health and welfare at work perspective.
- The nature and complexity of the products or services.
- The qualifications and experience of each new employee and how this might alter the induction content.
- The availability of the designated manager responsible for development and delivery of the induction training programme at a departmental level.

Typical areas covered in induction programmes include:
- Accepting P45s from new employees and passing these on to whoever is responsible for payroll.
- Clocking-in/out procedures, if applicable.
- Where to keep personal belongings such as coats, handbags, etc.
- Where the toilets are located.
- Break times and facilities for obtaining/consuming food on the premises.
- Car parking.
- Security arrangements.
- Introductions to immediate work colleagues and other directors/ managers.
- Introductions to suppliers, clients or other people relevant to the new employee's work.
- Company products or services.
- The company's ethos, goals, key objectives, charter, values, etc.
- The company's safety statement, including safety policy and work-related safety procedures.
- The company's HR manual or employee handbook.

In addition:
- Ensure that the employee is aware that they have become a valued member of the company's team.
- Provide time for the new employee(s) to read any induction material presented and to ask questions. Any questions or concerns expressed by a new employee during the induction training programme must be resolved before he/she starts work.

- Identify and appoint a mentor or coach from within the individual's immediate group of colleagues to assist the new employee in integrating as quickly and as pleasantly as possible.

- Explain the probationary period assessment approach and assure the employees that it will be participative and developmental, rather than a policing function.

These examples are not comprehensive and should be reviewed, added to or deleted, to suit company requirements.

Leaving employees to discover such important information for themselves places the company at risk, particularly with regard to safety matters.

Asking the new employee's work colleagues to look after this management function on an informal, or even formal, basis is not professional, does nothing to cement the employer/employee relationship and generally results in the employee picking up the wrong message or bad habits from 'old hands'.

If you consider the importance and the costs of recruitment, systematically managing the employee into the company will make good sense. It will create a better impression of the company, as well as demonstrating that the company, its directors and staff behave in a professional manner.

Induction programmes should be reviewed regularly, and updated as required.

PROBATION

Hiring a new employee is generally based on a number of different assessments, judgements and decision-making processes. For example, you will have reviewed the person's history contained in their CV or as detailed in your company job application form. You will have interviewed the person, perhaps several times, and even had a second or third opinion. In addition, you may have carried out one or more reference checks and you might have gone a step further and had an independent psychometric test to ensure that the person's work behaviour characteristics were in line with those demanded by the job requirements.

These elements of the recruiting process are all valid and useful ways of trying to ensure that you hire good employees, who will achieve the necessary results and blend in with the company ethos and with other employees. However, none of these techniques can guarantee that the person will actually be successful.

Therefore, a trial period to review actual performance *vis-à-vis* the job requirements is essential. Depending on the job complexity, a probationary period, varying between one and six months, is essential. The person's employment may be terminated at any time during this period, if they are deemed unsuitable.

It is essential that you define the terms of the probationary period in the new employee's contract of employment (you may have mentioned it at interview) and that you carry out several regular probationary period assessments for the new employee within this defined probationary period.

The new employee should be fully aware of what is required of him/her and that these requirements will be rated against actual performance over a number of assessments. The probationary period assessments should be formal, well-planned and regular and should measure the key performance requirements of the job, as well as the more regular work and environment requirements.

Sometimes, employees are hired to do a specific job, but get sidetracked into other work, because the employer's circumstances change or because they have other abilities that are called on. Although it is reasonable to require employees to be flexible to suit business changes, if the employer measures an employee against stated targets, without regard to such other work or changes in duties and responsibilities, the employee may not receive a fair probationary assessment. So, fairness and consistency are important. Being flexible must be a two-way process.

It is essential for the manager who carries out the assessment to share the results of the probationary period assessment with the new employee. This participation allows the new employee to understand, and to explain, any shortfall in performance. It is important to listen to such views and to give consideration to the person's position. The manager may modify his/her view, having considered the employee's input and may make changes that support the new employee more effectively to achieve an acceptable performance level, which should, in any case, be the core objective of the exercise.

Figure 11 shows a template probationary period assessment form, which you can review and modify to suit your particular company requirements.

The manager directly responsible for the performance of the new employee should complete this form. Any course of action to train, or retrain, or provide other support, or make changes to the employee's duties or responsibilities, should be recorded on the form for future reference. Specific performance improvement requirements and the next review date should also be recorded on the form. All this information should be explained and confirmed in writing to the employee concerned.

The manager and the employee should sign the form once completed, confirming that the contents have been discussed, a plan agreed and a new review date set.

Typical headings for a probationary period assessment form include:

- Job knowledge.
- Key skills.
- Quality of work.
- Quantity of work.
- Co-operation.
- Punctuality and attendance.
- Initiative.
- Internal relationships.
- General behaviour.

In addition to the basic headings, you should list the most important skills, competencies and objectives that the new employee must achieve to be successful in the job. All of these factors can be given point values in relation to their importance to the job and can then be rated against the maximum score.

FIGURE 11: PROBATIONARY PERIOD ASSESSMENT FORM

Name of Employee: _____ Job Title: _____

Commencement Date: _____ Assessment No: _____

Assessment Date: _____ Assessed by: _____

Circle your chosen selection and multiply your scores in the three key factors by 2.

	Pts	10	8	6	4	2
		How well does this employee understand the job requirements?				
Job Knowledge		Thoroughly understands all aspects of the job	More than adequate knowledge of the job	Has sufficient knowledge of some aspects of the job	Insufficient knowledge of some aspects of the job	Continually in need of instruction
		Is the employee's work accurate, satisfactory and consistent?				
Quality of Work		Consistently accurate and compliant	Careful person, seldom requires correction	Average acceptable work standard	Occasionally careless, needs checking & correction	Regularly inaccurate & careless, must be monitored
		Does the employee produce good quality product or services consistently?				
Quantity of Work		Maintains consistently high above-average output	Usually does more than expected	Average work rate performance	Slightly below average, needs prompting & supervision	Needs to be told what to do constantly and needs constant supervision
		How dependable is the employee in reporting and staying on the job?				
Depend-ability		Consistently reliable, dependable person, anxious to get job done	Generally reliable, can be depended on to get the job done	Average level of dependability, occasionally late or absent	Below average, sometimes late, sometimes makes errors of judgement	Unreliable, fails to do what is required, attendance poor
		Does the employee work without direction, contribute ideas & innovations?				
Initiative		Self-starter, very innovative, always looking for ways to contribute	Proceeds with little direction and makes regular useful suggestions	Does regular work without prompting, occasional suggestions	Relies on others, rarely makes any suggestions	Must be told exactly what to do, dislikes making decisions, needs direction

	Pts	10	8	6	4	2
Respons-ibility		**Does the employee accept and adequately attend to job responsibilities?**				
		Accepts all responsibility & responds well to emergency situations	Conscientiously tries to fulfil the responsibilities of the job	Accepts the basic responsibilities of the job	Does work reluctantly, has to be monitored	Indifferent attitude, shifts responsibility to others, dodges work
Co-operation		**Does the employee respond well to others needing support or assistance?**				
		Exceptionally willing and helpful, good team player	Frequently offers to help out when necessary	Gets on reasonably well with staff, occasionally lends a hand	Co-operation must always be sought, is never volunteered	Rejects all requests for help or support, most unco-operative, sometimes nasty
TOTAL POINTS						

Recorded Comments
Employee's Comments

_____
_____
_____

Employer's Comments

_____
_____
_____

Additional Information

_____
_____

Recommendations

_____
_____

Next Assessment Date: _____

Employee's Signature: _____ Date: _____
Employer's Signature: _____ Date: _____

Instructions

Purpose of this form

To identify any performance weaknesses and to take actions to assist the employee to achieve the necessary standard of performance within the probationary period. Alternatively, if the employee fails to reach the desired performance level, after receiving management support, and their employment is subsequently terminated before the probationary period is completed, the probationary reports are a professional record of the process and decision-making factors.

Who assesses the employee?

The employee's immediate supervisor or manager, or a director or owner of the company, as appropriate. This designated or agreed person should complete all the assessments throughout the probationary period for consistency.

How often should assessments be carried out?

Ideally, the employee should be assessed on a monthly basis, starting four weeks after their commencement date. However, assessments can also be carried out weekly, if necessary. Where there is a high level of complexity, or where the impact of poor performance could be either dangerous or could severely damage the company's credibility, more regular assessments and retraining might be essential. Consistency of application is good for the employee and employer alike and ensures fair process.

How do I use this form?

◊ The designated assessor should initially determine the key factors for success in the job. Use the job description as the basis to decide on the key responsibilities.

◊ This form is a generic template. Therefore, if physical output is a key factor, quantity of work would be the appropriate heading under which to assess the individual's performance. Each key job requirement should be looked at in this way.

◊ The form allows you to weight the three most important factors for each job. This quickly helps you to focus on the person's relevant performance factors *vis-à-vis* the key job requirements. For example, you may decide for a particular job that responsibility, initiative and dependability are the three most important factors. You score the individual as usual and whatever score appears under these three key criteria are multiplied by a factor of 2.

◊ If you score an employee as being particularly successful on all counts, this amounts to 100 points (10 for each of the 7 factors plus the double score for each of the three key factors: $(10 \times 7) + (10 \times 3) = 70 + 30 = 100$). Therefore, applying this principle for all assessments, the scores are out of a potential of 100 points.

◊ The assessor must share the results with the employee, listen and record the employee's views and then independently consider whether the employee's comments in any way alter the assessment. The results of this review should also be shared.

◊ The decisions of the assessor and the employee's comments must be recorded following this assessment in the space provided, as well as any additional observations. Such comments can be very relevant later, if there are any differences in views.

You may wish to define a minimum score, below which an employee is deemed unsatisfactory and unlikely to be able to make the necessary improvements during the balance of the probationary period. The person may be terminated during the probationary period, if they fail to achieve this basic performance standard.

Alternatively, if the person is above the minimum, but below the acceptable level for confirmation of full-time employment, you must explain the shortfall in performance to the employee and agree on what the employee must do to improve the performance to an acceptable level. It may also be necessary to define what the employer must do to assist the person to achieve the required performance standards. This could include training or re-training, clearer job definition or a review of what the individual is actually doing as distinct from what the job description states they should be doing.

A little effort at this point may make all the difference to raising the employee's understanding of the job and its key performance requirements. This may be all that is needed for you to be happy with the person's performance. With a little careful management, the next probationary review might then be satisfactory.

It is important that any problems or shortfalls in performance are identified during the probationary period, rather than later. Retaining an employee after the probationary period, without such critical performance analysis, could result in a range of problems at a later stage, if the need to dismiss the employee arises.

On occasions, you may wish to extend a person's probationary period to give you an opportunity for further review. Extending the probationary period is useful when the employee is performing reasonably well on most of the key factors but is still below an overall acceptable performance standard.

Additionally, if a new employee had an accident and was legitimately absent on sick leave, it would be unreasonable to rate them before they had an opportunity to prove themselves. Extending the probationary period by the same length of time as their sick leave demonstrates the company's positive employee relations policy and will be seen to be fair and equitable. While there are many reasons for extending the probationary review period, the general rule is to be fair and reasonable. If in doubt, extend the probationary period, quantify the shortfall, agree on another review date and record the details.

At the end of the probationary period, the manager will complete a final probationary period assessment. If he/she is satisfied that the new employee is operating to an acceptable level of performance and behaviour standards, he/she must sign the form confirming acceptance and then advise the appropriate company officer to confirm the successful completion of the probation period and thus the full-time employment status of the employee.

It is important that the probationary period does not reach, or extend beyond, 11 months, as employees with 12 months' service may claim unfair dismissal against an employer under the Unfair Dismissal Acts 1977-2001, if subsequently dismissed. Employees may also claim unfair dismissal for an employment period of less than 12 months under the Industrial Relations Acts 1946-2004.

Clearly-defined probationary periods, where careful and recorded assessments have been carried out, normally will contribute significantly to validating the company's professional processing of the employee and will protect the company against unfair dismissal claims.

HUMAN RESOURCE MANUAL / EMPLOYEE HANDBOOK

This document is a summary of all policies, practices and procedures in operation in the company with regard to people. It may have different titles – for example, it may be referred to as the company handbook, procedures manual, employee handbook or Human Resource manual. In some unionised companies, many of the practices and procedures are enshrined in the company/union agreement. However, these agreements generally do not include all the company's policies and procedures affecting all staff, so it is sensible to have a company handbook summarising such policies and procedures.

This section looks at the typical contents of a company HR manual (or whatever other title seems most appropriate for you) and provides a brief explanation of what the headings should refer to. These are examples and may not suit the requirements of every company, so it is important for managers to delete or add suitable subject matter to meet their organisation's specific needs.

The HR manual should be seen by managers as a support tool, which is a valuable aspect of POCM, and which brings clarity and consistency to how people are managed in a range of circumstances.

People need to know, and have a right to know, the rules and regulations, processes and entitlements that affect them at work. Not knowing these important facts can cause fear for some employees, which is de-motivational. Although having an HR manual in place is not a direct contributor to the motivation of staff, its absence can be demotivational.

It is important to refer to the HR manual in any letter of appointment or contract of employment. In doing so, confirm that the employee is subject to the terms and conditions outlined in the letter or contract **and** the HR manual, including any updates and modifications in the manual that occur from time to time. However, it is important that such changes are flagged to all employees and, in some cases, it may be essential for them to be involved in the development process, depending on the impact of the changes or additions on their terms and conditions.

Typical Contents

Introduction

Explain briefly the company's view on why the HR manual is important and how it contributes to the company's overall people-related policies.

New employees like to understand the type of company they have joined, how it has evolved and where it is going. They generally like to share this information with family and friends, to demonstrate that they have made a good choice in joining a developing and professionally-run company.

The Introduction should give an overview of the HR policies and procedures to which employees are subject. All employees should be encouraged to address any queries to their immediate manager or supervisor, and the HR manual should express the company's desire that an employee receive a timely and satisfactory response to such queries.

Company charter

This is the main policy statement, which should be crafted by the Board of Directors or the Chief Executive, setting out the mission statement, vision, ideals, principles and standard of behaviours with regard to how the company's directors and managers relate professionally to their staff and clients. It provides clear definitions, objectives and the key principles that address standards of respect, dignity, honesty, communications, responsibility, integrity and leadership. These are basic requirements and senior company officials must define these in plain, simple and understandable language.

Only principles that can be clearly maintained and honoured should be stated. It is more damaging to state principles that senior executives constantly bend and break, than to omit them. Such procedures or principles will have no meaning or value, will not be respected and will contribute nothing to the company. Managers' abuse of the principles will change an employee's perspective and trust in company management.

Ideally, the charter should be positive, motivational and inspiring, but also practical and honest. It does not have to be long: a page or half-page of something meaningful is better than several pages of unattainable drivel.

Operational policies and procedures

The real working end of the HR manual begins here. Try and make the sequence logical – for example, start at recruitment. Typical subjects include:

- **Recruitment and selection process:** This should cover job descriptions and personnel specifications, vacancies and advertising, selection and assessment of candidates, the interview process, offers of employment, advising unsuccessful candidates, induction training and the probationary period.

- **Remuneration and benefits:** Detail methods of payment, overtime and shift work rates, pension schemes (including Personal Retirement Savings Accounts – PRSAs) bonus schemes, health insurance, company car, travel expenses, etc.

- **Training and development:** How the company investigates training needs, internal and external training, study and examination leave, financial support, personal development opportunities and promotions.

- **Performance:** Appraisals, timing or frequency, documentation and appeals.

- **Hours of work:** Normal hours of work, breaks and rest periods, breastfeeding breaks, safety and legal restrictions, night work, shift work, attendance, punctuality and records.

- **Employee leave:** Annual leave for full-time, part-time and temporary staff, leave allocation procedures, public holidays, absence reporting, sick pay scheme (if in operation), long-term absence, return to work, leave entitlements and procedures for maternity, adoptive, carer's, parental, *force majeure* leave and jury service, compassionate leave policy and any other special leave, if relevant.

- **Resignation/termination:** Minimum notice, lay-off and short-time working, dismissals, redundancy and retirement.

- **Security:** Access rights, right to search staff and personal property, use of surveillance equipment, dealing with theft and lost property.

- **Employee relations:** Commitment to employees, communications systems, managing equality and diversity, dealing with personal problems and records.

- **Behaviour at work:** Key standards of behaviour, confidentiality, honesty, personal conduct, personal hygiene, personal appearance, uniforms, confidentiality, use of staff restaurant/canteen, phones, mobile phones, email and Internet, customer care policy, dealing with complaints and maintaining quality standards.

- **Problem resolution:** Grievance and disciplinary procedures.

- **Health, safety and welfare:** Health and safety policy, reference to safety statement and where it can be accessed, anti-bullying, anti-harassment and anti-sexual harassment policies and procedures.

PERSONNEL RECORDS

Introduction

As a starting point, it is necessary to have an individual file for each and every employee (including managers and supervisors). While employee records are moving towards electronic files, it is still important to have physical records of all the actual hard copy items and exchanges with the employee. It may be important to have these documents available in the event of a claim by an employee against the company. The file may be the key to proving or disproving a critical aspect of a case. These generally contain signatures of confirmation of acceptance by the employer and employee of any stated terms and conditions.

An employee's file might include:

- Letter of application and/or CV, other letters and contracts, safety and work-related training, holidays, working hours, etc.

- Performance-related information, including a record of what the person is good at and where they need to improve, what were the agreed targets, the timescale for review and the subsequent results.

- Personal matters, which could include medical support requirements.

- Grievance and disciplinary matters.

- Attendance information, including medical certificates related to absences.

- Accident investigation reports, doctors and specialists reports. Safety representative reports, photographs and other forms of evidence including witnesses' statements.

Responsibility for Employee Records

Responsibility for employee records should lie with a senior person in the company, usually the person who has responsibility for HR issues.

Generally, in larger companies with a HR department, the HR Manager is responsible for the maintenance and security of such records. The files are maintained by the HR Manager and his/her assistant or secretary and nobody else should have access to these files, with the exception of the chief executive. So, in a company that has no HR Manager, the chief executive appears to be the most logical person to monitor and manage these records.

Storing Employee Records

The hard copy material should be under lock and key in the office of a senior executive, or their assistant or secretary, and the soft copy material should be stored on the computer of such senior staff with good password control procedures. It is advisable to maintain regular backups of any relevant soft copy material. These backups should be stored at a different, but confidential and secure, location, in case of an accident, such as a fire.

Procedures

Employees should be aware of company procedures regarding the type of records maintained, the method of storing the records and the security and confidentiality of these arrangements.

Managers, supervisors or others responsible for employees should also be aware of their responsibility with regard to completing forms, maintaining copies for the HR files and handing these over within clear timeframes to the person in charge of the records, to ensure there is no loss or damage to the documents. Such procedures should be in writing and form an integral part of managers' or supervisors' responsibilities and training.

Employees may wish to have copies of their file material from time to time, or in the event of a discovery requirement associated with a claim. Therefore, the files should be maintained properly – ideally, in chronological sequence for easier reading. Sometimes, documents are just deposited in an envelope file and, in the event of an issue arising that requires file research, time is wasted as everything has to be placed in date order first. Filing as the documents become available will save time and there is less chance of the documents accidentally falling out when the files are being moved. It may sound obvious and simple but it does make a significant difference on that one occasion when it really matters that the files are up-to-date and accurate.

COMMUNICATIONS

Introduction

Communications is probably one of the most important aspects of motivation, which in turn is one of the most important aspects of people management. Motivation is multifaceted and communications is at the core of any successful motivational policy.

Many companies pride themselves on the standard of, and commitment to, their communications policy and procedures. Other companies believe in telling the staff as little as possible. Some senior managers have been known to state, 'The less they know, the better', or 'I would only open a can of worms if I let them know what was really going on'. You have probably heard many similar comments including the 'mushroom management philosophy' (keep them in the dark and give them as much fertiliser as possible!).

In essence, regular communications on matters that could impact either positively or negatively on the company and its employees helps strengthen the employer/employee relationship. Employees have wide-ranging responsibilities and financial commitments and cannot afford surprises that could damage their income and affect their financial and family commitments.

There are many ways to consider this topic of communications. It is always a good idea to start with yourself. For example, ask yourself, if I was on the receiving end, would I be interested in knowing:

- What the prospects were for my future employment status?
- About any expansion plans, so that I could consider promotion opportunities?
- Whether there was the possibility of redundancies due to new competition in the market place, so that I could begin to seek alternative employment?

The list is endless, but if you answered 'Yes', to any of these, it is reasonable to assume that your employees would have similar feelings and concerns about the key aspects of their employment and how it could affect their future.

Policy

Communications requires a policy statement, supported by clear practices and procedures. These should outline the purpose and principles and also the regular practices and procedures for managers to follow uniformly throughout the company.

Start by looking at the existing communication style. Ask, how do we communicate at the moment? Consider the following:

- Who in the company is currently the main communicator?
- What are our informal and formal communications practices?
- How structured is our approach to communications?
- Do we consider the implications of our communications?
- Do we have several managers in the company communicating with staff?
- Do we have several managers contradicting one another in their communications statements? Is there inconsistency in how we communicate?
- Do our managers collectively agree on what is to be communicated and how it is to be communicated?
- Do we have any examples of where our communications practices were beneficial or where they could have been beneficial, if we had communicated?
- Do we know how our employees feel about our communications style and how they would rate managers' communications abilities?
- Do we need to train someone in communications to run the communications process?

Key ingredients of good communication

- Ensure all employees are regularly informed about changes and general issues in a consistent way, with as much advance notice as possible.
- Contentious changes affecting employees should not be applied by *diktat*, without a communications session at which comments are listened to and genuinely given management consideration.
- Ensure communications are a genuine two-way process. Listening is as important as providing information.
- Getting the departments or teams together on major issues or regular monthly briefings is effective. The team players are familiar with each other and participation should be high. The manager must be aware of the need for the two-way process and not dominate the dialogue.
- The regular and structured communication should apply regardless of whether the employees are members of a trade union.

Planning communications sessions and topics

Each company must decide on what practice best suits its circumstances. The following approach is just one example:

- Key issues are aired at management meetings and key communications issues are identified.

- A particular manager may be designated to develop the communications presentation package on the subject matter.

- This is copied and presented to each manager for departmental dissemination presentations.

- This process is geared to ensure consistency in the presentation of the key information.

- Interaction and two-way dialogue is encouraged and, generally, a second manager supports the presenting manager in note-taking for further consideration of the employees' views.

Other Communications Techniques

In addition to the communications sessions mentioned above, other methods should operate in tandem to maximise the process and principles. The following are examples of other communications methods – some of these are only practiced in larger companies with diverse staffing, complex communications challenges and, generally, significant time and resource budgets. However, all managers should consider these methods and consider how they might be adapted to their own situation. The methods include:

- Monthly newsletters.

- Intranet forums.

- Noticeboards.

- Working/breakfast meetings.

- Working/communications lunch breaks.

- The open door policy.

- Quarterly communications sessions, with the chief executive in attendance and ready to engage in question-and-answer session.

- Feedback and redesign of communications practice to ensure interest and relevance.

- Feedback method related to questions raised.

Management Responsibility

Not all managers have the same communications abilities, so serious consideration should be given to providing an in-house training programme in communications skills for all managers. It is useful for the managers to address the issues together, if they are to apply the same policies. The interaction can be productive and helps to develop a consistent approach from the group. The stronger communicators will come to the fore and the weaker communicators can access them for advice as needed – and should be encouraged to do so.

Managers are required to engage with employees on regular operational, performance and training issues in the usual way on a daily basis, requiring interpersonal communications skills at a micro level. Although such skills are equally important, this section is focused primarily on the broader issues that require special presentation, feedback and discussion at a company-wide or departmental level.

Summary

There is a relationship between communications, motivation, honesty, trust and, on the other hand, commitment, flexibility, loyalty and performance. Getting them all right, all of the time, is a little like winning the lottery. However, as managers, this is exactly what is expected of us. We need to get these things right, as often as possible. This requires management application, an understanding of the value of getting it right and a commitment to the policies, practices and procedures we design and implement to make it so.

Building a high-trust relationship between employees and managers creates an environment with more potential to be successful. It will have greater levels of co-operation, will be more dependable in times of crisis, will have little or no industrial relations disputes or need for third party intervention. In essence, such companies perform more effectively than those with a low trust environment.

REMUNERATION

Introduction

Compensations and benefits, remuneration packages and other similar terms all amount to the same thing in terms of the basic objective – that is, to reward people for their work in a way that motivates them to join the company, to perform productively, at a cost that the company's business can support.

How we manage this depends on a variety of considerations, such as company and national culture, job types and complexity, skill-set availability, fair comparison with the companies we compete with for labour, and equitable internal relativities. Each company has its own unique needs and challenges in developing and maintaining an effective remuneration process.

Establishing Pay Rates

The company must have a good understanding of the internal and external relativities between jobs. A job evaluation system (see earlier) will help in defining the internal relativities between each occupation in terms of value.

The internal relativities must also be considered in the light of external considerations, to ensure that remuneration is appropriate, relative to the local labour catchment area. For example, if a craftsperson is positioned on a grade that, based on the evaluation system, pays less than the local market rate, it will be next to impossible to recruit a suitable candidates to fill vacancies. On the other hand, it is not appropriate to have some categories outside the grading structure, as this will not be perceived as fair.

To overcome this situation, employers generally carry out a local survey to discover the average established rate for key jobs, often jobs at strategic points on a scale – for example, the job at the lowest value and the job at the highest value, if similar jobs are available for comparison in the local labour area. This benchmarking approach then can be used to set the main rates for the internal jobs and, from this, to extrapolate logical and fair differentials for the other points and jobs on the grading scale.

This logical and fair approach, in itself, may not be sufficient to attract and hold the interest of suitable candidates. Employers need to consider alternative approaches to compensation, such as benefits and performance-related payments and bonuses. The right combination to suit the company's financial and cultural status should be carefully identified and applied. Such options are considered later in this section.

Wages & Salaries

Payment in return for work or services, made to employees carrying out manual work on a daily, hourly, weekly, or on a piece-work basis is usually called a wage. A salary is a fixed regular payment made by an employer, often monthly, for professional, administrative or office work.

Deductions

The employee's gross pay, less any deductions, is their take-home or net pay.

An employee's wage or salary is normally subject to deduction of Income Tax (PAYE) and Pay Related Social Insurance (PRSI).

Examples of other possible deductions from gross pay:

- Health insurance contributions.

- Pension contributions.

- Sports and social contributions.

- Trade union subscriptions.

- Savings schemes.

Other than as required by law, such as PAYE and PRSI, an employer may not make deductions from wages or salary, or receive payment from their employees, unless stipulated in the employee's contract of employment or where the employee confirms any agreed deductions in writing. Records of such written permission for deductions must be retained by the payroll department, or external payroll service provider, and on the employee's personnel file. The employee is also entitled to his/her own copy of any such documentation.

However, there are special restrictions in relation to deductions, or payments received, that arise from:

- Any act or omission of the employee (including suspension without pay, fines for damage to company property, etc).

- The supply to the employee by the employer of goods or services necessary to their employment.

Employees have the right, under the Payment of Wages Act 1991, to complain to a Rights Commissioner against an unlawful deduction or payment.

Details of gross pay calculations, and all deductions, must be itemised on a pay slip. It is a legal requirement that employers provide all employees with regular statements of their wages or salaries and any deductions from gross pay. As an employer, ensure that these statements remain confidential.

Methods of Payment

Wage or salary payments can be made weekly, monthly or otherwise to employees. The company has the discretion to make the payment into a bank account, by cheque or by cash.

The employee's rate of pay is normally in accordance with the company's salary structure, or as specified in collective agreements with employee groups, such as trade unions.

Wage and salaries can be subject to increases in accordance with national pay agreements or, in their absence, by direct negotiation with staff.

The gross amount, method of payment and frequency of payment must be detailed in the employee's contract of employment. Any changes to this arrangement must be agreed with the employee and confirmed in writing.

Overtime & Unsocial Hours

Any payment procedures related to additional hours of work or for unsocial hours, such as shift work, should be set out in contracts of employment or detailed in the company HR manual or employee handbook.

Many companies operate a procedure where employees receive premium rates for additional hours worked beyond the standard contract hours of work. For example, where employees work a standard five-day week from Monday to Friday, they may be paid the following premium rates:

- Time-and-a-half for hours worked after normal finishing time (up to midnight) from Monday to Friday.
- Double time for all hours worked (midnight to 7 am, Sundays, public holidays, etc).

Some companies offer time off in lieu, instead of monetary payment. In other companies, a reasonable amount of overtime is expected to be carried out by employees to maintain work continuity and is built into salaries.

Pay during Holidays & Sick Leave

Employees' entitlements to paid holidays are defined in the Organisation of Working Time Act 1997. This payment for annual leave must be given in advance, calculated at the normal weekly, monthly or other rate.

There is no entitlement in Irish law for an employee to be paid while off work, due to sickness. However, many companies administer sick pay procedures for short-term absence. If your company decides to implement such a scheme, be very clear on the policy and procedures and ensure that they are set out in the employee's contract of employment and/or detailed in the company HR manual or employee handbook.

Some companies operate a sick pay scheme for employees who are absent due to certified illness for long periods of time. This may be linked to an insurance scheme. Generally, such sick pay schemes operate in tandem with social welfare benefits.

Employers are required to provide time off under the Adoptive Leave Acts 1995 & 2005, the Carer's Leave Act 2001, the Maternity Protection Acts 1994 & 2005 and the Parental Leave Acts 1998 & 2006, but there is no provision to pay employees during this leave. The only exceptions are:

- *Force majeure* leave provided under the Parental Leave Acts 1998 & 2006.
- Leave for jury duty as set out under the Juries Act 1976.

Minimum Wage

The National Minimum Wage Act 2000 provides that an experienced adult worker must be paid an average hourly rate of not less than €8.30 per hour (from 1 January 2007, increasing to €8.65 from 1 July 2007). The minimum wage rate is reviewed on a regular basis by the Department of Enterprise Trade & Employment (see www.entemp.ie).

Lower rates may apply in certain circumstances – for example, where an employee is under the age of 18, for first-time job entrants or those engaged in structured training or study.

Performance Management

Companies that operate a performance management system should relate its operating guidelines to business needs and sound motivational principles.

Ideally, when creating pay and other reward policies, thought should be given to how various categories of employees are managed, with particular emphasis on the relationship between motivation and performance.

Some employees are managed by the operational process itself, as they must service a flow that has a stated throughput. This does not apply to administrative, supervisory or management jobs. Therefore, clear objectives must be identified for these jobs and appropriate timelines for achievement determined, or agreed with the employee.

The assessing manager's objective is not to discover the faults in others but to improve performance in a joint development process. Therefore, performance management must be a motivational process. This means discovering any blockages to achieving targets and the resolution of such issues. Such discussions, decisions and agreements must be recorded and the employee copied with the details. Clarity and fair application is critical.

While performance management is an aspect of the remuneration process, it is also a regular management activity (see later in this chapter).

Equality & Discrimination

Employers should ensure that all employees are treated fairly and equally. The Employment Equality Acts 1998 & 2004 prohibit discrimination between employees on: gender; marital status; family status; sexual orientation; religion; age; disability; race; or membership of the traveller community.

An employee may make a formal complaint under equality legislation to the Equality Tribunal, if he/she believes that an employer has discriminated against them on any of the above grounds.

Employee Benefits

Additional benefits, if applicable, must be detailed in the employee's employment contract. Remember that financial-related benefits may have implications for taxation – for example, benefit-in-kind.

Pensions schemes

Some organisations operate a company-wide pension scheme. Most company pension schemes are contributory – that is, employees contribute a percentage of salary. Pension contributions can be deducted from the employee's wages, with the consent of the employee, and paid to the pension management company.

Personal Retirement Savings Accounts (PRSA)

While it is a requirement for the company to have access for employees to a PRSA scheme, it is not compulsory for employees to subscribe, nor is it compulsory for employers to contribute to PRSAs. However, your company should strongly recommend that employees set up a PRSA, especially if you do not operate a company pension scheme.

Health insurance

Your company may also provide an employee contribution private health insurance scheme. Health insurance premiums can be deducted from the employee's wages, again with the consent of the employee, and payments are then made to the health insurance company.

Other financial benefits
These include bonus, sales commission, company car, travel allowance, company mobile phone, company laptop, meal allowances, childcare, etc.

Non-financial benefits
A combination of approaches to remuneration is required to adequately motivate employees. The more senior the position, the more important it is to develop a suitable motivational package. This can involve multiple reward factors. Companies try to achieve a motivational balance between the wage or salary and the other non-financial benefits. Getting this blend of motivators right is important to ensure the successful achievement of business objectives.

Generally, non-financial reward is based on the recognition of a person's achievement – for example, reaching or exceeding targets, implementation of beneficial innovations or above average performance.

People need challenges and achievements. Companies that provide opportunities for employees to go beyond the constraints of the job and relate specific non-financial rewards for achievement, in addition to fair base pay, will create a motivation package that addresses typical human needs. This motivational process tends to escalate proactive engagement of employees with the job in hand, and the company as a whole, by recognising their abilities and intelligence and providing encouragement to develop further.

Examples of non-financial reward include achievement awards (public recognition), decision-making autonomy (shows trust in their abilities), special development (training raises promotional opportunities) and involvement in special projects (recognises that they have the capacity for more demanding input, as well as their intellectual capacity).

The development of this style of motivation can embrace formal and informal approaches. It can allow managers and supervisors the autonomy for immediate recognition for an individual or team who have achieved a difficult target requiring special effort and flexibility – for example, by providing a gift voucher for a local restaurant or other immediate recognition response. Obviously, consistency of application of such rewards must be viewed within the context of the impact on those who are not in receipt of such rewards. Getting a balanced approach is critical.

The value of a simple 'Thank you', 'I really appreciate that' or 'That was a job well done' can be underestimated. However, over-use or abuse can have the opposite effect and can cause demotivation and offence. Achievement award plaques become meaningless after a while, unless the company's standards are clear and the awards do not come easy. In fact, such awards can be an embarrassment, if they do not relate to an achievement that is genuinely perceived by an individual's colleagues as well deserved and truly earned.

There are many different and innovative ways of rewarding excellence and employers should consider which best fits their needs and culture. If in doubt about how to develop such a scheme, or how to set standards for various employee categories or work environments, get some advice first.

FIGURE 12: REMUNERATION CHART

These (and other factors) must be taken into account when considering remuneration and rewards. The factors will vary from company to company and from year to year, depending on changing circumstances and level of importance. Consider all possible headings that are relevant to your company, rate and prioritise each and develop a suitable model that provides maximum motivation, fair reward and employee confidence.

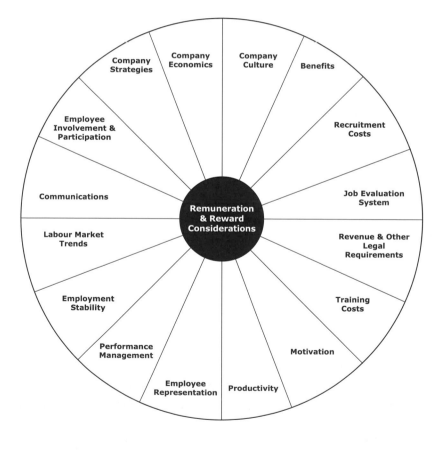

WORKING HOURS

The Organisation of Working Time Act 1997 sets out the rights of employees in respect of rest, maximum working time and holidays. These rights are governed by regulations made under this Act, as well as by other legally binding collective agreements.

Safety, Health & Welfare

The Organisation of Working Time Act 1997 sets out standards that protect employees from risks to their safety and health from working excessive hours without proper opportunities for rest, relaxation and for social and personal interactions.

The Safety, Health & Welfare at Work Act 2005 also places a duty of care on the employer to safeguard the health, safety and welfare of employees while at work. Neither the employer nor the employee may make arrangements that, in any way, place an employee at risk from working excessive hours.

Legislation

The following legislation provides protection for employees concerning working times and breaks:

- The Organisation of Working Time Act 1997.
- The Protection of Young Persons (Employment) Act 1996.

Because of their importance, employers should review both Acts mentioned above – summaries are available in **Chapter 4**.

Maximum Working Hours

The legislation permits no more than a maximum average working week of 48 hours for all non-exempt employees, averaged over an appropriate period (four, six, or 12-month periods, as appropriate).

Exempt employees include doctors, those in the transport industry and others who are responsible for deciding their own working hours.

There are specific requirements for young persons, regarding working hours and opportunities for rest, which are defined in **Chapter 4**.

Break Periods

In summary, employees are entitled to:

- **Daily rest:** 11 consecutive hours' break in a 24-hour period.

- **Weekly rest:** One period of 24 hours' unbroken rest within a week. This must be preceded by an 11-hour consecutive rest period.

- **Rest break:** 15 minutes where more than 4.5 hours have been worked; 30 minutes where 6 hours have been worked, which may include the first break period. Shop workers who work more than 6 hours, and whose hours of work include the hours 11.30 am to 2.30 pm, must be allowed a break of one hour between 11.30 am to 2.30 pm.

Shift Work

The Organisation of Working Time Act 1997 provides an automatic exemption for shift workers from the daily and weekly minimum rest periods above, when they are involved in shift change-over or on split shifts. However, there is a provision for these categories of employees to have compensatory rest periods scheduled within a reasonable time following such shifts. Employers should consider regularising such arrangements, so that there is no ambiguity. Such information can be included in the contract of employment or in the HR manual or employee handbook.

Maintenance of Records

Employers are required, under the Organisation of Working Time Act 1997, to create records for each employee concerning their hours of work and related details. These records must be maintained for a period of up to three years, even if the employee leaves the company.

More generally, employers should maintain a whole range of information on each employee's personnel file (see **Personnel Records** earlier). This makes good sense, as occasionally issues arise and claims are made against employers that can sometimes be dealt with very quickly and effectively, if the records are in place.

Payment for Additional Hours

Employers need to have procedures set out in the employment contract, or in the HR manual or employee handbook, that clearly state the arrangements for authorisation and payment of such hours.

If the employee is contracted for part-time work or full-time work, there should be ceilings or parameters when overtime rates apply. For example, full-time permanent employees who work a 37.5-hour week, Monday to Friday, from 9.00 a.m. to 5.30 p.m. each day, generally have overtime rates as follows:

- Time-and-a-half for all additional hours after normal finishing time, Monday to Friday.

- Time and a half for Saturday up to 1.00 pm and double time thereafter.

- Double time for all hours worked on Sunday.

Employers may have other arrangements, as agreed – for example, time off in lieu, flexitime, etc.

EMPLOYEE LEAVE

There are legislative requirements that define the minimum entitlements for employees with regard to annual leave, public holidays, holiday pay and that also ensure employees have reasonable opportunity to take such leave. In addition to these statutory requirements, there are other aspects to holidays and absences, which are also important from a HR best practice perspective.

Generally, employers in Ireland, particularly the larger companies, move ahead of the basic demands of the legislative requirements, based on a proactive policy approach to employee relations that contributes to good employer/employee relations, positive motivation and high performance.

Employer Objectives

Employers require their staff to regularly achieve a high level of performance and wish to ensure that their expertise and abilities are used fully for the benefit of the company. To achieve this maximum performance level, the employees must be capable of doing the work, must have a good attitude towards the work and the company, and must not be overly fatigued or stressed. Professional managers are aware that employees need to be well-motivated to maintain a consistent and satisfactory performance level.

Employee Relations Policy & Procedure

To ensure that productive motivational practices are developed, understood and applied, the employer needs to give careful thought and planning to the company's overall HR policies, practices and procedures. This section shows how holidays and absence policies and procedures can contribute to the creation and maintenance of a well-motivated team and, consequently, a positive work environment.

Best Practice

In all dealings with employees, it is necessary to be honest and genuine at all times. Clear and precise rules and guidelines are not established just to manipulate employees or to control their every move. Clear rules make it easy for employees to understand what is expected of them and what they can expect from the employer. Having holiday and absence rules will help the employee to plan with their families and friends how best to use their breaks. This means that the employee can prepare and enjoy holidays during the year and return to work in a fresh and healthy state of mind and body.

It is good practice to schedule holidays well in advance and to facilitate as many employees as possible with their preferred holiday dates. A fair process needs to be clearly defined, where employees can apply and schedule holidays. Where there is a continuous operational process, there should also be a selection process based on clear and fair rules. When too many employees request the same leave period, the selection process may have to include criteria, such as commencement dates or annual holiday rota systems, to ensure fair process. Employees will accept that they cannot have certain holiday leave, if the procedures and selection process are clear and applied equitably.

Many companies have a regular shut-down period each year (such as in August or around Christmas) and employees can plan around this practice well in advance. Early scheduling will provide the opportunity to those who were unable to get their preferred leave period to seek suitable alternatives, without incurring additional costs.

Safety, Health & Welfare

Holidays are critical to sustaining the mental and physical health and well-being of the employees at work and the employer has a statutory obligation and duty of care requirement with regard to each and every employee.

Employees suffering from fatigue or stress resulting from overwork can become prone, or exposed, to risks at work. This should be borne in mind when designing and operating fair holiday scheduling procedures. It goes without saying that job descriptions are equally important in job content design to ensure proper opportunity for rest breaks.

Where an employee is unreasonably denied proper holiday leave or other rest periods, and sustains an accident at work, the employer may be exposed to litigation costs and related awards.

Rest

Hours of work and holiday requirements, within the terms of the Organisation of Working Time Act 1997, recognise the need for regular rest for employees. Rest in this context means sufficient time off for the person to eat, get adequate rest or sleep, an opportunity to socialise, etc. Such rest is an important facet of achieving a healthy balance between working, social and personal life needs.

The proactive employer will ensure that employees' work requirements, opportunity for rest during the working week and holidays are scheduled so as to be compliant with, or better than, the minimum legislative requirements as a basic and safe working policy.

Some employers see such requirements as a nuisance, others see it as a pragmatic method of ensuring that their employees are fit, healthy, energised and fully capable of making a good contribution to the company.

Maintenance of Records

As mentioned before (see **Personnel Records**), every employee should have an individual file, which is specific to his/her employment history with the company. Employers are required, under the Organisation of Working Time Act 1997, to create records for each employee, concerning their hours of work and related details. These records must be maintained for a period of up to three years, even if the employee leaves the company.

Annual Leave

All employees are entitled to annual leave, which is determined by actual time worked. The Organisation of Working Time Act 1997 provides that, subject to a maximum of four working weeks, employees are entitled to:

- Four weeks' leave in a leave year in which the employee works at least 1,365 hours; or
- One-third of a working week in leave per calendar month that the employee works at least 117 hours; or
- 8% of the hours that an employee works in a leave year.

If more than one calculation applies, the employee should be awarded annual holiday leave based on whichever calculation gives the greatest result.

Some employers provide additional annual leave days. This is entirely discretionary, but must be detailed in the employee's contract of employment. Such additional leave may form part of a company/trade union agreement. Sometimes, such leave is service- or performance-related – for example, some companies award an additional day of leave for every five years of service with the company. Such policies may be useful in terms of making the company as attractive as possible – for example, where there has been a pattern of high labour turnover.

However, although employees will be pleased to receive additional benefits, they will always find it unreasonable if you propose reducing these back to statutory requirements when competition threatens and costs become prohibitive. In fact, any proposed reduction will generally result in a claim for compensation for loss of entitlements and has a de-motivating effect.

The statutory leave year runs from 1 April to 31 March. However, employers may use a different 12-month period – for example, 1 January to 31 December – provided that the same leave year is applied consistently.

Employees are entitled to be paid in advance on the day they are to finish work, prior to commencing their annual leave. Obviously, most employees depend on their holiday pay at this time and there is an obligation on the employer to ensure that they are paid.

Payment for annual leave

If the employee's normal pay is calculated solely on the basis of an hourly rate or fixed payment, then they will receive this amount for any week of annual leave or, for less than a week, on a *pro rata* basis.

Holiday pay for employees whose weekly pay includes commission or other performance-related payment must be based on their average earnings, excluding any pay for overtime. The calculation must be based on the 13 weeks immediately preceding the commencement of holiday leave.

If, for whatever reason, the employee did not work during the 13-week period immediately preceding the commencement of holiday leave, the calculation period used is based on the 13 weeks ending on the day on which time was last worked by the employee before the annual leave commences.

Authorising annual leave

Each company must decide on its specific internal approval procedures for authorising holiday leave, related to the needs of the business. This may be on a departmental basis, with the local manager being the authorising person. The manager selected would be responsible for ensuring that the department can operate effectively with a particular holiday roster and with minimum cover requirements.

Where various departments provide cross-departmental cover, and where employees are generally shared, one person should be selected as the authorising manager to ensure both that departments are adequately covered and that holiday scheduling is based on fair process. To avoid issues, a participative approach and consensus is recommended.

After eight months of work with an employer, the employee is entitled to an unbroken period of two weeks' annual leave, which may include one or more public holidays. An employment regulation order, registered employment agreement, collective agreement or any other agreement between the employer and employee may specify an arrangement different to this provision, provided that it is fair and reasonable.

Carry-over of annual leave

Generally, neither employers nor employees are allowed to defer holidays into the next annual leave year, except in special circumstances, such as in an emergency, where the temporary deferment of the holidays is crucial to the business. In such cases, the leave due to the employee concerned should be taken within the following six months.

Payment in lieu of annual leave

Employers are not allowed to trade off holidays for additional payments. To do so would contravene the Organisation of Working Time Act 1997 and would make the employer liable to sanction. Additionally, it would place the employee at risk from a health perspective and, thus, would contravene the Safety, Health & Welfare at Work Act 2005.

There are special circumstances, where a key employee may be required to forego scheduled holidays because of an emergency at work. However, there are many considerations regarding such requirements – for example, adequate compensation, rescheduled holiday leave and whether the person had already scheduled and paid for a holiday trip and the loss that would ensue. Compensation for such loss would be a practical solution. However, the holiday cancellation may disrupt the employee's family life and some consideration should be given to genuine 'damage limitation' in terms of motivation, fair play and key employee stability when assessing adequate compensation. Ideally, the person should be scheduled to take leave at the earliest opportunity following whatever special circumstances caused the postponement.

Employee illness during annual leave

In the event of an employee becoming ill during their scheduled annual holidays, he/she can request the employer to reschedule the holidays to a later date. This request must be supported by a medical certificate covering the period of the illness, as soon as possible, either during or immediately following the illness or return to work.

Annual leave entitlements for former employees

Since holiday leave is an accrued entitlement based on previous working time, it is important that to ensure that all outstanding entitlements, including payment for holidays accrued but not taken, are resolved with the employee before or on the date of termination of employment. This also applies in the event of a dismissal based on gross misconduct.

Shut-down or rostered annual leave

Depending on the nature of the business, each employer must decide on whether it is possible or practical to close the company entirely for a period of annual leave. The alternative is to stagger holidays so as to remain open and provide regular services to clients.

If an annual shut-down is possible, it makes it easy for both the employer and employee to plan around the preferred shut-down period. Such shut-downs are generally scheduled to occur within the schools' annual summer holidays so that employees may schedule family holidays.

However, this may not suit all employees, and there may be situations where employees request holidays outside the employer's preferred shut-down period. This can cause industrial relations issues, if preferential treatment is given to one or more employees. It is essential for good employee relations that the decision-making process regarding holiday leave is clear, fair and equitable and that the employer listens to, and understands, the views of the employees. Nonetheless, it is ultimately the employer's choice, as the needs of the business are central to its survival and development.

Obviously, the main consideration that an employer must address is whether, if the business shuts down for two weeks' leave, regular clients will source their needs elsewhere and not come back to the company after the holiday break? If this is a possibility, then the decision must be to stay open and roster the holidays. This might mean the provision of a skeleton staff service or a complete staffing requirement with temporary cover as necessary. Rostered holidays may mean additional unavoidable costs for temporary cover for some or all employees on leave.

The company may also have fixed annual holidays whereby the company selects set days, either on a regular basis annually or which change each year (for example, Good Friday, Christmas Eve and New Year's Eve) and which are not public holidays. These arrangements should be detailed in the employee's contract of employment, and in the HR manual or employee handbook.

Consultation regarding leave

Under the Organisation of Working Time Act 1997, employees, or their trade unions, must be consulted at least one month in advance of any dates selected by the employer for annual leave. It is more practical and more motivational to do so as early as possible to allow employees to avail of the best booking opportunities.

Public Holidays

The Organisation of Working Time Act 1997 provides for nine public holidays:

1. New Year's Day (1 January).
2. St. Patrick's Day (17 March).
3. Easter Monday.
4. First Monday in May.
5. First Monday in June.
6. First Monday in August.
7. Last Monday in October.
8. Christmas Day (25 December).
9. St. Stephen's Day (26 December).

The term "Bank Holiday" is often used to describe these nine public holidays, as well other days, such as Good Friday (the Friday before Easter Sunday). However, only the nine days above have legal standing – employees have no entitlement in law to other days off.

All full-time employees are automatically entitled to payment for public holidays. Other employees (for example, part-time and casual workers) qualify for public holiday entitlement, provided they have worked at least 40 hours during the five weeks ending on the day immediately preceding a public holiday. Part-time employees are entitled to public holiday entitlements on a *pro rata* basis.

If the public holiday falls on a day on which the employee normally works, the employee is entitled to one of the following, at the employer's discretion:

- A paid day off on the public holiday.
- A paid day off within a month.
- An extra day's annual leave.
- An additional day's pay.

If the public holiday falls on a day on which the employee does not normally work, he/she is entitled to 20% of their normal weekly rate of remuneration for that day. If an employee is required to work on a public holiday (for example, in a continuous process operation), their entitlement is as follows, as the employer may decide:

- A paid day off within a month.
- An extra day's annual leave.
- An additional day's pay.

However, if the requirement to work on a public holiday is not part of the employee's regular work, then overtime rates apply.

An employee may request their employer, at least 21 days prior to a public holiday, to determine which of the public holiday entitlement approaches is to be applied. The employer is required to provide notification of the entitlement at least 14 days before the public holiday. Failure to do so automatically entitles the employee to a paid day off on that public holiday. Ideally, you should regularise the procedure and include it in the HR manual or employee handbook.

Public holiday entitlements for former employees

Where an employee ceased to be employed during the week ending on the day before the public holiday, and the employee has worked for the four weeks preceding that week, he/she is entitled to receive a normal day's pay for that public holiday.

In the event of death, this amount is combined with any other entitlements due to any next of kin.

Absence from work

An employee is not entitled to a public holiday, if he/she is absent:

- Due to an injury sustained in an occupational accident, beyond 52 consecutive weeks.

- Due to an injury sustained in a non-occupational accident, beyond 26 consecutive weeks.

- For any other absence authorised by the employer (including lay-off), beyond 13 consecutive weeks.

- By reason of a strike.

Employees who are absent on statutory leave (maternity, adoptive, parental or carer's leave) maintain their public holiday entitlement for the duration of the leave. However, employees on carer's leave maintain this entitlement only for the first 13 weeks of their leave.

Statutory Leave

Statutory leave legislation provides entitlements and protection for employees to take leave from work in relation to family matters. Such leave can be paid or unpaid, depending on the legislation. A summary of the provisions of statutory leave legalisation is outlined below – see **Chapter 4** for a *précis* of each Act.

There may be social welfare benefits available for employees on statutory leave, subject to qualifying conditions. Further details are available from the Department of Social & Family Affairs (www.welfare.ie).

Some companies may offer leave above and beyond that laid down in employment legislation. Such practices may be positive in employee relations terms but can be a costly precedent. It is important, therefore, to be clear on why you wish to put such additional benefits in place and to understand the long-term impact. Consider the possibility of a downturn in business and the ramifications of your policy and procedures on costs.

The procedure regarding statutory leave should be made available to employees in written format, ideally in your company's HR manual or employee handbook. If you are preparing a policy and procedure for the first time, you should ensure that it complies with legislation as well as established custom and practice within the company. All employees should be treated equally and consistently with regard to statutory leave entitlements.

As long as the procedures for requesting and taking statutory leave are clearly and correctly stated, you should not encounter difficulties. However, you may wish to add the following statement to the written policies:

> Any abuse or breaches of the company's procedures regarding statutory leave is considered serious and will be dealt with under the company's disciplinary procedures.

Adoptive leave

Employees are entitled to a minimum of 24 consecutive weeks of *unpaid* leave (for leave commencing on or after 1 March 2007; otherwise, 20 weeks).

Employees may also take up to 16 consecutive weeks' additional *unpaid* adoptive leave (for leave commencing on or after 1 March 2007; otherwise, 16 weeks). The additional leave must commence immediately after the end of the adoptive leave and is subject to the employee providing the statutory written notifications to the employer.

There is no service requirement. All employees who adopt children are entitled to adoptive leave, regardless of their length of service. However, an employee will not be entitled to adoptive leave if he/she fails to provide written notification or certificates to his/her employer within the time limits as required under adoptive leave legislation.

An employee is entitled to paid time off to attend certain pre-adoption classes and meetings that he/she is obliged to attend within the State as part of the pre-adoption process (such as meetings with social workers). This is subject to the employee providing the correct written notification to the company, as required under adoptive leave legislation.

While on adoptive leave, the employee retains certain rights:

- Annual leave and public holiday entitlements that accrue to an employee during adoptive leave will be granted in accordance with the terms of the Organisation of Working Time Act 1997.

- Service continuity is maintained, along with other employment rights, and the adoptive leave period is included as reckonable service (for example, for calculating redundancy or other entitlements).

- The employee retains the right to return to the same or equivalent and suitable work, including location and pay, on terms not substantially less favourable.

- Training, probation or apprenticeship, interrupted by adoptive leave, is temporarily suspended until after the leave period.

- The employee cannot be suspended, receive a notice of termination, or be terminated while on adoptive leave. If an employee has been suspended or has received a termination notice before his/her adoptive leave begins, which is due to expire during the period of adoptive leave, it should be extended by the period of the adoptive leave.

Maternity leave

From 1 March 2007, maternity leave is 26 weeks (but only for employees who commence maternity leave on or after that date; otherwise, 22 weeks). At least two of those weeks must be taken before the expected date of the birth and the maternity leave period should finish no earlier than four weeks after the date of the birth.

From 1 March 2007, employees are entitled to take 16 weeks of additional maternity leave (for leave commencing on or after that date; otherwise 12 weeks). This additional leave must commence immediately after the end of the maternity leave period and is subject to the employee providing the statutory written notifications to the employer.

Maternity leave applies to all female employees, whether permanent or temporary, full-time or part-time, regardless of their length of service. However, an employee will not be entitled to maternity leave if she fails to provide written notification or certificates within the time limits set out in maternity leave legislation. Employees employed under a fixed term contract are covered by maternity legislation, up to the date the contract of employment is due to expire.

Regulations under safety legislation require an employer to conduct a risk assessment of the employee's place of work with regard to pregnant employees, employees who have recently given birth or employees who are breastfeeding. Under maternity legislation, if the employer and the employee agree that the inherent risks of the job cannot be removed, and if a transfer to more suitable work is not possible, the employee is entitled to health and safety leave. The employer only has to pay an employee on such health and safety leave for the first 21 days. Thereafter, the employee should apply to the Department of Social & Family Affairs for health and safety benefit.

An expectant employee is entitled to **paid** time off work to attend one set of ante-natal classes (other than the last three classes in such a set). An expectant father has a once-off right to **paid** time off to attend the last two ante-natal classes in a set of such classes attended by the expectant mother of his child. Such leave is subject to the employee having provided written notification of the dates and times of the classes.

An employee is also entitled to **paid** time off for ante-natal and post-natal care appointments, once he/she has provided the employer with the statutory written notification. Employees are entitled to as much time off as necessary to attend to such visits, including the travel time to and from such appointments.

For up to six months after the birth, an employee who is breastfeeding is entitled to:

- **Paid** time off work, to facilitate breastfeeding (where facilities are provided in the workplace); or

- A reduction in her working hours, without loss of pay, to facilitate breastfeeding (where facilities are not provided in the workplace).

This time off, or the reduction in working hours, may comprise one break of 60 minutes or two breaks of 30 minutes' duration each, three breaks of 20 minutes' duration each, or any number and duration of breaks as may be agreed between the employee and her manager.

Companies are not required to provide breastfeeding facilities, if the provision of such facilities gives rise to more than a nominal cost. To date, case law indicates that nominal cost is not a fixed sum but is assessed on the basis of company size and turnover, and that the particular circumstances will be evaluated in each case.

The employee maintains the following rights while on maternity leave:

- Annual leave and public holiday entitlements that accrue during the maternity leave period can be added on at the end of the employee's period of maternity leave.

- The employee's service continuity and all other employment rights are maintained; and the maternity leave taken is included as reckonable service.

- The employee retains the right to return to the same or equivalent and suitable work, location and pay, on terms not substantially less favourable.

- Training, probation or apprenticeship periods, interrupted by maternity leave, may be temporarily suspended until after the maternity leave period.

The Unfair Dismissals Acts 1977-2001 protect employees from dismissal on the grounds of pregnancy, giving birth, breastfeeding or any connected matter. Employees who exercise, or propose to exercise, a right under maternity legislation to any form of protective leave or absence due to natal care are also protected against dismissal which is deemed as unfair. In these circumstances, the employee does not have to have one year's continuous service to be protected by the Unfair Dismissals Acts 1977-2001.

Parental leave

An employee, who is a natural or adoptive parent, is entitled to 14 weeks' unpaid leave, provided that they have followed the statutory notification procedures and have one year's continuous service with the company.

Employees with less than one year's service but more than three months' service, are entitled to *pro rata* parental leave entitlements – that is, one week per month worked.

Employees employed on a part-time basis can take *pro rata* parental leave, calculated based on the number of hours they worked in the 14-week period prior to the proposed commencement of the parental leave.

Employees employed under a fixed-term contract are also entitled to parental leave. However, if the contract is due to expire during the period of parental leave, parental leave entitlements also expire on the same day. There is no entitlement to return to work for such employees.

Parental leave can be taken in respect of a natural or adopted child before the child reaches eight years of age or, if the child is disabled, up to 16 years of age.

Parental leave may be taken as a continuous block of 14 weeks, in two separate periods (each period is subject to a minimum of six continuous weeks) or, by agreement between the company and employee, as a number of broken periods (in weeks, days or even hours).

The company and the employee jointly must prepare a parental leave agreement, which should state the agreed terms of the leave period. This agreement cannot be changed, except by joint agreement.

The employee maintains the following rights while on parental leave:

- Any annual leave and public holiday entitlements that accumulate during an employee's period of parental leave can be added to the leave period.
- Service continuity is maintained, as are all employment rights, and the parental leave taken is included as reckonable service.

- The employee retains the right to return to the same or equivalent and suitable work, location and pay, on terms not substantially less favourable.

- Training, probation or apprenticeship, interrupted by parental leave, is temporarily suspended until after the leave period.

Force majeure leave

Force majeure leave is defined in the Parental Leave Acts 1998 & 2006 as leave for situations where, for urgent family reasons, owing to illness or injury of an individual specified below, the **immediate** presence of the employee is **indispensable**:

1. A child or an adopted child of the employee.

2. The husband / wife / spouse of the employee.

3. The parent or grandparent of the employee.

4. The brother or sister of the employee.

5. A person for whom the employee has a duty of care.

6. A person other than specified in 1 to 5 above, who resides with the employee in a relationship of domestic dependency if, in the event of injury or illness, one reasonably relies on the other to make arrangements for the provision of care (including same-sex partners).

Force majeure leave is **paid** leave and is separate to parental leave. The maximum entitlement is three days' paid leave in any one year or five days' paid leave over three years.

There is no service requirement. All employees are entitled to *force majeure* leave, regardless of the length of service.

The employee maintains all his/her rights while absent on *force majeure* leave.

Carer's leave

Employees are entitled to take **unpaid** leave to provide full-time care for an eligible person in need, for a minimum period of 13 weeks, up to a maximum of 104 weeks.

The person being cared for must satisfy the eligibility requirements of the Department of Social & Family Affairs. Only employees with at least one year's continuous service are eligible to avail of the entitlements and protection of the Carer's Leave Act 2001. The employee must also provide written notification or certificates within the time limits, as set out in the legislation.

Carer's leave may be taken, by agreement between the employee and the company, in one block of 104 weeks or in several separate blocks of time, the total duration of which amounts to no more than 104 weeks.

The company and the employee jointly must prepare a carer's leave agreement, which should state the agreed terms of the leave period. This agreement cannot be changed, except by joint agreement.

While on carer's leave, the employee retains the following rights:

- The employee's service continuity and all employment rights are maintained, and the carer's leave taken is included as reckonable service.

- The employee has no right to remuneration, superannuation benefits or contributions in respect of the employment while they are absent from work due to carer's leave.

- Annual leave and public holiday entitlements accrue only in respect of the first 13 weeks of carer's leave. Any annual leave hours or days that accumulate can be added on at the end of the carer's leave period.

- The employee retains the right to return to the same or equivalent and suitable work, location and pay, on terms not substantially less favourable.

- Training, probation or apprenticeship periods, interrupted by carer's leave, may be temporarily suspended until after the carer's leave period.

Juror's leave

Jury service is compulsory for all citizens between the ages of 18 and 70 years listed on the Register of Electors, under the Juries Act 1976. The categories of people who do not have to undertake jury service are listed in the Act.

All employees of the company are entitled to **paid** leave while undertaking jury service, for the duration of the absence. Therefore, there is no interruption to an employee's contract of employment and he/she maintains all his/her rights while absent on juror's leave.

The length of time a juror is required for jury service varies, usually between four days to two weeks. The expected time period will be stated in the summons.

If an employee's absence from work could have a serious impact on the business, the employer may apply to the court to have the jury service deferred. Such an application must not be intended to prevent civic duty, so genuine evidence of the reasoning will be important.

Non-statutory Leave

This leave is entirely at the discretion of the company. Generally, larger companies provide more non-statutory leave entitlements than smaller companies, as part of their employee relations and motivational policies.

For non-statutory leave, there is a danger in each case being judged on its own merit at the discretion of management. This may lead to bias and discrimination, either accidental or otherwise, which causes de-motivation, anger and, possibly, inequality claims. It is better to develop a clear policy and to include it in the company's HR manual or employee handbook. If there is any abuse of the policy, the case can be processed by company management on the basis of disciplinary procedures.

Compassionate or bereavement leave

Allowing compassionate leave is optional, but most companies allow time off on compassionate grounds for the death of a spouse or blood relative (parent, sibling or child).

Generally up to three days' *paid* leave is allowed in the event of the death of a member of the employee's immediate family (spouse, parent, sibling or child). Some companies even give the employee time off in the event of the death of a blood relative of his/her spouse – usually, one day's *paid* leave, but can be up to three days' paid leave.

For all other bereavements, such as the death of friends, neighbours or other relatives not already specified, some companies grant one day's *paid* leave.

Additional time off without pay may be authorised by the company. If a funeral takes place on a non-working day or during annual leave, an employee is not entitled to time off or payment in lieu.

The employee should be asked to provide written confirmation of such leave to the company as soon as is reasonably practicable. The written notice should contain the reason for the leave, the commencement date of the leave and the date of return to work. This notice should then be retained in the employee's personnel file.

Special leave

Companies occasionally grant *unpaid* leave to employees in special circumstances, at the discretion of the company. Generally, there is a service requirement of at least one year.

The employee should be asked to apply in writing to his/her immediate manager, stating the date(s) of, and reason for, the proposed leave, with as much notice as possible. Reasons for such special leave may include:

- Education or study.
- Travel.
- Purchasing or constructing a new house.
- Lifestyle change.
- Career break.
- Wedding leave.

There are many possible reasons for an employee to request special leave of absence. It may be useful for the company to list what may or may not be acceptable under certain circumstances, to ensure consistency of decision-making.

The manager must also consider the impact of the employee's absence on the company. He/she should take into consideration whether a replacement person will be required for the duration of the leave and whether the cost is greater than having the employee remain at work.

If the impact of the leave causes excessive disruption or costs, or places services, customers or product at risk, the leave may not be possible. If the manager believes that the leave will not cause any significant inconvenience or disruption and is prepared to approve the leave, a written agreement should be drawn up, stating the terms and conditions under which the leave of absence is permitted.

A minimum written notice period, stating the intended date of return to work, should form part of the special leave period agreement. This must be signed by both the manager and the employee requesting the leave and a copy should be retained on file and another one given to the employee.

Regardless of the foregoing best practice approach, this is very much a discretionary practice, as managers tend to judge each case on merit and favoured employees who have some important value to the department or company may receive special leeway. This, of course, leads to unequal treatment of employees, not intentionally, but often as a consequence of motivational needs. Managers should be careful to apply such discretionary powers as equitably as possible to avoid inequality claims.

Paternity leave
Most countries in the EU now have paid paternity leave enshrined in their legislation. This currently ranges from two days in Spain and Luxembourg to two weeks in the UK and France.

Under maternity legislation, there is a once-off entitlement for an expectant father to *paid* time off to attend two ante-natal classes with the expectant mother (the last two classes in a set).

The other statutory entitlement for a father under maternity legislation is special leave in the event of the mother's death.

There is no statutory entitlement for a father to take paid time off work when his child is born, often referred to as paternity leave. However, a father can make a request to take *unpaid* parental leave under the Parental Leave Acts 1998 & 2006. An employee, who is a natural or adoptive parent, is entitled to 14 weeks' *unpaid* leave, once he/she has provided the employer with the statutory written notification and has one year's continuous service.

ABSENTEEISM

Definition

An employee is absent when he/she is not available to do work, as and when expected or contracted. The absence may be excused or unexcused, which, of course, will affect the employer's response.

There are legitimate reasons for some absences, some of which are defined under employment legislation, such as:

- Annual leave.
- Adoptive leave.
- Carer's leave.
- *Force majeure* leave.
- Maternity leave.
- Parental leave.
- Public holiday leave.

There are also other special leave arrangements that are agreed between employers and employees.

In general, the company should still satisfy itself that there are no abuses of statutory leave entitlements.

Causes

There are many genuine reasons for absenteeism, but regular trends in such behaviour must be addressed, managed and resolved. Some companies may agree on a certain level of flexibility regarding attendance criteria, because of an employee's personal health requirements.

Some employees may drift into poor attendance, due to a personal issue that causes the poor attendance pattern. On discovery of this, the manager should agree a specific timeframe for review of the issues and the employee's support requirements. Other employees may have no particular personal problem, other than a difficulty in getting out of bed! **Figure 13** gives examples of internal and external, and avoidable and unavoidable, causes of absenteeism.

FIGURE 13: CAUSES OF ABSENTEEISM

	Avoidable	Unavoidable
Internal	Badly-constructed jobs. Poor safety controls. Poor working conditions. Bullying and harassment. Lack of job clarity. Insufficient training. Poor relationships with management or colleagues. Job instability.	Change in working methods. Departmental transfers resulting from redundancies. Heavy physical work inherent in the job leading to fatigue. Heavy mental based work inherent in the job leading to pressure and stress.
External	Football matches. Hangovers and alcoholism. Sunny days. Minor aches and pains. Laziness.	Physical illness. Mental illness. Deaths in family. Career changes. Inheritance. Need to help with family business.

Dealing properly with all these cases is critical. Poor attendance can result in real losses for the company. Attendance records can be a good barometer of attitude within the company. Poor attendance, coupled with a growing labour turnover, is certainly indicative of such motivational issues.

Offending employees may be dismissed, thus eliminating the problem – but at a cost, the cost of rehiring and retraining, which can be quite high.

Some companies provide assistance for employees who have personal difficulties that are exclusively external in nature. However, the employee may perceive this as welcome support or unwelcome interference. A good employee relations-oriented company will certainly have some support structure in place that can help in some way to reduce absenteeism, while building the employer-to-employee relationship.

Overall, it is important for the company to have a policy and procedure that managers and supervisors apply in a consistent and fair way. The objective is to minimise the adverse effects of poor attendance by the application of fair control procedures.

Costs

Recent surveys indicate that Irish employees are absent eight days in a year, on average, at an estimated national cost of €150 million to €1 billion *per annum*. In each company, management is responsible for minimising the negative impact on the company, through reasonable and practical controls.

The most obvious and immediate cost of absenteeism is the payment of staff who are absent from work, where the company operates a sick pay scheme. However, the other costs are not always immediately noticeable and are sometimes difficult to identify, let alone quantify – for example:

- Lost time and production.

- Diminished productivity and quality. Management may have to scale back operations or shut down lines due to the reduction in staffing levels.

- Administrative costs associated with rescheduling staff or hiring temporary cover.

- Additional payroll costs for temporary staff to cover absent employees.

- Training costs associated with introducing temporary staff.

- Outsourcing the work at a higher cost.

- Working additional hours at premium overtime rates.

- Insurance claims and legal fees associated with employees who are absent due to an accident at work.

- Management time to cater for operational changes.

Long-term Absence

Employees with particular difficulties may be absent for long periods of time, due to a personal illness or a serious illness of a close family member. The most important action for the company is to maintain contact with the individual and have regular discussions on their status. Again, there must be no badgering or harassment of the employee. From a motivational perspective, a supporting role involving two-way communications, understanding and empathy has a more productive long-term impact on employee relations. It is important that the person understands that he/she is valued by the company and that their job is open when they are in a position to return to work.

The company might also help the person to assess possible alternatives that combine work with being available for the family member (if that is the reason for the absence) – including working part-time, sharing the burden with another family member, working outside normal hours, working from home during a care period, etc.

If suffering from illness, the person may have to be referred to the company doctor periodically for a medical review.

Occasionally an employee is unable to return to work at all, due to the seriousness of his/her illness. Some companies have a plan in place for early retirement. On the other hand, the person may just fail to return and have on-going entitlement to social welfare benefits.

Records

It is obvious that a company must have a way of recording timekeeping and attendance, if it is to be controlled. Some jobs operate on the basis of trust, some are controlled by performance. For example, in the latter case, once the job is done within the planned timescale or within a predefined cost, it does not matter whether the person started exactly on time or worked later to make up. This does not apply to every job and such flexibility needs to be carefully monitored. You may wish to have a consistent monitoring method or may opt to have certain jobs linked to clocking in and out. Some companies require all employees, including the senior managers, to clock in and out as a demonstration of equitable and consistent treatment. This is not always realistic nor is it perceived as consistent, as managers may have a range of legitimate reasons for being off-site, so it is often seen as a 'window-dressing'.

The recording method is important. It should not be demeaning or manipulative. It should be practical, fair, equitable and accurate.

Some companies may find it useful or necessary to have different methods of dealing with absences under various headings – for example, illness related, and non-illness related, absences, the former having a support-based element, the latter being more focused on management control procedures.

Managing Absenteeism

Duty of care

Under safety, health and welfare legislation, the employer has a duty of care for all employees' well-being. So, you must ensure that relevant and appropriate safety practices and procedures are in place and any physical or mental strains inherent in the jobs are eliminated or reduced to a minimum. This will include safety training and the avoidance of accidents at work.

Sick pay schemes

Good employee relations policy and practice tends to have some form of sick pay scheme in place. There is a fear that, when a company puts such a scheme in operation, the level of absence will increase. So the proactive HR approach in itself can cause absence problems. It is therefore important for companies to implement the control features and absence costing at the same time as the employee benefits and to demonstrate that these are being managed.

Disciplinary action

In cases of an employee being regularly absent on grounds of illness, the company should focus on understanding the reasons for the absences and on assisting or supporting the employee to professionally deal with the issue.

However, even when following a proactive and supportive effort, disciplinary action may be the only way left for an employer to deal with an employee who has a track record of habitual lateness and absence.

It is not a good policy to treat all lateness and absence in a like manner regardless of the reason, nor is it practical. It may seem equitable, but some flexibility or leniency is required from time in relation to a person's circumstances. There may be personal reasons for the poor track record; some of the issues causing the poor attendance may be out of the employee's immediate control – for example, a sick child.

All cases of poor attendance should be reviewed and managed individually. Where there appears to be no legitimate reason for habitual lateness and/or absenteeism, the company must process the issue through the disciplinary procedures. This process can result eventually in the dismissal of the employee. There should be incremental steps in the disciplinary procedures that allow sufficient time for the individual to amend their attendance performance.

It is important that employees are fully aware of all matters concerning the attendance procedures and also how they can be processed through the disciplinary procedures; the final result being dismissal.

Preventative actions

Some companies have high levels of absenteeism that can be attributed to the nature of the work and the environment. Heavy industry, with an unavoidable poor working environment, generally results in higher levels of absenteeism. Such organisations need to be particularly proactive with regard to safety, health and welfare and need to invest significantly in preventative measures to avoid absenteeism. These measures can include having regular check-ups, on-site professional safety and nursing staff who monitor the environment, and work practices to reduce exposure to hazards and make improvements. Job content analysis (see earlier) – engineering out the difficult aspects of the duties and responsibilities of an occupation that tends to contribute to poor attendance or labour turnover – can be useful here.

Such companies may also have regular visits by a doctor to assess individuals who are habitually exposed to dust and fumes, or who have to wear safety equipment. Their work-related illnesses and other complaints can be checked and actions taken to reduce and eliminate risks and avoid the necessity for absence due to illness.

These practices may be totally unnecessary in some industries and only partially relevant in others. It is up to the company to ascertain what preventative measures are appropriate and relevant for the work and environment for each occupation. For example, some chemical-based companies use carcinogenic materials – for them, under safety legislation, it is imperative to have protections and detailed safety procedures in force, including regular assessment by a company-nominated doctor and regular tests at hospitals. Other companies may be in businesses where there is very limited health-related exposure for employees – for example, retail distribution of lightweight products.

All companies, however, are exposed to potential absenteeism, with all the associated costs – thus a strategic management solution is required. Any management control procedure is a preventative measure or deterrent.

Back to work interviews

Any process or procedure that incorporates a direct follow-through interview with employees following an absence will generally lead to reduction in poor attendance. No one likes to be interviewed concerning their absence, particularly when the absence was not for a reasonable, recognised or legitimate reason. However, avoid brow-beating or badgering employees on their return to work. This simply has a further negative effect and de-motivates most employees who may already have a problem.

A standard procedure involving a meeting (however brief) applied consistently to all staff, and where there is a record made of the reason for the absence, will register with staff and will be perceived as reasonable and acceptable. The meeting can be supportive, as well as investigative, in nature. It is important for management to understand the nature of the absences, so as to be in a position to accurately cost the absence in each case. As part of any control practices and procedures, such information is an important aspect for communicating with the employee, so that they also will appreciate the impact of their poor attendance on the company. This can be expressed in different formats, such the impact on other staff, the team, the customers, the costs, etc.

Confirmation of fitness to resume work

Despite the fact that the supervisor or manager may be very anxious to get an employee back to work, particularly if the person is a key performer, there is a need to ensure that the person is fit to resume normal working, under the duty of care requirements of safety legislation.

If the person is out sick with flu, and the turn-around time is approximately two weeks, it is probable that they will be fit to resume within the anticipated time frame. On the other hand, if a person is absent due to some other, more serious ailment, such as injuries sustained in car crash or having suffered a stroke or heart attack, then the formal fitness to return to work procedure is extremely important.

In all cases of assessing return to work fitness, the level of risk involved in the occupation must be taken into account. It is usual for companies to require the employee to present a doctor's certificate, stating that they are fit to resume normal work.

Key hit list for managing absenteeism

- Ensure the company has a clear attendance policy and procedures and that all employees understand their duties and responsibilities and how these are integrated into the procedures.

- Ensure that each manager or supervisor is trained in the company's attendance management practices, understand their responsibilities and regularly report on the status of attendance in their department, the actions taken and the results.

- Cost all types of absence in the company and share this information with all employees.

- Be fair and equitable, but also flexible, in dealing with personal matters.

- Plan all holiday leave carefully and ensure employees take their allocated leave as scheduled.

- Make sure that employees who are not on leave are not over-worked and stressed, which can lead to absenteeism.

- Provide employees with comfortable working environments, so they can be more productive. The environment should be designed to help maintain employees at work, rather than causing them to be absent from work due to fatigue, stress or injury.

- Provide as many opportunities as possible for employees to work within flexible working practices, to suit their work-life balance needs.

- Carry out regular assessments with employees and use attendance records to help you understand the main causes of poor attendance; then develop flexible solutions with employees.

- Be proactive with employees who call in sick. Set up a standard questionnaire, possibly with assistance of a company doctor, to ascertain the seriousness of the illness, the possible action and follow-up and the expected duration of the absence.

- Include attendance as one of the key factors in each employee's annual formal performance assessment.

TRAINING & DEVELOPMENT

Definition

Training means the transfer of knowledge and/or skills from a source (for example, a person, book, tape, video, course, etc) to another person, for the purpose of raising that person's level of knowledge and/or skills and, when applied in a work context, with the aim of raising the performance of the individual in a specific task or occupation in qualitative and quantitative terms.

Background

There is sometimes some confusion regarding the purpose and application of training, development and even education. In essence, they are all involved in the acquisition or the transfer of knowledge and skills from one person to another.

Education

Education is generally how we describe our pre-work schooling. It is a broad presentation of knowledge and, generally, does not address formally the application of such knowledge into skills. Students tend to develop different interests, as they try to absorb very broad-based information topics. As they acquire this knowledge, they may or may not empathise with the subject matter. Their motivation or objective is to remember the information, in order for them to repeat it and pass exams. This, in turn, may or may not help them to be specific in choosing courses that will lead them to their chosen career.

Training

Training can be applied in a work or sport/recreational context and, in both contexts, means the raising of abilities through the acquisition of specific knowledge and skills. The repetitious practising of the skills develops the abilities to be consistent and reliable in performance terms.

Training is applied very specifically in a work context: to ensure the best use of resources by raising the abilities of an individual to achieve maximum quality and throughput, with the minimum of waste. It is very much targeted at occupational and business needs in relation to bridging the gap between an individual's existing knowledge and skill-sets and those required by the company to achieve predetermined results.

Development

Development, on the other hand, looks more on the individual, their career and potential. Some companies invest in the future of employees, beyond their immediate occupational needs.

Often the developmental courses being subsidised by the company have no immediate link with the job and prepares the individual for other occupations either in the company or externally. Although this policy has very obvious pros and cons, it is certainly motivational.

However, in this ever-changing world, the 'job for life' concept is all but gone (perhaps with the exception of the public sector) and employees generally like some change and challenge. Companies, therefore, must be prepared to lose talent, as well as recruit new talent, if they wish to stay fresh and vibrant.

Learning

The education, training and development approaches require the trainee or student to absorb and to learn. Effective learning is a constituent part of any training programme. In a work context, this learning through training must be transferable to the individual's work. The trainer must have skill-sets that engage, enthuse and motivate the participants. Effective learning in a training approach is not the mechanical repetition of information but, of necessity, must incorporate understanding and application in relation to a business objective.

In a work context

Of the three approaches (education, development and training), training is the most appropriate for the average employer, as the function is specifically geared towards assisting the company to achieve business-related objectives.

Training can be costly, so ideally all employees would arrive into the company fully-trained and capable of carrying out their jobs to maximum performance levels. Although this is not realistically sustainable for all occupations and work environments, it is not a bad starting point. Consider, for example, how far you should go in your recruitment practices to ensure that the maximum knowledge and skill-sets are acquired for each occupation.

Nonetheless, regardless of any recruitment policy, the external market affecting the company, the changes in technology and labour turnover of experienced staff all impact in some way on a company's need to have a level of training in the company. If such changes are a reality for your company, and training is an inevitable requirement for maintaining and improving performance, then the training function should be given professional attention.

The Constituent Parts of Training

All occupations require varying degrees of knowledge, skill and attitude to accomplish their duties and responsibilities or to achieve predicted results:

- **Knowledge:** This is the key information required to be able to carry out a task or do a job – what specifically needs to be done, how it must be done, in what sequence, what equipment (if any) is required, how it is operated, what safety practices and equipment are required, what can go wrong and how to avoid this or make corrections.

- **Skill:** The physical and mental abilities needed to apply the knowledge required to achieve the results, in conjunction with predetermined safety, quality and performance standards.

- **Attitude:** Attitude is not as easy to define as the knowledge and skill requirements of a job. One can teach and help a person to develop certain skills and one can provide information regarding the knowledge requirements of a job. However, you cannot train someone to have the right attitude. Attitude, therefore, is an inner state of mind. This state of mind alters how we think, feel and behave. If we want to do something, but are short on the knowledge or skill, our positive 'can do, will do' attitude will help us to overcome the knowledge and skill shortfall reasonably quickly. However, if we do not wish to do something, our attitude being negative for whatever reason, our work rate will be poor and we may make more mistakes. This one factor (attitude), therefore, for which we cannot provide training, can have a significant impact on a person's performance at work. How we, as managers, treat people will have an impact on their attitude. We can have a positive effect on an individual's attitude, if we understand and apply positive motivational influencers.

Training means increasing a person's specific knowledge and/or skills to enable them to do something to a defined level of competence, which they were unable to do previously. So, measuring the 'before' and 'after' is important to confirm the success or otherwise of a training programme.

In essence, training is a process that identifies the key ingredients of knowledge, skill and attitude required for an occupation, and compares these with the level of such abilities in a potential (or existing) job-holder. The trainer identifies the gap between what the job-holder (or trainee) has and what they need, then develops and delivers a training programme to bridge this gap, incrementally providing the knowledge of what must be done, explaining and demonstrating the specific skills, providing supervised practice and monitoring the results under a range of headings, until the defined abilities are achieved by the trainee.

FIGURE 14: TRAINING CYCLE CHART

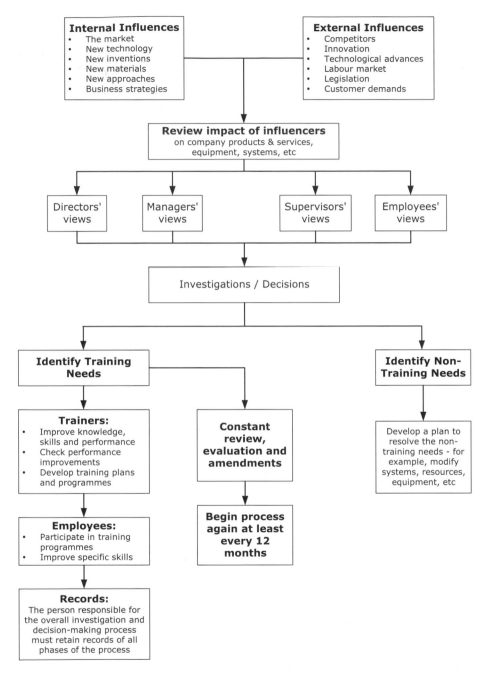

Identification of Training Needs

Introduction

Training is a management responsibility requiring careful and professional analysis and decision-making. It is a necessary process in most companies and, while often costly, generally saves the company money. The annual cycle of identifying training needs and applying training solutions to address business needs, problems and objectives must be approached systematically. The training cycle chart (see **Figure 14**) outlines the various steps required.

An investigation of training needs (ITN) (sometimes called a training needs analysis (TNA)) is a formal attempt to ensure that training is specifically directed to help resolve business issues. An ITN, ideally, should be part of the broader total business-based performance and development assessment. This overall business assessment and decision-making process must have regard to the employee element and the current pool of expertise in the company, as well as to on-going developments in the business that change the demands on all resources, including Human Resources.

This is a management exercise and, ideally, should involve all managers and other staff who have specialist knowledge of the market trends and the associated demands on employees. The chief executive should hold a central, controlling role and should organise and chair any meetings, providing the basic direction within which other managers can carry out their own assessments of needs.

The ITN exercise must focus on the overall organisational needs, the departmental or section needs and the individual needs of employees. It is a strategic business process that identifies existing or potential business changes and the related skill-set gaps. The exercise will uncover both training and non-training needs.

Step 1: What information and where to get it

- Training needs analysis is about identifying gaps in knowledge, skill and performance and coming up with a plan to fill the gaps.

- You will need to know the chief executive's intentions for the company over the next 12 months (the main plan), including the key priorities.

- This can lead you to various other departments and managers to help identify specific needs.

- Plan activities to ensure that you have ample time to interview, analyse and make decisions.

- Consider what relevant information already exists and where to access it.

- Decide on how you will gather the information – for example, by interviews, questionnaires, workplace observation or records.

- Compare the current position with how things need to be at a given point in the future. The overall plan will provide the framework for the future and outline what the future needs to look like.

- Can you and the other managers articulate this at ground level, or do you need specialist assistance?

- You will uncover needs under headings such as:

  - **Job skill training:** Compare what job skills people have against the job skills required. This can involve both knowledge and skills inputs.

  - **Job performance training:** Compare the level of performance people are achieving against the desired level of performance required. This may uncover productivity improvement needs.

  - **Training to respond to external demands:** For example, new competitive products or services, changes in requirements resulting from changes in new or amended legislation or new safety requirements.

  - **Training to meet business changes and objectives:** For example, new equipment, new products, new methods or new customer service procedures.

Step 2: Develop the training plan

- Identify appropriate training approaches to suit the gaps and performance objectives – for example, in-house and/or external training, off-the-job and/or on-the-job training, mentoring or coaching – and schedule the training.

- The plan will include who to train, what to train them in, when to train them, how to train them and how to measure the training effectiveness.

- How much will it cost? It is important to understand the cost and what is necessary as a result to justify the return on investment (ROI).

- Be sure you understand the employees' or trainees' expectations, as well as management's.

- You may need to get acceptance and approval for your training plan and secure the necessary resources and support to make it happen.

Documentation

The ITN exercise is all about research, investigation, discussion, innovation and planning. You will need to go through this process systematically on a regular basis to ensure the best use of resources to secure the future of the company. Develop check-sheets to record all discoveries for prioritising and decisions. The investigation of training needs will help you to systematically document your findings, decisions, actions, measurement and costs.

Specific Training Requirements

After you have determined the overall business direction and related training focus, you can break this down by department and by person. You will need to state clearly why the training needs to be undertaken, who should carry it out and when the training is to take place. You should also attempt to estimate and control the costs and be specific in identifying the expected results of the training in quality and performance terms.

Informal Training Approach

Sometimes, training is not conducted in a formal manner and the training amounts to little more than watching and copying another employee. Professional trainers generally refer to this as 'sitting by Nellie' training.

'Sitting by Nellie' training is fraught with problems and risks, which vary according to the nature of the work involved. The biggest and most significant risk relates to an employee's exposure within a safety, health and welfare context. The Safety, Health & Welfare at Work Act 2005 places responsibility for training employees with the employer, so as to ensure that they are safe while carrying out their duties and responsibilities. A casual attitude to training employees, therefore, is risky, to say the least.

Employers must have a designated training person (who is adequately skilled in providing training), either internally or externally, who is aware of the safety training requirements, aware of training methods and is able to incorporate safety training elements into all aspects of work within the company and to build such safety awareness training into the various work or performance-related training programmes.

Systematic Training Approach

The opposite to 'sitting by Nellie' is systematic training. As the term suggests it is a structured approach, requiring the trainer to break the job down into knowledge and skill elements and to incorporate the necessary safety standards and proper use of all related plant, equipment, safety aids and procedures. Ideally, trainers should be trained in this professional training method. If employees are not trained properly, or if the trainers do not have the competence to develop systematic training programmes for the job in hand, and there is an accident, the company may be liable.

Apart from the obvious safety requirements, employees who are not as competent as you would wish place the company's quality standards, image and revenue at risk. A systematic approach to bringing their abilities up to a high level of competence is both cost-effective and necessary for the business to be successful and to ensure credibility with the customer.

Training the Trainers

In general, and where feasible, training should be provided internally by management and other staff as appropriate. In such circumstances, the trainers will be required to undergo special training to become trainers. Trainer skills include communications, influencing, supporting, encouraging, organisation, structure and, of course, a systematic training approach to the transfer of knowledge and skills. Alternatively, you may wish to hire external training specialists. It is also important to know how you are going to evaluate the trainers' performance.

When selecting an external training consultant, be specific about your needs and expected results:

- Confirm their track record and expertise in the area required.
- Check references.
- Verify accredited training, if required.
- Check out return on investment (ROI).
- Involve the supplier in programme design.
- Involve the supplier in assessing results.
- Use agreed criteria for assessing the learning transfer precisely to your needs.

Evaluation of Training

All employees undergoing company-nominated training, either internal or external, should be assessed to ensure that the training has been successful and that the desired changes or improvements in performance are achieved, as required. The trainees should also be required to provide their evaluation of the training – for example, did it meet their needs, was it too difficult, are they satisfied with their new competencies, what was their rating of the trainer, etc. You may find it useful to develop a standard evaluation form to be completed by each trainee, focusing on key objectives or change requirements, to capture this information.

The immediate supervisor or manager should assess the performance of each employee undergoing training, retraining or development. The trainee should participate in the assessment.

When planning the training, set review times and ensure all are aware of these review times and criteria during each programme.

Retain training records on training files and on the trainee's personnel record.

Policy

Employers should prepare a written policy and procedure statement for the training function. The purpose is to provide direction and consistency for all employees. It need not be a weighty document, but it should address all key training-related issues for your company. It should integrate into the recruitment, performance management/motivation policies and, above all, address the business needs. It should also be integrated into the company's HR manual or employee handbook.

Summary

The training process is an on-going management cycle. Once you have identified the needs, implemented training programmes and assessed the effectiveness of any training, the information obtained should be amalgamated with any other relevant information arising from what has occurred since the last training period. This forms the basis of a new training plan for the next period.

Evaluation is critical throughout the various stages of the process. Be sure to:

- Assess and identify the need.
- Establish clear objectives and timescales.
- Plan each aspect of the training.
- Define costs.
- Execute the training (get participants' views, expectations and satisfaction levels on the programme).
- Define clear measurements to assess improvement changes.
- Collect specific performance improvement data on pre-stated criteria.
- Review the performance results - did the training pay for itself and achieve the desired results?
- Keep good records for future reference.
- Recommence the training analysis cycle.

PERFORMANCE MANAGEMENT

Definition

Performance management involves managers working proactively with employees, in a systematic way to raise individual and/or group performance under specific headings applicable to their individual jobs and/or team work, having regard to business needs and positive motivational principles.

Sources of Poor Performance

Poor performance is costly and impacts negatively on the company in terms of costs, environment, attitude, confidence, trust, employee stability, customer service, productivity and profitability. Although the causes of poor performance can vary from person to person and company to company, the key causes, generally uncovered when assessing poor performance, include (but are not limited to):

- Poor recruitment and selection practices.
- An individual's attitude (influenced by business or personal issues).
- The working environment.
- Lack of particular knowledge or skills.
- Poor training.
- Poor equipment.
- Poor systems.
- Bad management.
- Lack of clarity regarding standards and also of duties and responsibilities.
- Fear of making a mistake.
- Fear of the manager.

It is management's responsibility to understand the nature of such causes, the negative impact they have on the company and to take actions that will resolve issues and bring about beneficial changes in performance.

However, sometimes it is the manager himself/herself who may be the main cause of the performance shortfall. Depending on each manager's qualifications, training and development in the role, their understanding of motivational concepts, empathy and understanding of people and the impact of their actions and style, they will be either a positive or negative contributor to their direct reports' standard of performance.

This, of course, applies right up to the chief executive. The approach, attitude and style demonstrated by the chief executive generally will be reflected by other managers. The chief executive's own style may even de-motivate the very managers on whom the company is relying to raise performance and achieve key business results through their staff.

A clear statement by the chief executive, fully supported by all the company's managers and which adequately outlines the company's principles and approach to people and how they are managed, can be a solid foundation upon which all related performance management actions are based.

Motivation

At the core of performance is motivation. You will probably have come across someone who is highly competent and skilled at his/her occupation but whose performance leaves something to be desired. It is probably a question of the individual's motivation, his/her state of mind or attitude. But, what is affecting this motivation? More than likely, it will be one or more of those causes mentioned above.

There are many motivational theorists who can help us shape our thinking as managers and some of their philosophical ideas will be mentioned briefly in this section. However, sometimes a manager's honest statement of how they themselves would like to be managed, developed and motivated would be a good and practical starting point.

Managers who have studied motivational concepts will remember McGregor's *Theory X and Theory Y Managers*. The *Theory X Manager* believes that people are lazy by nature and must be reprimanded or 'hauled over the coals' in order to get them to work. The *Theory Y Manager* represents the opposite view and believes that treating people as we would like to be treated ourselves – in a humane way, with respect, dignity, support and practical encouragement – is much more effective. Generally, the modern HR Manager is a believer, promoter and advocate of the *Theory Y* approach.

Review the motivation theories of Hertzberg, Maslow, Taylor and McGregor. They are the old classics of management motivational philosophy but are still legitimate concepts today and certainly provide food for thought.

Performance Appraisals

At the outset, the manager provides the resources to enable the person to do the job to clear standards that must be defined in the job description. The person must work to achieve such standards of quality and quantity. So this is a two-way arrangement and both participants need to understand the constituent parts. The performance appraisal is a method of measuring the actual occurrences against these pre-defined criteria.

This relationship ideally requires the manager and the employee to work together to achieve the best results. Mutual identification of strengths and weaknesses is progressive and beneficial and it is particularly beneficial when this is genuinely operated as a two-way process. The objective is then to build on the strengths, and to agree on actions to reduce the weaknesses through a structured approach to improve knowledge and skills and remove any other barriers discovered during the process. These can be expressed as training and non-training needs and actions.

This joint approach requires good leadership qualities in the manager in terms of communication, strategic planning, analysis and providing a supportive role for those required to raise their performance in relation to the weaknesses identified.

Many managers find this annual round of performance appraisal sessions cumbersome and tedious. It is perceived by many managers as one of the more uncomfortable or unpleasant management functions. This is generally because there is a lack of clarity in the principles and procedures involved and a failure to assess and plan the developmental actions.

Some managers see the exercise as the annual chastising of below-standard performers rather than as a developmental opportunity. This management attitude needs to change; otherwise, the process will result in further deterioration in performance, as employees become demotivated through what they perceive as poor management practice.

Managers are not required to find performance shortfalls for every employee, as a matter of form. The analysis must represent an honest assessment based on facts. It must also involve the views of the person being appraised, who should also see the exercise as a personal developmental opportunity for himself/herself. An open-ended discussion, where the manager moves beyond recrimination into an educational and developmental mode, is more successful and helps to build a high level of trust between managers and their employees.

How we advise a person of a shortfall in standards of performance can have a demotivational impact on the individual – in other words, the exact opposite of what we wish to achieve. So communication and full engagement with the person, setting out the terms of discussion in advance and identifying the ideal objectives we would like to achieve in a mutual exercise would greatly help to avoid a demotivational result.

The policies and procedures we develop as managers provide the framework for our performance management practices. It is critical for managers not to carry out any appraisals until the policies, principles and procedures are discussed and agreed by all those responsible for the application of the performance management and appraisal process.

Managers have the greatest effect on their employees' performance and company productivity. Inexperienced managers, or managers with a personality that is not conducive to working positively with others, can have an adverse impact on the attitudes of others. Consequently, before considering the analysis of all employees in any formal performance analysis structure, the chief executive should assess management abilities and styles. If the chief executive is unsure about how best to do this, then commissioning an external consultant will help to ensure that the approach in use in the company reflects best practice.

Depending on the nature of the work, the performance appraisal methods or systems applied can be complex or simple, focused or general. However, it is preferable that the approach is positive and proactive and operated as a joint effort rather than a one-way complaints mechanism. Any documentation used should be used to focus the discussion and as a tool to assist with the identification of a jointly-agreed plan for change.

Two simple systems are suggested here to help encourage a systematic approach to performance management – one for jobs with a high proportion of repetitious duties (referred to below as **System 1**) and the other for jobs with higher degrees of decision-making latitude (**System 2**).

System 1

Even in a direct, focused approach, where the manager provides a list of issues for discussion related to performance shortfalls that can be directly related to the individual's actions, it can still be beneficial to adopt a counselling or coaching approach to discuss these shortfalls, rather than a chastising attitude. The discussion therefore is two-way, with the objective of uncovering what may have contributed to below-standard performance and what joint actions the participants could take to improve the performance during the next period.

The manager should prepare for the performance appraisal session by completing a prompt chart (see **Figure 15**), which outlines various work-related headings (factors) and a range of differentiating standards of performance. In the example, five standard ratings are used – 10, 8, 6, 4 and 2. This makes the process easier, as the manager can simply tick off the appropriate rating for each heading, based on the rationale for each score.

FIGURE 15: PERFORMANCE MANAGEMENT PROMPT CHART – SYSTEM 1

Points Values	X	10	8	6	4	2
X = weightings		How well does this employee understand the job requirements?				
Job Knowledge		Thoroughly understands all aspects of the job	More than adequate knowledge of the job	Sufficient knowledge of some aspects of the job	Insufficient knowledge of some aspects of the job	Continually in need of instruction
Points value?		Is the employee's work accurate, satisfactory and consistent?				
Quality of Work		Consistently accurate standards & is compliant	Careful person seldom requires correction	Average acceptable work standard	Occasionally careless, needs checking & correction	Regularly inaccurate & careless, must be monitored
Points value?		Insert appropriate question to reflect the work-related factor heading.				
Other work-related factors		Ensure each of the rating explanations is adequately described	....	....	....	....

Instructions

1. The designated assessor initially should determine the key factors for success in the job, using the job description as a basis.

2. This form is a generic template. Therefore, if physical output is a key factor, then quantity of work would be the appropriate heading under which to assess the individual's performance. Each key job requirement should be looked at in this way.

3. The form allows you to weight the three most important factors for each job. This quickly helps you to focus on the person's relevant performance factors vis-à-vis the key job requirements. For example, you may decide that, for a particular job, **responsibility**, **initiative** and **dependability** are the three most important factors. You score the individual within the range suggested and whatever score appears under these three key criteria might be multiplied by a factor of 2. For example, if you scored an employee as being particularly successful on all counts, this would amount to 100 points – 70 for each of the seven factors plus the double score for each of the three key factors. Therefore, applying this principle for all assessments, the scores are out of a potential of 100 points.

There are other considerations that can be built into the performance appraisal meeting, which help the manager and the employee to get a better understanding of the status of the performance, what can be done to consolidate the positives and whether further development or resources can be used to reduce any weaknesses that were jointly identified and agreed during the performance appraisal process. These considerations should be documented in the appraisal form.

System 2

This is for managerial, supervisory and administrative type jobs. The spirit and intent of the appraisal meetings is the same as for **System 1**, but the appraisal documentation prompts the assessor using different criteria and requires more careful consideration of objectives.

In many cases, the objectives for such categories can only be expressed as generalisations, rather than as a scoring method. However, there still must be clear and achievable targets against which the individual's performance can be measured.

When designing and agreeing objectives, which may be measured several times during the usual 12-month appraisal period, avoid ambiguous statements, that can be difficult to assess or which can result in misunderstandings due to different perspectives on either side.

The objective for the manager is to motivate and develop the individual and to improve performance where it is really needed. Getting this philosophical approach clear in everyone's mind is important, as any other application of the system will be de-motivational.

The prompt chart in **Figure 16** helps the manager to focus on the critical areas of the employee's performance. As in the example for **System 1** (**Figure 15**), the factors should be adjusted to suit the occupation and organisational culture.

FIGURE 16: PERFORMANCE MANAGEMENT PROMPT CHART – SYSTEM 2

Managers may find this a useful prompt to define strengths and weaknesses. The manager must enter his/her rating and write explanations in the comments section. This requires more analytical time and effort than System 1, as the employees in these occupations have more latitude or freedom to act (albeit within some controls or guidelines).

4 = Excellent   3 = Good   2 = Acceptable   1 = Unacceptable

Performance Factors		Rating	Comments
Quality	Finished assignments within the employee's scope of responsibility are satisfactorily completed.		
Job Understanding	Consider the person's level of understanding of their main responsibilities and how they affect others. Is there sufficient understanding?		
Relationship with Others	Readily accepts assignments, suggestions or criticism from manager / supervisor; works effectively with others - uses courtesy and tact in dealings with others at all levels; willing to help.		
Initiative	Self-starter, seeks additional responsibility and performs additional tasks without being asked; pays close attention to the job at hand and uses time effectively; proposes job improvements; receptive to new ideas; shows interest in further development within the company.		
Other	People management, communication, dealing with conflict, etc		

System 2 very much focuses on a joint investigative discussion to determine what is going right, what could be better and how the participants can work together to resolve issues and/or achieve productive change. It is trying to find common ground or agreement to achieve what the participants decide are the most desirable factors in raising performance.

This analysis can be done by identifying key performance questions:

- The positives - what is working well at present?
- Why is it working well?
- What is the ideal?
- What is not quite right yet?
- What resources, information or changes would we need to make it better than it is?

The manager acts as a guide or coach to help uncover important issues and identify solutions.

The agreed performance management plan and the appropriate review dates should then be documented in the appraisal form.

Preparation for the performance appraisal

Ensure that there is clarity from the chief executive down to supervisors as to the policies, principles and procedures of the company's performance management approach. These should be clearly stated in writing.

Take time to prepare an individual assessment in advance for each person you intend to meet and work with on the joint performance assessment exercise. Give adequate notice to each person about the performance management meeting, the content and the approach and what is expected of them. It is important to explain that it is a positive and beneficial process, aimed at achieving lasting improvements for employees and the company.

The performance appraisal meeting

The environment should be private and comfortable and free from any distraction or interruption.

Welcome the person to the meeting and ensure they are aware that it is a two-way process and that they have the freedom to express their views in a safe and developmental environment and are genuinely encouraged to do so.

Have general performance-related questions prepared, but listen carefully to the answers. This listening approach is more akin to the style of a counsellor or management coach. The old approach would be for the manager just to tell the person what was wrong with them and then what they must do about it. This was often followed up with an 'or else' statement, which guaranteed that the person went home demotivated! This is not the objective. In that style, you are bringing a specific issue to the individual to get them to admit failure or force them to accept particular targets. If such a serious state exists with an employee, surely it should have been dealt with before the performance appraisal meeting – possibly within the company's disciplinary procedures?

The performance management approach set out here is a joint search for what is important and relevant for the individual and for the company.

Managers should seek to train themselves in such skills before considering embarking on a one-to-one performance management session. As a listener, you may be surprised to discover interesting facts about performance issues that you had not considered. Things are not always as they first appear. Proactive listening means asking questions during the session that will provide useful information for developing productive changes.

While it is a proactive approach, agreement is not always possible. The meeting can be suspended while the participants reflect on the content that has arisen. The manager still has responsibility for ensuring the positive nature of the sessions, while maintaining clear sight of the business changes that are necessary. Several sessions might be necessary to achieve the required result. Investment in the joint proactive approach is worthwhile, but requires patience, understanding and innovation.

The final outcome will be that the participants agree what they must do for one another to achieve certain productive changes within an agreed timeframe. Setting clear objectives is necessary and practical, although these may need to be expressed in generalities occasionally, depending on the circumstances and occupation.

The manager, of course, is not finished there. The rules of engagement require the manager to understand fully what he/she must do to support the individual. Also, the manager must check back to ensure that the support structures are adequate and working as agreed at the performance management meeting. Set review dates to assess how the joint efforts are working with regard to the agreed objectives, where they might be falling down and what, if anything, should be done to make further corrections to ensure the achievement of what was agreed.

Summary

Performance management is not an annual event. It is a regular aspect of management life. It is too late to take corrective action when things go off target. Incremental adjustments are what keep people on target.

There are a variety of styles and systems available and you will need to find a suitable approach for your company. You can develop your own approach using these criteria or you can adapt another system to suit your needs. Keep the system as simple as possible and use it as a prompter for an honest, but developmental, discussion.

TERMINATION OF EMPLOYMENT

Introduction

There are many reasons for resignations and dismissals in companies but, in either case, it is important for the employer to ensure that there are clear procedures established for dealing with the situation and that these procedures are applied consistently, fairly and impartially. It is also important that these procedures are legally correct.

You may never have dealt with a complete investigation or dismissal procedure in the past, or you may have dismissed an employee without following all the suggested steps in this section. In doing so, you may have experienced no resistance or received no subsequent claim for unfair dismissal. Therefore, when you consider the steps below, you may feel that the procedures seem long, tedious, unwieldy or even unnecessary. This is not so, these procedures have evolved, based on legal precedent and each step is important.

Cases have been lost due to the omission of any one of these procedural steps. The steps need not be drawn out over a long period of time, although, in certain circumstances, this might be necessary. An employer must consider the circumstances of the issue, the facts and evidence, the individual concerned and the complexity of the issue. All of these considerations will contribute to the process timescale.

In all cases where a termination of employment is related to a disciplinary issue, the procedures applied must reflect the requirements of the laws of natural justice (see **Chapter 2**). Anyone retrospectively assessing your procedures will measure all that you have done against these basic laws.

Notice Periods

An employee, or the employer, may terminate the employee's employment by providing notice within the terms of the employee's contract of employment. In addition, the Minimum Notice & Terms of Employment Acts 1973-2001 set out the minimum periods of notice required, in relation to the employee's length of service with the company, as shown in **Figure 17**.

Nonetheless, the company, or the employee, may waive the right to notice and/or accept payment in lieu of notice, by agreement.

FIGURE 17: MINIMUM STATUTORY NOTICE PERIODS

Length of Service	Minimum Notice Period
13 weeks to 2 years	1 week
2 years to 5 years	2 weeks
5 years to 10 years	4 weeks
10 years to 15 years	6 weeks
More than 15 years	8 weeks

Resignations

Employees resign for a wide range of reasons – some positive and some negative. It is important for employers to understand why staff resign.

An employer may be overjoyed to 'see the back' of some problematic individual, who they were unable to motivate or failed to process through any disciplinary procedures and who had a disruptive influence on others; conversely, there are occasions when an employer would prefer that a person did not leave the company.

Knowing the reason why someone has decided to leave, generally for a valid reason (for example, more money, better prospects or family relocation) provides the employer with the opportunity to discuss the situation with the employee, and possibly to develop an equally valid reason for the individual to change their mind and remain with the company. However, employers can also discover, only after the employee has left, that the employee had a complaint, grievance or claim against the company. It could be concerning an accident at work, or because an individual believes that the employer has been non-compliant with some aspect of the employment contract or with some legislative requirement. If the relationship was poor before the resignation, the reason for the resignation may be solely related to the employee seeking compensation, or because the employee feels less exposed while pursuing a claim for compensation when outside the company.

Ideally, employers should create a working environment that helps to minimise resignations of employees whom they value. In companies with good employee relations, employees are seen as an important resource that holds the pool of skill-sets necessary for the maintenance and development of the business, and which has cost a significant amount of money and time to assemble and develop. Generally, the costs involved in replacing these skill-sets are much higher than investing in proactive employee relations measures and employee development strategies to keep them.

Procedures in respect of a resignation

- The employee should be asked to provide a written resignation for the company's records, before any other action is taken.

- Ensure the correct calculation of the individual's legal entitlements to pay, holiday pay, pension rights, the provision of a P45 on time, etc.

- Sign off all necessary documentation.

- Hold an exit interview with the leaver, to assess how he/she feels about the company, its products, the environment, its policies, etc.

- Maintain all HR and payroll records associated with the individual, for the appropriate period (which varies from Act to Act, and sometimes within an Act for different types of records). The method of storage should be clear and the person responsible defined.

Redundancy

Redundancy is essentially a dismissal from employment. The Redundancy Payments Acts 1967-2003:

- Provide definitions for dismissal on the grounds of redundancy.

- Define the minimum statutory redundancy payments for employees in relation to their weekly remuneration and to their length of service with the company.

- Place payment and procedural obligations on employers.

Custom and practice in Ireland

While the terms of redundancy payments are clearly defined in the Acts, some companies pay more than these basic requirements. Such additional payments are negotiated directly between the company and its employees, through their representatives or with the assistance of the Labour Relations Commission, Rights Commissioner or the Labour Court, depending on circumstances.

Whether negotiated directly or through third parties, it can be difficult to reach agreement on a suitable and affordable redundancy package. Negotiations often include issues concerning the selections of employees, other than on a basis of a 'last in, first out' policy. Establishing the selection criteria generally requires negotiation and the consideration of other options such as retraining and redeployment. Some employers who have a need to reduce staff through redundancy often allow employees to volunteer, rather than to be selected for redundancy on the basis of 'last in, first out'. However, voluntary redundancy is not always possible, as the employer may need to retain certain expertise within the company, if it is to continue in business following the redundancies.

The financial circumstances of some companies may prevent them from offering redundancy payment terms greater than those provided for by law. Employees may challenge this position through the national industrial relations procedures based on custom and practice, either within the company, the industry or locality.

Employers should be aware that, in the event of third party investigations, despite evidence that the company has problems and may not have sufficient funds to pay amounts greater than statutory entitlements, recommendations may still be made, following an industrial relations hearing, to pay in excess of the statutory amounts. Of course, the employer may appeal such a decision.

Legitimate reasons for redundancy

A redundancy occurs where a dismissal is wholly or mainly because:

1. The employer has ceased, or intends to cease, to carry out the business for the purpose of which the employee is employed, or to carry out that business in the place where the employee was/is employed (company closure or relocation).

2. The requirements of the organisation for employees to carry out work of a particular kind in the place where the employee was employed have ceased or diminished, or are expected to do so (or the company ceases to do the work for which the employee was employed, due to deteriorating business or fall-off in orders).

3. The employer has decided to carry on the business with fewer or no employees, whether by requiring the employee's work to be done by other employees or otherwise (reorganisation or doing work in a different way, including outsourcing the work on contract or the introduction of new technology).

4. The employer has decided that the employee's work should be done in a different manner, for which the employee is not sufficiently qualified or trained (change in work demand, where the knowledge and skill requirements are deemed to be greater than the employee's capabilities).

5. The employer has decided that the employee's work should be done by a person who is also capable of doing other work for which the employee is not sufficiently qualified or trained.

Essential requirements for redundancy

It has been pointed out by the Employment Appeals Tribunal (EAT) that two important characteristics are present in all five of the legitimate reasons for redundancy:

1. **Impartiality**: The reason for a dismissal relates to the job, not to the individual employee.

2. **Change**: An alteration in the workplace, ranging from a complete or partial shutdown to changes due to decreases in volume or activity, changes in technology or in the nature of how a job is done.

Incorrect grounds for redundancy

If redundancy is due to one of the automatically unfair or incorrect grounds listed in Section 6 of the Unfair Dismissals Acts 1977-2001, the redundancy is not legitimate. A dismissal or redundancy is seen as unfair if it results wholly or mainly from one or more of the following:

- Trade union membership or activities.
- Religious or political opinions.
- Involvement of the employee in civil proceedings (whether actual, threatened or proposed) against his/her employer.
- Involvement of the employee in criminal proceedings (whether actual, threatened or proposed) against his/her employer.
- Race, colour or sexual orientation.
- Age.
- Membership of the travelling community.
- Matters relating to pregnancy.
- Not a genuine redundancy situation and/or improper and unfair procedures for selection were applied.
- Exercise of statutory leave rights (adoptive, carer's, maternity or parental).

It is up to the employee to prove that the dismissal was not on the basis of a legitimate redundancy, if he/she decides to pursue an unfair dismissal or wrongful dismissal case.

Selection for redundancy

The selection process must be fair and non-discriminatory (not biased on the grounds of gender, age, marital status, family status, sexual orientation, religion, race, disability or membership of the travelling community).

Ensure that the records that you rely upon for selecting employees are available and accurate. The selection process, if not on the basis of 'last in, first out' should be fair, equitable and objective and there must be adequate records or other evidence to support the decision-making.

In the event of a claim, the Employment Appeals Tribunal (EAT) will look at whether an employer used objective criteria to come to a decision about who was selected for redundancy. It is important to be able to explain and to prove the details about which employees are to remain, their level of importance in terms of knowledge and skills retention and the impact on the company, if they were to go. Knowing that the selection processes could result in a challenge or dispute, employers should give serious consideration to these issues before commencing the selection process, rather than being instructed to do so by the EAT in the event of a dispute. Using the opportunity to get rid of a problematic employee *via* the stated procedural method for selection will not be seen as fair practice, no matter how well the case is made. So, being 'squeaky-clean' in your selection process is strongly advised.

Notice periods

Redundancies of fewer employees than the numbers described in the collective redundancy section (**following**), require the employer to issue notice in accordance with the minimum notice periods set out in the Minimum Notice & Terms of Employment (Information) Acts 1994 & 2001 (see **Figure 17**).

The employer may give written notification of redundancy directly to the employee or post the notice to his/her home address.

It is good employee relations practice to discuss the situation, as far in advance as possible, regardless of the level of redundancies, with all employees in the company, and particularly with those who might be directly affected. Ideally, people should not be subjected to sudden shocks or surprises. They need time to plan and to take corrective action. The impact of redundancy can be devastating for your employees and their families. Careful handling and support for employees will be appreciated. This will also be appreciated by those remaining in the company. It could also make a substantial difference to employee relations and stability, if the company's circumstances were to improve at a later date and the redundant employees are requested to re-apply for their former positions because their skill sets become imperative. (It can happen.)

Employer's rebate

An employer who pays the correct statutory redundancy lump sum entitlement to an eligible employee is entitled to a 60% rebate from the Social

Insurance Fund. An employer paying more than the statutory amount will still only be entitled to this set percentage of the statutory amount.

Documentation

The employer and employee must complete the appropriate redundancy payment documentation, which is available from the Department of Enterprise, Trade & Employment.

In order to claim a employer's rebate, the RP50 form must be fully completed and signed by the employer and by the employee(s) being made redundant. The employer must submit the form to the Department of Enterprise, Trade & Employment within six months of the employee(s) receiving their lump sum.

Redundancy payment entitlements

- The employee is entitled to a lump sum payment, based on length of service and his/her weekly rate of remuneration at the time the employer declares the redundancy.

- The employer must pay the total lump sum due to the employee not later than the date of termination of employment.

- Since the introduction of the Redundancy Payments (Amendment) Act 2003, the redundancy payment (lump sum payment) is two weeks' remuneration multiplied by the number of years' service (from the age of 16 onwards) plus one week's remuneration. For all employees, weekly remuneration for the purposes of calculating the lump sum is capped at €600 per week.

- Remuneration is wider than just wages or salary, and could include company car, lunch expenses, clothing allowance, etc. For the purposes of a redundancy payment, convert all such benefits-in-kind into a cash value and amalgamate these with the wage or salary, subject to the €600 maximum.

- All statutory redundancy payments are tax-free.

Collective Redundancies

Collective redundancies definitions and procedures are defined in the Protection of Employment Act 1977, which enacted an EU directive.

A collective redundancy occurs when a certain number of employees are made redundant within a 30-day period. The number that qualifies as a collective redundancy depends on the size of the organisation:

- Five redundancies in a company employing from 20 to 49 employees.

- Ten redundancies in a company employing from 50 to 99 employees.
- 10% redundancies in a company employing from 100 to 299 employees.
- Thirty redundancies in a company employing more than 300 employees.

Collective redundancy procedures

Where there is to be multiple or collective redundancies, the employer must inform the Department of Enterprise, Trade & Employment, in writing, at least 30 days before the intended redundancies. This notice must contain:

- Name and address of the employer.
- Indication of the type of employer (sole trader, partnership or company).
- The reason(s) for the proposed collective redundancies.
- Address where the collective redundancies are proposed.
- The period during which the collective redundancies are proposed to take place.
- The number and category (or description) of employees normally employed.
- The number and category (or description) of employees who are being made redundant.
- The names and addresses of the trade unions or staff associations representing employees affected by the proposed redundancies and with whom it has been the practice of the employer to conduct collective bargaining negotiations.
- The date on which consultations with each trade union or staff association commenced and the progress achieved to date in those consultations.

Except in the case of bankruptcy or winding-up proceeding, no redundancies can take place during this 30-day notification period.

The 30-day notification period does not affect the employee's right to the relevant period of notice under the Minimum Notice & Terms of Employment Acts 1973-2001 (see **Figure 17**) and the Redundancy Payment Acts 1967-2003. Nor does it affect the employee's right to notice as outlined in his/her contract of employment. No waiver of the provision of the Acts is allowed, even by agreement.

In selecting employees for collective redundancy, care must be taken to ensure that there is no unfair selection (see earlier), in order to avoid any claim under the Unfair Dismissals Acts 1977-2001.

Employee representatives

In the event of collective redundancies, an employer must consult with the employees or representatives of the employees at least 30 days before the intended redundancies.

Representatives are defined as trade unions, staff associations or other bodies that hold negotiation licences and with which it has been the practice of the employer to conduct collective bargaining negotiations.

Where no trade union or staff association exists to represent the employees, representatives (employees from within the organisation) can be chosen by the employees to represent them in any negotiations with their employer. The employer is required to provide arrangements for employees to select their own representatives, including facilities for employees to meet and elect representatives, either during or after working hours. For example, an employer might provide meeting facilities for one hour before the normal daily finish time, allowing the employees to continue the meeting after hours.

Consultation process

Where there is to be multiple or collective redundancies, an employer must consult with the employees or their representatives at least 30 days before the intended redundancies. The employees or their representatives must also receive a copy of the notice sent to the Minister for Enterprise, Trade & Employment.

The objective of the consultative process is to allow the employees to express their views and, if possible, to discuss ways of avoiding or reducing the effect of the redundancies. The consultations may explore options other than redundancies – for example:

- Reducing the number of employees affected.
- Mitigating their circumstances by redeployment or retraining.
- The possibility of employees going on short-time or taking a reduction in salary.

Where redundancies are unavoidable, the consultation must include:

- The selection criteria and process to be used as the basis for selecting employees for redundancy.
- Voluntary redundancy packages.
- The timing of the redundancies.

Information

Employers are obliged to provide in writing to the employee representatives the same information as they are required to send to the Minister for Enterprise, Trade & Employment (see above).

In addition, they must provide the method for calculating any redundancy payments, other than the statutory minimum payment defined under the Redundancy Payments Acts. However, it makes good communications sense to detail all payments, itemised under their respective categorisation, to avoid any ambiguity.

Lay-off and Short-time Working

Under the Redundancy Payments Acts 1967-2003, and subject to qualifying conditions, an employee who has been laid-off, or is on short-time working hours, may be entitled to claim redundancy, once the period of lay-off or short-time has continued for longer than four consecutive weeks or at least six weeks over a period of 13 consecutive weeks.

The employee must serve notice to the employer of intention to claim statutory redundancy, no later than four weeks after the end of a lay-off or short-time period.

In such a situation, the employer may serve a counter notice that there will be at least 13 weeks' work commencing within a period of four weeks from the date of the employee's claim for statutory redundancy, This counter notice must be served on the employee within seven days of receipt of the claim for redundancy. If the employer is unable to give such an undertaking, the employee will be entitled to redundancy, subject to the normal qualifying conditions and statutory payments.

Lay-off

Lay-off is defined in Section 11 of the Redundancy Payment Act 1967, as a temporary situation where an employee's employment is suspended, when the employer is unable to provide work but has a reasonable belief that the situation will not be permanent.

The employer is required to provide notice of lay-off to the employee, prior to the cessation of employment.

Short-time working

Short-time is also defined in Section 11 of the Redundancy Payment Act 1967. For example, the employee receives less than half of his/her normal weekly remuneration or his/her number of hours of work are reduced to less than half the normal weekly hours, due to a reduction in the amount of work to be done. This must be a temporary situation.

The employer is required to provide notice of short-time working to the employee, prior to the reduction in working hours.

Documentation

The RP9 form is used for lay-off or short-term situations.

Part A is completed when an employer wishes to notify an employee of temporary lay-off or short-time.

An employee may use Part B of the RP9 form to notify the company of his/her intention to claim a redundancy lump sum payment in a lay-off or short-time working situation.

If an employer wishes to serve a counter notice to the redundancy claim, Part C of the RP9 form should be completed.

Outplacement

Outplacement describes a temporary support service for employees whose employment is being terminated. There is no legal obligation on an employer to provide any outplacement services for any category of employee. It is purely a voluntary act or policy decision by the employer.

The service was introduced to Ireland through the large multinational US-based companies when implementing redundancies. Initially, the service was used to support senior employees, who were affected by redundancy or whose performance was not satisfactory. The provision of such services has spread to other categories of employees. Human Resource managers, in general, perceive outplacement services as a positive and proactive employee relations practice.

The outplacement specialist deals with each person on an individual basis, to help them to cope, adjust or plan to source new employment. The individual service is very important, as everyone has different circumstances, financial responsibilities, abilities, desires, preferences, fears, worries, skill-sets, options, ideas, etc, which need to be identified. The outplacement specialist will provide the individual with the tools to develop a comprehensive campaign to source alternative employment or other income.

The outplacement specialist:

- Interviews and assesses the person's skill-sets and helps identify his/her main employment preferences and possibilities.

- Provides assistance with the preparation of a Curriculum Vitae for the individual, highlighting the person's expertise in terms of their formal education, knowledge and skills that they have acquired in each of their employments to date. The specialist also identifies any weaknesses in an employee's Curriculum Vitae and suggests any immediate or longer-term solution, including training, etc.

- Carries out a psychometric analysis of the person to identify the individual's key traits and to understand his/her subconscious work-related preferences, personality traits, strengths and weaknesses. This is a very valuable analysis and helps the person to overcome any difficulties such as communications, flexibility, decision-making, etc and provides valuable information to help the person to match these traits to jobs where they might be 'best suited'.

- Carries out mock interviews with the employee to help improve interviewing abilities and raise confidence.

- Prepares generic letters of application for the individual for various job types.

- Assists with job searches.

- Answers the person's questions, including advice concerning the best use of any monies arising from a redundancy or other termination settlement.

- Uses a variety of developmental tools to help the individual to develop and regain confidence and reduce any fears.

The costs of outplacement services varies in relation to the preferred service requirements, the status of the employee concerned and the number of employees involved.

Dismissals

In all dismissal cases, it is important that the employer follows the company's internal procedures for terminating the employment or, in the case of redundancy, follows the correct procedure under the terms of the Redundancy Payments Acts 1967-2003.

Dismissals are much more complex situations than retirement or resignations and could result in difficulties for the employer, if not handled correctly.

Dismissals related to redundancy are relatively straightforward, but must still be procedurally correct.

Dismissals involving disciplinary matters can become complex and can result in litigation.

Dismissals related to disciplinary matters

This section relates to misdemeanours, gross misconduct, employer investigations and procedures associated with investigations and dismissals.

At all stages throughout the investigation and termination procedures, the employer must keep detailed notes of every meeting and every piece of evidence gained or statement made or submitted by the employee and their representatives and any other witnesses, including management's own statements and any interactions with the employee in question.

Arriving at a dismissal decision can be a complex matter. If it is related to behaviour or performance issues, it is important that the investigative, decision-making and notification sequence is explained to the person involved and that their rights under the laws of natural justice are upheld. These requirements are critical. These procedures and the laws of natural justice are dealt within this chapter.

Phase 1: Becoming aware of an issue

When you become aware of an issue, you must ascertain the apparent seriousness of the issue, based on the preliminary information available, before an investigation commences. This should be done in two steps:

1. Is there a disciplinary issue to be addressed?
2. Is the issue a gross misconduct matter?

If the matter is serious – for example, if it falls within one or more of the company's definitions of gross misconduct – the person may be **suspended with pay**, pending the results of an impartial investigation. Suspending someone **without pay** during an investigation means that you are penalising him/her, before they have been found guilty. Inevitably, this will be cited later as evidence of bias against the employee, if he/she decides to make a claim against your decision. Indeed, there must be a good reason for suspending someone with pay pending an investigation, as they may feel that they are missing the opportunity to communicate with their witnesses during the initial investigative process while they are suspended.

It is important that you ensure that your procedures and documentation are reasonable. In the event of an issue arising, where you have little or no previous hands-on experience, it is advisable to seek assistance. Copy your adviser immediately with all procedures and documentation received, together with a summary statement of the issue to be investigated. It is acceptable to proceed with the initial steps in the investigation process before receiving a solicitor's comments, once you ensure that the employee's rights are being honoured within the laws of natural justice at all times.

If the employer considers that the matter is serious, and that it would be practical to conduct the investigation without the presence of the employee under investigation, the employee should be placed on temporary suspension with pay, pending the results of the investigation. This does not mean that they are not going to be consulted. It just means that they will be dealt with separately, following the initial internal inquiries. Such initial enquiries must be documented, and the employee to be investigated is entitled to access such information.

Phase 2: The laws of natural justice – employees' rights and the investigation process

The employee is considered innocent, until it is proven otherwise. Even if the matter appears a 'cut and dry' case, it is necessary to go through the investigative process systematically, including interviewing the accused before any final decision is taken.

There are clear steps to be followed here:

- The employee being suspended with pay is notified, in writing at the earliest possible opportunity, of this decision and the reason for it.
- The employee must be made aware of the issue and all the relevant details.
- The employee must have a genuine right of reply to the issue.
- The employee must have the right of representation with regard to the issue.
- The employee must have the right of appeal following any employer decision.

You are required to take statements from those involved, including the accused and witnesses, if available, and then consider all the information. If in doubt, seek additional information. Develop a list of relevant questions that need to be asked. Write all the information down, do not rely on memory. If your subsequent decision is challenged, you must be able to rely on the written information to support your decision-making process and be able to demonstrate a reasonable logic for your decisions.

Phase 3: Notification of the conclusion of the investigation and reflection time

When the employee's rights are addressed, and you subsequently come to a decision (for example, dismissal), the employee must be made aware of this decision and the reason for it, before any action is actually taken.

For example, you may state that you have concluded the investigation and believe that the person was 'guilty' of whatever offence they are being investigated for. You state that, for this gross misconduct offence, the standard sanction is dismissal. However, before deciding on the actual sanction, the employee must be advised that they may consider their position and make any additional submissions they wish within a reasonable period of time – for example, the following day – so that you can consider such additional information before reaching a final decision. This is an important step in the procedure.

The following day, the employee is requested to attend a meeting with his/her representative and is asked by you whether they wish to make any further submissions regarding the issue.

If any information is offered, you may schedule another meeting, at your discretion. This is to allow a reasonable period for the employer to reflect on any extra evidence presented.

Any such information arising must be recorded and considered by you to see whether it changes the nature of the evidence received to date and, as a consequence, affects the original decision or the standard sanction for the offence. This could take an hour or a day – the timing is again at your discretion. However, it would be prudent to err on the cautious side, when allowing a sufficient amount of time to give a full and fair consideration of the information presented.

If, following the period of reflection, you believe that any such additional information does not have any major impact on the decision, you can then advise the employee accordingly.

If there is a standard sanction for the misdemeanour, this standard sanction for the offence should be explained to the person concerned. The employee is then given a further opportunity, in conjunction with his/her representative, to make any representations regarding the level of sanction to be taken by the company – either at this meeting, or after a short break, or on the following day, at your discretion.

When you are satisfied that the individual has completed their defence, are satisfied that you have completely analysed all the evidence available, have come to a rational, unbiased decision and observed the final steps in the process above, then the employee may be dismissed.

Phase 4: Termination meeting
You invite the individual and their representative or witness, as they choose, to attend a meeting, which may be on or off the premises. You may wish, for example, to take a conference room in a hotel for such a meeting rather than

use a company office. This would be a particular consideration where privacy is difficult or where the employee requests such privacy.

You explain the above procedure and the nature of the decision, based on the facts and statements taken, including any additional information provided by the employee. You state your final conclusion, having regard to all these facts.

At this point, and depending on the nature of the issue for which the person is being dismissed, you may consider alternatives or even any representations by the employee's representative regarding the sanction to be taken. Every case is different and you should consider such submissions. There is no obligation on you to accept such requests but it would be considered appropriate at least to give consideration to any proposals presented.

It is advisable to explain the appeals process to the person involved and their representative. For example, the accused should know who has the authority to dismiss in the company and whether there is a more senior person to whom an appeal can be referred, prior to the action being taken.

Phase 5: Internal appeals

If, at this stage, the employee being dismissed makes a submission to appeal the dismissal, the procedures should be clear and followed carefully

The appeal is generally reviewed by a person other than the individual who made the decision to dismiss. The same fair process must be applied within the laws of natural justice. However, if the employee makes such an appeal but provides no new grounds or evidence, you may feel that full consideration was given to all evidence presented and no further consideration is required. If this is the case, this position should be stated in writing to the employee. Alternatively, if the person's appeal is based on their opinion that not all the evidence was properly reviewed or that the interpretation of that evidence is incorrect, then it is important to ensure that the evidence is reviewed again by a person other than the original manager/investigator.

It can happen that new evidence does arise that can change your decision or that the interpretation of the original evidence was incorrect for some reason.

Phase 6: Termination procedures

Assuming that no additional evidence has changed the facts, and the issue requires dismissal, the administrative termination procedures at this point are similar to resignations (see earlier) with regard to the person's accrued entitlements, pay, etc.

Phase 7: External appeals

The employee still may believe that the decision is incorrect, or that the procedures were flawed, and has the right to appeal the company's decision to a Rights Commissioner, or the Employment Appeals Tribunal. Alternatively, the employee may decide to take a High Court case for wrongful dismissal against the company.

Costs

Unfair dismissal claims carry a maximum award against the employer of an amount based on the dismissed employee's annual pay for two years.

Wrongful dismissals cases have no upper limitation on damages. The costs of processing and losing an unfair dismissal or a wrongful dismissals case are considerable. Consequently, the correct procedures for investigation and dismissal should be observed at all times.

It seems that it is becoming increasingly difficult to dismiss a person from work, regardless of the cause. There are more and more steps appearing in the investigative and dismissals procedures and solicitors and barristers are tending to add steps in the process 'just to be sure'. Therefore, if in doubt, seek professional advice. Remember that it is cheaper to add another step in the process if you are in the slightest doubt, or if the employee is adamant that they are innocent. Even having an independent third party to assess the evidence and process, where the employee thinks that process has been unfair, is a demonstration of your desire to be impartial. Such costs can be reasonable and far less than fighting a claim for unfair dismissals.

Providing References

Dealing with requests for references is becoming increasingly difficult for managers. In the past, we may have given a verbal 'thumbs up' (or down) on a particular individual spontaneously and without reflecting too deeply on the impact of our words. This is no longer prudent and the ramifications for the manager and the company are becoming more complex.

A reference is, by nature, judgemental and prone to interpretations and challenges. Consequently, it is not something to be decided upon without due consideration of some or all of the following:

- Currently, there is no obligation under Irish employment law to provide a reference, either verbally or in writing for any employee, either to them directly or to a prospective employer. So the company policy could be that it supplies no references for any employee. The provision of references is a matter of company policy and procedure. However, make sure it is applied consistently. Do not refuse for one employee who was not all that good and then agree to provide a reference for another whom you feel was a model employee. If that became public knowledge, you might have a claim from the one you refused, based on inequality or victimisation.

- If you do decide to supply references, a person in the company who is familiar with the risks involved and who has access to personnel files should be charged with the job of providing references within guidelines.

- The most important consideration in deciding to issue a reference to an employee or to a prospective employer is accuracy.

- The employer should be in a position to defend all references, if necessary, using company records.

- Keep records of each individual's performance and of any references issued based on such performance records.

- An employee can make a claim against you under civil, common or constitutional law for allegedly depriving him or her of the right to work, on the basis of false information that may have been provided by you to a prospective employer. This might be based on the suspicion that you provided a poor reference. However, the employee could request a review of all the documentation at your premises and at the prospective employer's premises, with regard to interview notes, etc under disclosure. As mentioned above, the quality of your evidence is important. It could make the difference between having to pay damages and not.

- While such cases may seem few and far between, it is at least important for you to know what can happen, so that you can develop suitable policies, practices and procedures for your company.

Fairness and reasonableness

Employees are entitled to human dignity, honesty and respect. The more one considers the logic behind a reference policy, the more obvious it is that references are an individual thing. For example, if you decide to provide only a basic reference to all employees, you must decide whether this is fair on employees who have been exceptionally co-operative, flexible and regular high performers. The employer would prefer these high performers to stay with the company but, in general, would not want to block their progress if they decided to leave. Providing a good reference to high performers is showing respect for their efforts, their commitment and the contribution that they made to the company during their service period. And refusing to give any reference on the basis that it might backfire at some future date may seem fair and reasonable to you, but the good employee may think otherwise.

To be completely fair, each employee needs to get a reference that most accurately reflects their performance and behaviour.

Dealing with requests for references

References may be requested by existing and former employees and by prospective employers, in writing or verbally. You are under no obligation to respond either way, but you must decide how you are going to handle such requests in a consistent and fair manner. Issue a policy and procedure statement and ensure that all those responsible for the application of such policies and procedures are in compliance.

Issuing an accurate reference directly to an employee on the day they leave is probably the most effective way of ensuring that the information you provide is up-to-date, fresh in everyone's mind and that the documents to support the information are readily available and are then properly filed for future reference. The manager responsible for issuing references should decide what information you wish to share and under what circumstances.

Summary

A formal employee reference policy with clear procedures is essential for the following reasons:

- To be fair to all your employees and, possibly, to other employers.

- To acknowledge good performers.

- To be in a position to defend your position, if required.

- To ensure fair and equitable treatment of all employees.

- To ensure that you know why you are issuing a good employee with a good reference.

- To ensure that you are clear about why you are not going to issue a reference, or are only prepared to issue a basic reference.

- To ensure all management and supervisory staff understand the reference procedures and who is responsible for their preparation and final signatures.

- When you provide a reference, you are providing a service to your former employee and also to the requesting employer. You are verifying information, based on your specific experience with the employee in question, so good records are essential.

- You may wish to include your policy and procedures regarding references in the HR manual, employee handbook or even in the contract of employment.

Retirement

When we think of retirement, we normally associate this with a pension scheme. However not all companies have pension schemes in place and some may not even have any particular procedures regarding retirement.

Ideally, every employee would have a pension scheme and a set age for retirement, possibly with some special considerations for employees wishing to work on and who have skill-sets that the employer would be happy to retain. Alternatively, it might also be relevant to have early retirement options for employees.

Until the company is in a position to develop such policies, the minimum requirement is to have a process in place to provide employees with access to pension suppliers for the purpose of establishing a Personal Retirement Savings Account (PRSA).

A PRSA is an investment vehicle used for long-term retirement provision by employees, self-employed, homemakers, carers, unemployed and any other category of person. If employees sign up for such savings accounts, the employer is also obliged to assist with making deductions and payments to the pension companies. These are statutory requirements under the terms of the Pensions (Amendment) Act 2002. Employers may work in conjunction with the pension providers to supplement the employee saving contribution, although there is no statutory requirement on them to do so.

Apart from the monetary considerations of retirement, which is of course a very important consideration, there is also the question of how the employee will deal with the actual retirement itself – the sudden availability of time, being at home seven days a week, loss of social contact with friends and work colleagues. Many employees, even those with good pension schemes, can find it difficult to adjust to retirement. Their partners also find it difficult to have them 'under their feet' on a daily basis. You can help your employees who are due to retire to consider and plan for these changes, to allow for an easier and more productive transition.

Some employees may have a second job that they can continue; others may have a long and well-established hobby or interest, which they are looking forward to immersing themselves in. However, there are some employees who dread retirement day and who would prefer to stay on. These employees may have no partner or few friends and may also be afraid of the impending loneliness. All these considerations are valid and the good employer will be aware of the related stress on employees facing such circumstances.

At a minimum, you could develop an internal support structure that could involve employees, on a voluntary basis, to provide self-help group support for retiring colleagues. External consultants could be used to assist the preparation of terms of reference for such support groups. Employees may wish to contribute to the development of retirement presentations, including activity options following retirement.

In the UK, the working-men's clubs helped maintain continuity with colleagues following their retirement. There are very few of these clubs in Ireland, in comparison with the UK. We have all heard of individuals 'fading away' once they left their employment, despite the fact that they were in good health and fulfilling a valuable role immediately before retirement. There are a number of reasons for this apparent loss of energy, enthusiasm and interest, including an apparent deterioration in self-worth. Being proactive in this area will be beneficial for retiring employees and will also be a very positive and motivational project for those non-retiring employees/volunteers who are willing to get involved.

CHAPTER 2

INDUSTRIAL

RELATIONS

INDUSTRIAL RELATIONS OVERVIEW

Employee Relations & Industrial Relations

It is important to note that the terms 'employee relations' and 'industrial relations' have two entirely different meanings:

- **Employee relations** refers to the proactive or developmental policies, practices and procedures (and the attitude toward employees) that help to consolidate a sound and non-confrontational relationship between the employer (manager, supervisor or other company representatives) and the employee.

- **Industrial relations** refers to the procedures that are used by the company and its employees to resolve issues or problems that occur, and which are, or could be, confrontational. Industrial relations, therefore, is reactive, as distinct from the proactive attributes associated with employee relations. When the industrial relations procedures fail, or are broken by either party, the parties can refer the issues to external arbitration, which has its own set of procedural requirements.

Employers who conduct their business with a distinct commitment to establishing and pursuing a good employee relations culture have a better chance of maintaining a stable environment, free from industrial relations disputes, work stoppages and other industrial relations actions. Companies with a track record of industrial relations disputes, strikes and other industrial relations actions find it more difficult to break the mould and to change the environment to a proactive employee relations culture. Once 'mutual trust' has been damaged, it is difficult, costly and time-consuming to repair.

This chapter is a practical guide to help employers to understand the process and approach to resolving issues, willingly or otherwise, through the industrial relations procedures.

Industrial Relations Actions

Industrial relations refers to the formal negotiating processes for the resolution of disputes at work.

Industrial relations actions can refer to the actions taken by an employee, or a group of employees, in dispute with a company. These actions can include a brief work stoppage, an all out strike, a 'go slow' while remaining at work, a picket at the entrance to the premises, and other actions designed to bring pressure to bear on the employer to acquiesce to certain demands, reasonable or otherwise.

If the employees are members of a trade union, a strike will either be officially recognised or not recognised by the union officials. If officially recognised, the strike notice, or notice of any other form of industrial relations action, must conform to specific notification regulations.

In some cases, the employer may be the one taking industrial action, in the form of a 'lock-out' of employees from the workplace.

Trade Union Involvement in Industrial Relations

Trade unions are a part of the Irish industrial relations process and play an important role within the industrial relations context. They represent individual members, and also groups of employees, in various industry-based negotiations and with the resolution of employee issues.

Company/union procedural agreements state the formal relationship between the employer and the employees and include details on how grievances and other issues are dealt with. If issues remain unresolved, a disputes procedure comes into play. This procedure is designed, in the first instance, to resolve an issue, while recognising the need to avoid business disruption, which could be detrimental to both the employer and employees.

The trade unions also participate with government and employers as social partners in Joint Industrial Councils, Joint Labour Committees, social partnership bargaining and on Employment Appeals Tribunals.

The trade unions' policy is to support business growth, while seeking to maintain reasonable rates of pay and good conditions for their members. This is frequently a dichotomy for trade union officials at local or industry level, when it is evident that the company or industry in question is going through a downturn in business.

Internal Procedures

Industrial relations processes are formal communications structures, with the specific aims of resolving issues and avoiding conflict. As an employer, you are advised to take a leadership role in the resolution of any dispute.

Issues concerning individuals should be heard by the employer, recorded, considered and a response provided as quickly as possible. Do not allow problems to fester. Remember that consistency and fairness is essential. You should be aware that any decision may become custom and practice for any similar issues arising in the future. So careful thought must be given to the repercussions of any decisions made. 'Buying out' a problem with a financial settlement could have far-reaching consequences, as the decision will inevitably be cited by other employees at a later stage and custom and practice is generally upheld in the third party industrial relations investigations.

Issues concerning groups of employees are even more important, as the costs can be considerable. If in doubt on any matter you believe to be important, check with your HR or industrial relations adviser.

Regardless of how well the procedures are designed, or how much the parties commit to the avoidance of disruption, unless the parties manage each issue carefully, there is always the possibility of a breakdown in the employer/employee relationship. This may lead to mistrust, and then conflict. Generally, such conflict has a negative impact on company performance. It is hard to repair such rifts, as the mutual trust to which the parties aspire is inevitably damaged. So conflict should be avoided by both sides, if they are to build a positive 'high trust' environment that can respond effectively to business demands.

Grievance procedure

The grievance procedure contains the mechanism for hearing complaints from employees and the appeals procedures (see **Figure 18**).

The appeals routes within a company will vary from company to company, generally influenced by the size of the company and its reporting hierarchy.

Grievance procedures are dealt with in more detail later in this chapter.

Disciplinary procedure

The disciplinary procedure is the vehicle for processing the employer's issues with staff. It is a formal structure with the specific aim of resolving people issues, such as advising employees of shortfalls in behaviour and/or performance (see **Figure 19**).

The employer provides written statements regarding the behaviour or performance shortfall and information about the decisions taken and the nature of future stages of the procedures. The employee must have the right of reply, the right to representation and the right of appeal within the laws of natural justice.

The disciplinary procedure allows for the employee to appeal decisions, internally and also externally, if the employee does not believe the employer's decision to be correct or fair.

The appeals route within a company will vary from company to company, depending on the size of the company and its reporting hierarchy.

Disciplinary procedures are dealt with in more detail later in this chapter.

FIGURE 18: GRIEVANCE PROCESS CHART

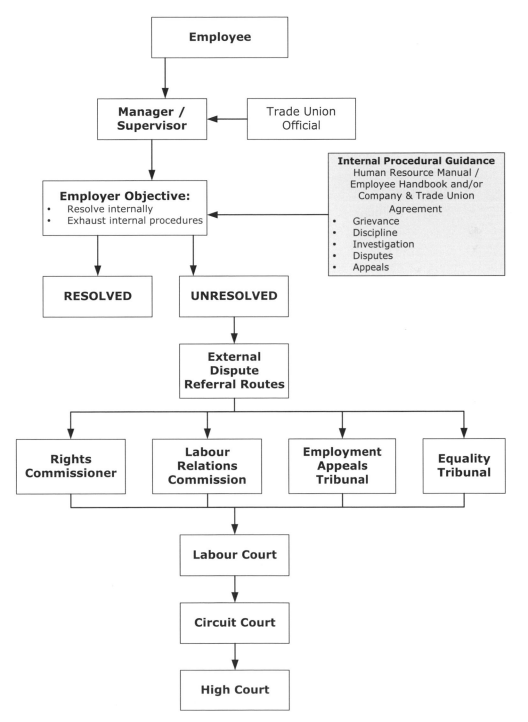

FIGURE 19: DISCIPLINARY PROCESS CHART

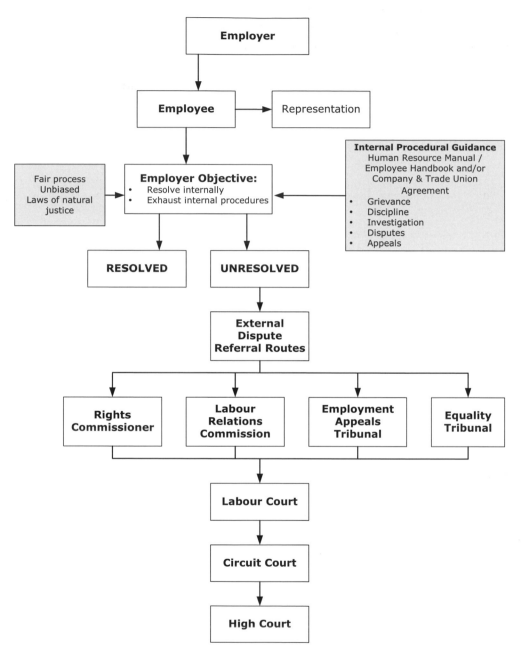

External Procedures

When the internal process fails to achieve an agreement as to how an issue is to be resolved, the parties may seek, either independently or jointly, the assistance of an appropriate body within the State's industrial relations support structure. These support structures include the Rights Commissioner Service, the Labour Relations Commission, the Equality Tribunal, the Employment Appeals Tribunal and the Labour Court.

Employment legislation

The Department of Enterprise, Trade & Employment, in conjunction with the European Union's input into social policies, develops and implements a wide range of employment legislation.

This legislation provides standards, rules and regulations for a wide range of issues affecting people at work. The legislation places obligations on employers and employees and defines entitlements for people at work under many headings. It also defines the appropriate industrial relations processes to be used for disputes, the different appeals mechanisms for each process and also the penalties for non-compliance with the employment legislation.

It is important for every employer:

- To have some understanding of how these three aspects of industrial relations affect their particular work environment.

- To know where to access information regarding the employer responsibility under each employment Act and to ensure company compliance with these laws.

- To know how to process industrial relations issues, both within the company and externally within the industrial relations mechanisms established by legislation.

THE LAWS OF NATURAL JUSTICE

An understanding and diligent application of the laws of natural justice is probably the most effective action an employer can take to ensure that employees are properly processed through any action in which they might be subject to some sanction or loss arising from a decision or judgement within the company. In addition, ensuring company compliance with the laws of natural justice is the best defence in many types of employee claim.

So, what are the laws of natural justice, where do you find them, where do they come from and what do they mean?

The expression, and indeed the basis of these laws, originates from the Romans. The Romans saw these laws as the basic legal principles that are required by nature, and which are so obvious that they should be applied universally without needing to be enacted into law. These few simple laws are the accepted basis of fair and equitable treatment in any set of circumstances where an accusation or suspicion is raised by one person against another and where a judgement must ensue. The laws of natural justice provide principles of fair process as a natural right.

The Romans had two primary natural laws:

1. *Audi alteram partem*: The right to be heard, or the right to hear the other side.
2. *Nemo judex in parte sua*: No person may judge their own case.

The key elements of the first of these laws of natural justice (the right to be heard) demands certain logical procedures. An accused person is innocent until proven guilty and therefore has the right to:

- Know precisely what they are accused of (ideally, this should be in writing to avoid ambiguity).
- Know the source of such accusations or allegations.
- Have reasonable time to prepare a defence.
- Know when they must present their defence.
- Respond to any allegations.
- Have representation.
- Review any evidence presented against them.
- Cross-examine any witnesses.
- Present witnesses in their defence.

- Appeal any judgement made against them.

The key elements of the second of these laws of natural justice (no person may judge their own case) are:

- An accused person must have an independent judge or arbitrator.

- The judge must be impartial and have no direct or indirect conflict of interest that might prejudice fair process. A judge or arbitrator must declare any potential vested interest or conflict of interest in a case and either bow out or have another impartial assessor decide whether he/she is eligible to judge.

- A person involved in arbitration of a case may not sit on any subsequent panel in a case that has been appealed.

- The judge must allow equitable time for the participants to present their positions and to challenge the position of their opponent.

- The accused person has the right to know what type of sanctions might be applied against him in relation to the particular issue if found 'guilty'.

- The person has the right to have their evidence considered and the judgement made only after all the evidence has been presented.

All grievance and disciplinary procedures should reflect fair process and must be applied in direct accordance with the laws of natural justice, which must be explained to employees. Many cases are lost by employers because the procedures were not applied correctly or because the procedures themselves were flawed.

A good way of making a personal judgment about your procedures is to ask yourself the question, 'If I was on the receiving end of this process, how would I wish to be treated?'.

GRIEVANCE PROCEDURES

The purpose of having a grievance procedure in your company is to resolve issues quickly and effectively (and, preferably, amicably), before they can have a negative impact on the employer/employee relationship and disrupt other aspects of the business. Grievance procedures are an important part of the proactive approach to creating a good employee relations environment, and:

- Provide clear rules and guidelines.

- Support good communications and honest dialogue.

- Prevent issues festering and becoming serious dispute items.

- Ensure consistent, equitable and fair process for all staff.

- Provide reasonable time frames for each step in the grievance process.

- Provide an appeals mechanism.

- Remove employees' fears.

- Support good employee relations.

- Can positively contribute to the 'bond of trust'.

How Grievance Procedures Work

Grievance procedures are like a pressure release valve, which acts to prevent the escalation of problems. In a company with a good employee relations environment, some of the issues raised will be resolved directly between the employee and his/her line manager – this should be the objective for all managers. However, once the matter needs to be addressed in a more formal way, then the procedures are an important support tool to help avoid confrontation while dealing with the issue. Therefore, managers must listen carefully to any grievances and ensure they are properly documented to avoid any confusion. It is important that the managers or supervisors handling the grievance do not become defensive or go on the offensive. The objective is to bring stability and resolution to all problems.

Some issues can be resolved almost immediately, through a common sense approach and without any fuss or confrontation. However, other issues may not be so easy to address and may extend beyond the immediate employee and his/her manager. In such cases, it is generally a good idea to allow the employee involved in the grievance to have a colleague or, where appropriate, an employee representative or trade union representative to accompany them. If the matter has escalated beyond the immediate employee/manager team, and the employee wishes to have someone present, it is obviously necessary for the employer to have a similar witness at the meeting.

Grievances should be resolved in the shortest possible period of time and as fairly as possible. All relevant details should be recorded and placed on the employee's personnel file.

The process

Step 1 in the sample grievance procedure (**Figure 20**) allows for the identification of the particular issue, its formal recording and for questions concerning the history, including dates, times, witnesses, etc. It also provides an immediate opportunity for the matter to be resolved, if at all possible. This first step may be a low-key chat between the employee and their manager or supervisor. Ideally, this should be sufficient to resolve most issues.

The purpose in recording the grievance is to ensure that the details are understood and that the first date of the first airing of the grievance is noted to ensure a reasonable processing time. However, this first step could be a verbal notification, at the discretion of the manager and depending on the complexity of the issue. Even a verbal notification should be noted in the individual's file.

If the decision or response of the individual's immediate manager is not acceptable to the employee, he/she then may refer the matter (already recorded in writing) to the next person in the line of command (**Step 2**). When the level two manager receives this appeal, he/she is obliged to investigate the matter directly with the employee and any others involved and must provide a decision (in writing, if considered necessary) to the employee in a timely manner – for example, not later than seven working days from the date of the appeal.

The remainder of the grievance procedure is simply the progression of the issue to higher levels within the company. The number of levels depends on the company's line of authority and the layers of management. This should be kept to a minimum level (for example, a maximum of five 'appeals' levels) as the company objective should be to resolve issues quickly.

These are the internal procedures. Of course, the employee may not be satisfied with the company's resolution proposal and may refer his/her case to a third party for a recommendation – for example, to the external industrial relations processes of the Labour Relations Commission, a Rights Commissioner or the Employment Appeals Tribunal. Cases can be appealed right up to the High Court.

FIGURE 20: GRIEVANCE PROCEDURE

The company accepts that, from time to time, situations will arise when employees have a problem with some aspect of their work, a management decision or a policy decision, which affects their work content or job description or at a personal level. When this occurs, it is in everyone's interest to have these issues investigated and resolved without delay. It is our intention that all employees be encouraged to use this procedure where necessary.

There are five stages to the process and they should be followed carefully and patiently. Meetings concerning the grievance procedures will take place in private and all details will be confidential. When stating grievances, an employee may request the attendance of a work colleague. Grievances should be resolved in the shortest possible period of time as fairly as possible and all relevant details should be recorded and placed on the employee's personnel file.

Step 1　The employee should raise the matter initially with his/her immediate manager. Ideally, the first informal meeting will be sufficient to resolve most issues. However, failing that, the employee is required to put the grievance in writing or to have assistance in doing so, if necessary. This will be a clear statement of the issue and will be dated. Having enquired into the employee's grievance, the manager will discuss it with the employee and will notify him/her of a decision within seven working days. If required, the employee may involve his/her representative or a colleague.

Step 2　If the decision of the employee's immediate manager is not acceptable to the employee, he/she may then refer the matter in writing to the next senior manager, who will investigate the matter directly with the employee and any others involved. The employee will receive a decision in writing not later than seven working days from receipt of his/her appeal.

Step 3　If the decision of the second manager is not acceptable to the employee, he/she may refer the matter in writing to next senior manager, who will investigate the matter directly with the employee and any others involved. The employee will receive a decision in writing not later than seven working days from receipt of his/her appeal.

Step 4　If the decision of the third manager is not acceptable to the employee, he/she may refer the matter in writing to the Chief Executive, who will investigate the matter directly with the employee and any others involved. The employee will receive a decision in writing not later than seven working days from receipt of his/her appeal.

Step 5　Where a grievance remains unresolved, the matter may be referred to the relevant industrial relations agency, as appropriate:
  ◊　A Rights Commissioner.
  ◊　The Employment Appeals Tribunal.
  ◊　The Equality Tribunal.
  ◊　The Labour Court.
  ◊　The Labour Relations Commission.

DISCIPLINARY PROCEDURES

Disciplinary procedures must provide a logical and just framework for the employer to investigate, process and resolve issues with employees, which are out of line with any company standards and rules required for the effective operation and regulation of the company's business, or which constitute unacceptable behaviour generally.

Employers pursuing a proactive employee relations strategy normally will work with a problem employee at an informal level, before embarking on the formal disciplinary route. However, regardless of how proactive a manager is, or how a company tries to be fair in the application of its HR policies, the formal route will be necessary from time to time.

Performance and behavioural issues that require the formal process are normally subject to disciplinary procedures and sanctions.

Unlike grievance procedures, disciplinary procedures should not be modified for faster processing. They are structured to provide a reasonable opportunity for the employee concerned to defend their position in relation to any allegation and to have sufficient time and support to make the necessary adjustments required to their performance or behaviour.

Similarly, in the likelihood of a matter being so serious that the employee's job is at risk, they must be allowed to defend themselves and be represented in such matters. Consequently, short-circuiting the procedures is not recommended, unless the issue is judged to be of a 'gross misconduct' status, in which case the procedures are accelerated but still within a clearly-defined structure and having regards to the individual's rights.

Internal procedures, therefore, should allow for the just, fair and equitable treatment of employees. Employees also have protection within the law against unjust treatment and may have their circumstances considered under employment legislation. Therefore, no disciplinary matter, and particularly not those falling within definitions of gross misconduct, should be taken lightly in terms of procedural processes.

Employees' Rights

Employees must be made aware of the disciplinary procedures and the reasoning or necessity for such procedures. The employee's rights within the laws of natural justice must be upheld at all times.

Within the disciplinary procedures, ensure that each employee is advised of the following important factors:

- The date, time and place of the meeting one working day in advance, if possible, or immediately in the case of gross misconduct. However, in the case of gross misconduct, the most appropriate action is to ask the person to leave the premises immediately, on the basis that they will continue to receive full pay pending the results of an investigation (see below).

- Who is to conduct the interview and who else will be present.

- The details of the alleged shortcomings or misconduct, in writing and with sufficient detail to enable the person to defend themselves.

- The right to be represented or accompanied by a work colleague or other appropriate person, at the discretion of the employee concerned.

- You must ask the individual whether they understand all that has been explained and ensure that they are ready for the meeting to go ahead.

- Another manager or witness, as appropriate, must accompany the manager conducting the interview.

- The right of reply – the opportunity to explain his/her actions or his/her view of the evidence, the right to make statements defending his/her position, the right to propose witnesses and the right to cross-examine company witnesses.

- The right to due consideration of his/her views and evidence.

- The right of appeal.

Issues Requiring Disciplinary Procedures

Examples of generally unacceptable behaviour warranting application of the disciplinary procedures can be divided into two basic categories: performance-related issues and behaviour-related issues – for example:

Performance-related issues	Behaviour-related issues
Failure to properly complete documentation procedures and/or falsification of such documents.	Rudeness to customers at any time – breaches of the customer care policy.
Giving false or misleading information on an employment application form.	Conduct that brings the company's reputation or credibility into disrepute.
Attendance issues.	Harassing colleagues or customers.
Regularly failing to comply with reasonable management instructions.	Stealing products or cash.
Regularly failing to achieve work-related targets.	Slovenly or unkempt appearance.

This is not an exhaustive list. You should develop a list relevant to your own business and include it in your company's disciplinary procedures.

Gross Misconduct

In cases of alleged gross misconduct, an employee may be suspended (***with pay***), pending a full investigation and prior to any disciplinary decision being made. Regardless of how obvious the misconduct appears to be, this period of suspension with pay, pending a formal investigation, is critical to demonstrate that the employer observed reasonable procedures within the laws of natural justice. Suspension without pay under such circumstances is likely to be perceived by the courts as being biased – that is, applying a punishment before adequate investigation and denying the employee's rights under the laws of natural justice, which essentially condemns the employee without trial.

The following are examples of gross misconduct offences warranting dismissal:

- Theft, fraud, or attempted theft or fraud, if proven to the company's satisfaction. This applies equally to the property of the company, suppliers, staff members, and others.

- Drunkenness during working hours.

- Failure to comply with the company safety and health procedures and the Safety, Health & Welfare at Work Act 2005 and subsequent amendments.

- Action or neglect of duty or responsibility that could prejudice the health and safety at work of any employee of the company.

- Physical violence directed at any other person.

- Making false allegations of personal accidents or injuries at work.

- Failure to comply with the company smoke-free workplace policy and the Public Health (Tobacco) Act 2002 and subsequent amendments.

- Being involved directly or indirectly in bullying, harassment, sexual harassment, abuse, intimidation or other demeaning behaviour toward others.

- Disclosure of confidential company information to any company or persons outside the company.

- Misappropriation of company funds.

- Wilful damage to company property or equipment belonging to the company's customers or suppliers.

- Inappropriate use of the Internet or email.

This is not an exhaustive list. Develop your own list to include any unacceptable circumstances or behaviour relevant to your business.

In all cases of gross misconduct, management must carry out a full investigation. At all times, the employee has the right to all details concerning the issue, the right of reply, the right of representation and the right of appeal prior to the application of sanctions. Employees should also be allowed to make any submissions related to the sanction, with regard to mitigating circumstances that might reduce the level of the proposed sanction.

Sanctions

The main objective of disciplinary procedures is to get the employee to adjust his/her behaviour or performance to the required standard willingly, not to inflict punishment.

Nonetheless, there are many reasons why an employee may not be able, or even want, to make the necessary adjustment – perhaps because of a shortfall in knowledge and skills, personality issues that affect attitude towards their manager or the company or a host of other reasons.

Skill shortfalls sometimes can be put right, if the employee is willing and motivated, and has the necessary abilities to improve knowledge and skills. However, if an employee's attitude is not right, it is particularly difficult to bring about productive change, and training and support may not achieve a sufficient improvement in performance.

Where the issue is not about skills, some employers take a very progressive view, that the person at least deserves an opportunity to put things right. Coaching, mentoring and counselling may help the employee to identify his/her problem and modify their behaviour. Unfortunately, the problem person can be his or her own worst enemy and may find it difficult to see the damage they are causing to themselves and their career, and the impact they are having on their colleagues.

Once the formal procedures have been activated, there are different sanctions that may be applied where the person is at fault and in relation to their previous record of offences and sanctions. The following are typical examples.

Suspension without pay

A suspension without pay is a serious form of punishment for a particular offence or performance shortcoming, and acts as a reminder that the employee ultimately faces dismissal, if they persist with the behaviour or performance issue.

Demotion

In certain circumstances, where an employee fails to satisfy the demands of the job, after standard training programmes and a reasonable time period, it may be possible to demote or transfer the person to other less demanding work.

The details of the actions to be taken should be discussed with the individual, prior to implementation. The individual should have the opportunity to have a colleague or representative present at such a meeting, and, ideally, the individual should be in agreement with the offer of alternative work. There is no obligation on the employer to provide alternative work and such decisions are solely at the employer's discretion.

The employee may not wish to be reassigned and may prefer dismissal, or request further training or time. An employer must give due consideration to an employee's response to a demotion proposal.

Dismissal

Any employee found to have committed a gross misconduct offence, in breach of company regulations and procedures, after fair and reasonable investigation, or who are unable to achieve the required level of job performance after all reasonable efforts have been made to support the employee to reach the desired performance level, may be dismissed from the company.

Losing one's job is a very serious matter, usually impacting on the person's ability to cover financial commitments. Therefore, dismissal should only be considered as a last resort, or when an issue is so serious that it would be detrimental to the company and its employees for the employee being processed under the disciplinary procedures to remain with the company.

It is important to ensure that the employee receives the appropriate period of notice as set out in the Minimum Notice & Terms of Employment Acts 1973-2001, or in his/her contract of employment if he/she is entitled to more than the statutory minimum. The company has the right to pay the employee in lieu of notice.

Appeals

Every employee in the company has the right to appeal any disciplinary action through their immediate manager, up to and including the chief executive.

If the person believes that he/she has been wronged and that he/she is not guilty of the offence alleged, he/she should have the right to appeal the sanction.

As the first level is rather low-key, the appeals mechanism could be restricted to a single appeal step. Each level of 'seriousness' should be reflected in the extent of the appeals procedures. However, some companies have systematic appeals procedures at every step in the disciplinary procedures. This comprehensive approach may have several steps, up to and including the chief executive, or a nomination by the chief executive of a senior manager or director to investigate the appeal on his/her behalf.

Larger companies have a greater capacity to deal with this rather complex procedural approach. However, they also may have a greater exposure and thus may need to feel confident of being absolutely correct on each phase of the procedural process. Therefore, you need to look at the following steps explained in **Figure 21** and develop a suitable appeals mechanism at each sanction level for your own situation.

At all stages of the disciplinary process, management must satisfy the test of reasonableness. As far as possible, and depending on the seriousness of the issue, the employee's record and any other relevant factors should be taken into consideration.

An employee has a number of days (seven days is reasonable) within which to make an appeal and the company must consider and respond to an appeal within a reasonable time period (for example, 14 days).

The courts are particularly diligent in ensuring that all possible avenues were considered by the company, that the laws of natural justice were fully observed, that the procedures were fully exhausted and that the decision was fair and equitable.

FIGURE 21: DISCIPLINARY PROCEDURE

Actions that are considered as misconduct, or performance-related issues, will be subject to clear procedural steps, along the following lines:

Stage 1: Formal warning

If an employee fails to meet the company's stated or agreed standards of behaviour or performance at work, he/she will receive a formal verbal warning from his/her immediate manager. This formal verbal warning will explain the reason(s) for the action and will include the possible consequences should there be no improvement. Verbal warnings are recorded on the employee's personal file and a copy is issued to the employee. The employee has the right to make any comments, explanations, etc, which may be accepted or rejected by the person's immediate manager. The immediate manager should listen and record any comments and agree on any support requirements.

Stage 2: Formal written warning

If the employee fails to meet the company requirements within the period stated in the first verbal (recorded) warning, or the improvement is not sufficient, a formal written warning will be issued by the employee's immediate manager. A copy will be retained in the employee's personal file. The employee has the right to make any comments, explanations, etc, which may be accepted or rejected by the person's immediate manager. The immediate manager will listen and record any comments and agree on any support requirements.

Stage 3: Final written warning

If the employee again fails to meet the company's requirements, as specified in the Stage 2 warning, the person's immediate manager will issue a final written warning. A copy will be retained in the employee's personal file. The employee has the right to make any comments, explanations, etc, which may be accepted or rejected by the person's immediate manager. The immediate manager will listen and record any comments and agree on any support requirements.

Stage 4: Suspension

If the employee again fails to meet the requirements, as specified in the Stage 3 warning, the person's immediate manager or a more senior manager will enforce a period of suspension. This will be without pay. The employee has the right to make any comments, explanations, etc, which may be accepted or rejected by the manager. The manager will listen and record any comments and agree on any support requirements. A written statement, including the background and facts warranting the suspension, will be issued to the employee and a copy will be retained on the employee's file. The duration of the suspension will be related to the offence and is at the discretion of the senior manager, having discussed and listened to the views of the employee's immediate manager.

On return to work, if the necessary improvements are achieved and no further warnings are issued within 12 months, the employee will revert to a clear record.

Stage 5: Dismissal

If the employee again fails to meet the requirements, as specified in the Stage 4 suspension/warning, the employee may be dismissed following the final investigation and decision-making sequence of the recommended dismissals procedure.

The employee must be advised of the decision to dismiss and be allowed the opportunity to appeal the decision and to make any other representation regarding the level of sanction and to present any arguments in this regard. The company must give due consideration to the submissions or verbal presentations made directly by the employee or his/her representatives and advise the employee within a reasonable timescale of the final decision. All such procedures should be exhausted before any sanction is activated.

When a decision to dismiss is taken, after it has been assessed that no satisfactory improvements have been achieved (or maintained), and except in circumstances justifying immediate termination of employment, the employee will be entitled to receive the appropriate period of notice. This notice is stated in the Minimum Notice & Terms of Employment Acts 1973-2001. The senior manager reserves the right to pay the employee in lieu of notice.

Appeals

The employee is entitled to appeal any such decision and also to refer his/her case to a third party for investigation.

INVESTIGATIONS

Most employers, at one time or another, are faced with the need to conduct an investigation into issues in their company concerning employees. The issue may be between an employee and a manager, or between an employee and another employee, but is generally related to performance or behavioural issues.

Generally, directors and managers who are not Human Resource professionals dislike having to engage in this work and have very little experience of how they should go about it. Sometimes, they put the issue on hold until they have time to deal with it, but really hoping it might resolve itself or just go away. Sometimes, but this is very seldom, it does go away – generally when the issue is minor or where it resulted from a genuine misunderstanding. Relying on this 'wait and see' approach is extremely risky and such inaction creates a dangerous precedent. Mostly, issues, problems or complaints that are left alone fester and things then go from bad to worse, often with serious consequences for all those involved, as well as damaging company performance.

Issues can have safety, health and welfare implications and the employer has a duty of care under existing safety legislation. So, people-related issues must be resolved in a reasonable timeframe and in a professional and equitable manner.

Employees have rights and, as an employer or manager, you are required to respect these. In the case of one employee complaining about the behaviour of another, you must ensure fair and equitable treatment of both employees. An investigation that is found to have been conducted in a biased manner – for example, following an investigation by a third party – is likely to result in a significant cost for the employer.

It is imperative, therefore, for the employer to ensure that internal investigative procedures are completely impartial and that investigations are conducted by managers within fair and just procedures. Because of the potentially serious actions that could arise from investigations, the investigation process should be carried out by a senior manager, ideally with some guidance from a human resource consultant, industrial relations professional, or a solicitor who specialises in employment law.

The Investigative Process

As a basic policy, all issues, complaints or allegations received formally or informally by an employer must be investigated *via* a process that is both fair and seen to be fair. The details must be recorded, decisions made, actions taken and those actions recorded on file, including any follow-through assessments. Investigations should commence as soon as possible following the discovery of any issue.

Issues that might require investigation and resolution include:

- A manager observes an employee removing property from the premises without authority.

- An employee complains that another employee has verbally abused a customer.

- An employee complains that another employee has been bullying and/or harassing them.

- An employee makes a formal complaint against a manager or director for bullying, harassment or intimidation.

- A customer complains that an employee has given him/her the wrong change and that the employee was abusive and dismissive when they complained to that employee.

- An employee complains of sexual harassment from a supervisor or colleague.

Key considerations

As an employer you are responsible for all aspects of such investigations.

The outcome of such investigations is very important, as they can impact on the company's image, atmosphere and performance. They can also affect the livelihood of one (or more) of your employees and so the investigation and decision-making process must be handled (and be seen to be handled) in a professional and impartial manner.

If a complaint has been made, it is very important that the complainant's rights are honoured, in addition to the rights of the person against whom the complaint has been made. Once again, the laws of natural justice apply.

Be as practical as possible in considering each step to be taken, in relation to the apparent seriousness of the case, while having regard to the level of seriousness in which the complainant or 'alleged injured party' perceives the issue.

No judgements should be made or actions taken until a full investigation of all the facts has been completed.

The Phases of an Investigation

Once you become aware of a complaint, issue or occurrence requiring investigation, there are six logical and sequential steps in the investigative process:

1. Investigation.
2. Interpretation.
3. Conclusions and sanctions.
4. Internal appeals.
5. Actions.
6. External appeals.

Phase 1: Investigation

Record the issue or complaint immediately and make a preliminary judgement as to the seriousness of the issue.

If it seems serious, the complainant should be asked to put the specifics of the complaint in writing.

Some issues may be perceived as being very serious. These are generally referred to as 'gross misconduct' issues and are generally considered to be grounds for instant or summary dismissal, subject to the results of an investigation. Examples of gross misconduct must be clearly stated in the company's disciplinary procedures.

The terms instant or summary dismissal do not mean the instantaneous and permanent termination of employment and removal of the employee from the premises. In the event of a gross misconduct issue, you must advise the employee against whom a complaint is made of the allegation. You may wish to commence an investigation immediately or you may take the view that the matter is both serious and complex and thus decide to suspend the employee on full pay pending the results of a preliminary investigation.

In other words, there is no prejudgement and there is no actual penalty for the employee. The suspension allows you to carry out a preliminary investigation only and may help to avoid an escalation of the issue. It also prevents further deterioration in the work environment or interference in the initial investigative process. Remember that investigations come first, decisions come later.

If the issue requires further investigation, appropriate investigators must be selected who can provide an impartial and unbiased investigation. It may even be necessary to engage an external independent investigator. It is recommended that you consider jointly agreeing the selection of an independent investigator with the employee against whom a complaint is made and his/her representative.

The investigative meeting should begin with a statement affirming the company's commitment to fair and impartial process, confirmed in writing and containing the following:

- Explain the need to carry out a full investigation into all issues, complaints and dangerous occurrences that arise in the company.

- Provide a copy of all the relevant details concerning the complaint or allegation made against the employee, including statements or documents that the company intends to rely upon.

- The employee's right of reply to these issues.

- The employee's right to be represented by a trade union official or accompanied by a colleague, as he/she wishes.

- The employee's responsibility to comply and co-operate with the investigative process. Explain that failure to comply with the investigation will be viewed by the company as insubordination and will warrant separate disciplinary consideration.

The investigator should outline the issue to the respondent and ask him/her to explain their position regarding the issue.

It may be necessary to interview witnesses and consider any relevant documentation. In the interests of fair process, both sides should be afforded the opportunity to question witnesses.

The investigator must record the full details of investigative meetings for later review, to aid decision-making and as a permanent record of the explanations in the event of the process being appealed to further third party investigations.

Phase 2: Interpretation
The investigator considers the facts, assesses the contributing factors, reviews the evidence and seeks clarification or additional information, if considered necessary.

Phase 3: Conclusions and sanctions
Once a full and fair investigation, recognising the rights of all concerned, has been completed, you must arrive at a conclusion and decide on an appropriate level of sanction for the offence, if necessary.

The investigation conclusions might be as shown in **Figure 22**.

FIGURE 22: INVESTIGATION CONCLUSIONS

Investigative Result	Minimum Action
There is insufficient evidence to warrant any disciplinary action against any employee and yet there was an unacceptable occurrence, which could have been damaging to the company.	Advise all employees involved in the process of the findings and issue a warning to all of the dangers or risks for the company and/or staff and reiterate that the company will not accept that particular behaviour.
An employee was found to be at fault, but it appears to be a genuine mistake.	The employee is given a verbal (recorded) warning if it is a first offence, a written warning on a similar second offence or a final warning on a third similar offence.
The employee involved is engaged habitually in disruptive behaviour or routinely breaches company procedures/rules and has once again been found to be guilty of acts that could have been damaging to the company or colleagues. The issue has been rated as a 'gross misconduct' offence. The previous occurrences and frequency, and the risks to which the company was exposed as a result of the employee's actions have been considered and taken into account.	A senior company official advises the employee that he/she has concluded his/her investigations, the matter has been rated as gross misconduct and the investigation finds the employee to be at fault. Because the matter warrants *instant dismissal* under the company's disciplinary procedures (which the employee must be aware of), the company wishes to offer the employee a chance to make any final submissions before it considers what action is appropriate in this case. The employer sets the time and date for this disciplinary hearing (which might be the following day) on which it will receive any submissions regarding the case or any submissions regarding the sanctions to be taken against the employee. The foregoing statements should be prepared in advance and a copy given to the employee in the form of an official company letter on headed paper and the term 'disciplinary hearing' should be used for the proposed meeting.

There are so many considerations when deciding on any sanction that it is impossible to list them all. However, the above scenarios indicate a number of different factors that need to be considered in investigations, in arriving at conclusions, in advising an employee of such conclusions and when making decisions, including:

- The severity of the issue.
- The quality of the evidence available.

- The company's stated policies, practices and procedures.

- The need for consistency within the company between similar cases and the application of procedures. Consider precedence or custom and practice.

- Any mitigating circumstances, including previous record, personal issues, etc.

- The need to record carefully all aspects of the investigation, including the statements of the accused and any witnesses.

- The need to communicate fully with the accused employee and to ensure that the employee understands his/her rights during all phases of the investigative process. This must include the respondent's right to cross-examine the complainant about the accusations made in writing and/or verbally to the investigator.

- Ensure the employee is aware that he/she may access an appeals procedure before any decision is implemented.

- The need to genuinely respect the employee's rights within the laws of natural justice at all phases of the investigation procedures.

- Following the final decision-making, ensuring that the respondent has a right of appeal to an external third party within the disciplinary process.

Phase 4: Internal appeals

If the employee decides to appeal a decision, in the first instance, you should require the employee to state, in writing, the basis of the appeal. It is not sufficient for the employee to request an appeal, unless there are reasonable grounds, such as new evidence or if the investigation itself is being challenged on procedural grounds.

Depending on such rationale, you may need to appoint another investigator to ensure fair process. On appeal, the respondent is entitled to a different investigator. This is generally a more senior person within the company than the person who conducted the initial investigation. Alternatively, an external investigator might need to be appointed.

Following any appeal hearings and the review of any additional and relevant evidence presented, you must consider whether the original interpretation is still valid. If not, then a new interpretation is developed and presented to the employee. If the original interpretation is still considered correct and fair, then this is conveyed to the employee.

Apart from the employee's right of appeal, he/she may also appeal the level of sanction, but must provide a statement of their rationale for any reduction of the sanction. Generally, an employee's representative will suggest a sanction reduction, based on the absence of other serious actions against the employee during his/her employment with the company.

If, and when, you reach the conclusion that the employee is guilty of an offence, and you are satisfied with the quality of the evidence, you must still ensure that the procedures continue to honour the laws of natural justice. This policy must be adhered to throughout the disciplinary hearing, the decision-making phase and the appeals procedures and before a formal termination of employment is activated. Any subsequent appeal of the issue, either through external industrial relations third parties or through the civil courts, will give careful consideration to the employer's application of such procedures.

Phase 5: Action

The employee must be advised of the conclusion of the investigation and the proposed level of sanction. He/she must be given the opportunity to make any additional comments or submissions regarding the level of sanction. If the employee does not wish to make an appeal, the sanction is applied.

The employee must also be made aware of the conclusions of the appeals process. If the decision is to apply the action against the employee, the reason(s) are put in writing and the appropriate disciplinary action is applied.

In the event of a dismissal, the person may be given payment in lieu of notice as the employer sees fit.

Phase 6: External appeals

Notwithstanding that the company applies fair procedure as outlined here, the employee has the right to refer the case to a third party such as a Rights Commissioner, the Employment Appeals Tribunal or to take a common law case against the employer as he/she feels or as recommended by a representative.

The parties may agree to refer the case to an agreed third party before the dismissal formally takes place. This may even be a stated procedural option in some companies.

Alternatively, you may be completely satisfied that the company process has been fair and equitable, and decide to proceed with the dismissal.

The employee, if eligible, may claim unfair dismissal, under the Unfair Dismissals Acts 1977-2001 or pursue a wrongful dismissals case under common law. The employee requires legitimate grounds for challenging the dismissal, for example:

- That he/she is innocent of the alleged offences or charges.

- That the evidence, on which the employer relied for the dismissal, is inaccurate.

- That the procedures applied by the employer denied him/her his/her rights under the laws of natural justice.
- That the sanctions applied are too severe.
- That the investigation was inadequate.

An employee may request an adjournment at any stage of the investigative process, if he/she feels that there is insufficient time for them to prepare a response to the allegations as presented by the company.

The Rights Commissioner or Employment Appeals Tribunal hears submissions, reviews information, asks questions, and considers evidence and witness statements. The Employment Appeals Tribunal takes witnesses' statements under oath. The company process is also reviewed by these external third parties to assess the fairness of internal procedures and the fairness of their application.

Third party investigations determine the legitimacy of the dismissal based on the evidence presented. Where an employer is found to have dismissed an employee unfairly, and depending on the circumstances, the recommendation or determination may require that the employee be re-instated, re-engaged and/or receive compensation of up to two years' remuneration.

Conclusion

There are a wide range of circumstances concerning employment-related problems and issues, which require investigation and action by employers. The example of the six-phase approach, outlined above, has been designed based on a gross misconduct issue. In the case of lesser issues or allegations, where the impact of the offence does not appear to be as severe, or where the employee in question has a good employment history, the level of detail and procedure can be adjusted accordingly.

Clear, well-understood disciplinary procedures will allow an immediate response to most issues and, after a rapid consideration of the details, the standard disciplinary sanctions can be applied. Nonetheless, in all cases warranting investigation that could result in a penalty or sanction against an employee, the laws of natural justice must apply and the onus of responsibility rests with the employer to ensure fair process throughout the procedures.

Many complaints not rated gross misconduct can be resolved speedily and without recourse to the phases outlined above, if the manager is willing to invest some time in discussing the issues with those involved and seeks common-sense solutions to which the parties can agree. Experienced judgement and intervention can often help to avoid the confrontation, and associated disruption and costs, created by the formal investigative process.

FIGURE 23: INVESTIGATION PROCESS CHART

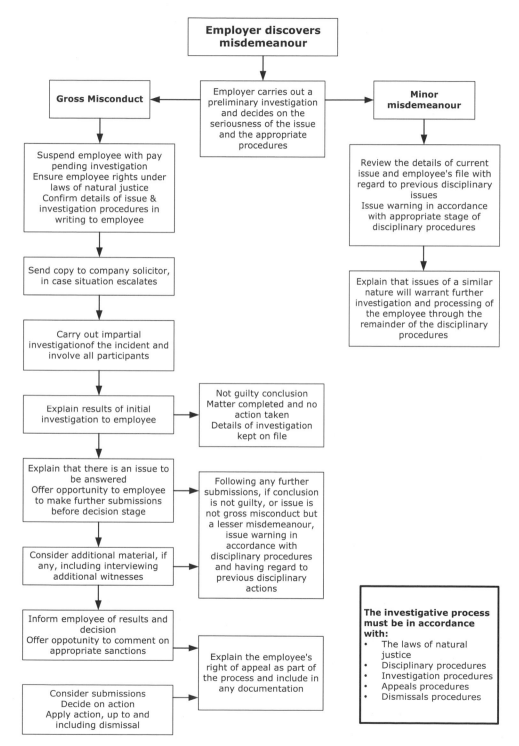

THE LABOUR RELATIONS COMMISSION

The Labour Relations Commission encourages employers, trade unions and employees to take a positive and constructive approach to industrial relations. It supports the introduction and use of consultation and negotiation procedures to resolve disputes that may arise in employment.

The parties to an industrial dispute should only resort to the LRC's services when internal procedures have been exhausted and when every effort has been made to resolve the issue in dispute.

Resolving issues through the company's internal procedures helps to consolidate the procedures and builds trust and confidence. Referring matters externally to the Labour Relations Commission or other external industrial relations processes works in opposition to sound employee relations trust-building policies and can become an abdication of responsibility.

Occasionally, however, the assistance of third party intervention may be the only option and the LRC officers are well-experienced and will provide professional help, direction and advice to resolve the issue as practically and as fairly as possible.

While the relevant procedures of the company or the LRC are being followed, the parties should refrain from any form of industrial action, such as go-slows, lock-outs or work stoppages.

Referral of cases to the Labour Relations Commission

The purpose in referring issues to the LRC is:

- To avoid a dispute escalating to a strike or other form of industrial action that could impact negatively on the company's business operations.
- To avoid any significant damage to the employer/employee relationship.
- To get expert and unbiased assistance to help analyse and resolve issues.
- To help interpret any policies, practices and procedures in force and how they were applied or should be applied.

The LRC provides the following specific services:

- Industrial relations conciliation service.
- Industrial relations advisory, development and research service.
- The Rights Commissioner service.
- Support to Joint Labour Committees and Joint Industrial Councils.

Conciliation Service

Conciliation is a voluntary mediation process, in which a professional mediator assists employers and their employees to resolve disputes when their efforts to do so have not succeeded. The process can be described as a facilitated search for agreement between disputing parties.

The LRC assigns a mediator, known as an Industrial Relations Officer (IRO), who acts as an independent, impartial chairperson in discussions and negotiations between the negotiating teams that represent the employer and the employees. The task of the IRO is to assist the teams in their efforts to reach a mutually acceptable settlement to their dispute.

The service is available to all employees and employers, except those specifically excluded by law (the army, police and prison services).

To use the service, employees need not be trade union members, nor do employers have to belong to a representative body. However, the parties to the dispute may appoint industrial relations specialists to help present their case.

The Labour Relations Commission's conciliation process

The process of conciliation begins when one (or both) disputing parties refers a case to the LRC, requesting assistance with the industrial relations dispute.

The LRC then contacts both parties to confirm that they are both willing to participate. Participation is entirely voluntary. As the outcome can have a stabilising influence, the parties are normally pleased to enter the process.

An IRO from the LRC will schedule and chair a joint meeting of the parties representing the employees and the employer, at which each side presents a brief synopsis of their current views on the issue.

The IRO then generally meets the parties separately in a side conference, seeking clarification of the information concerning the background to the issues and other related details and explores possibilities for a settlement. These meetings generally take place on the same day.

The IRO treats as confidential all information received during the course of conciliation. The IRO will not divulge this information to any other party unless expressly permitted to do so.

The conciliation process is informal and non-legalistic in practice. The parties are free to represent themselves or be represented by trade unions, by employer organisations or by other appropriate representatives such as HR advisers.

Legal representation at the conciliation conference is unnecessary and may, in fact, hamper the informal nature of the discussions. It is, after all, a joint effort to find a mutually agreeable win/win solution to differences of opinion or understanding. Resolution of the dispute is the main objective.

Generally, the parties wish to reach a satisfactory conclusion as speedily and as painlessly as possible.

There are two possible outcomes to the conciliation process:

1. Resolution of the dispute.

2. Continuing disagreement.

A settlement occurs either when the parties reach a mutually acceptable agreement in conciliation or where they accept a proposal for settlement that the IRO has put to them. The IRO will not offer a settlement proposal, unless the parties' negotiating teams are prepared to recommend that proposal for acceptance by the groups they represent. Regardless of the results of the meetings, the IRO generally brings the parties together to summarise at the end of the conference. The IRO may also adjourn the proceedings to allow the parties time to consider any proposals developed during the conference.

Where the process ends in continuing disagreement, the parties have the option of referring the dispute to the Labour Court for recommendation. Occasionally, the parties may find, through the conciliation process, a direction or formula that they can take to those they represent and work out a final agreement at a local level.

Referring industrial disputes to the Labour Court

The LRC refers cases to the Labour Court when it believes that 'no further efforts on the Commission's part will produce a settlement'.

Also, where one or both parties reject a recommendation proposed by the IRO for the resolution of a dispute, the IRO can refer the case to a full hearing of the Labour Court.

Industrial Relations Advisory, Development & Research Service

The Advisory, Development & Research Service of the LRC works with employers, employees and trade unions in non-dispute situations to develop effective industrial relations practices, procedures and structures that best meet their needs. This also can be done by the parties at local level. However, where there are significantly different views on what the correct procedures should be, the LRC can help with the assessment, recommendations and negotiation of revised procedures. The service is professional, independent, and impartial. Its executives are highly qualified and have extensive experience in Irish industrial relations practice.

Advisory, Development & Research services include:

• Diagnostic surveys.

- Joint working parties.
- Preventive mediation/facilitation.
- Partnership development policies.
- Education and training.
- Scrutiny of ballots.

Rights Commissioner

Under the auspices of the LRC, the Rights Commissioner service investigates cases under certain employment related Acts, in relation to individual cases rather than employee groups. Further information on the Rights Commissioner service is available in the next section.

Joint Labour Committees & Joint Industrial Councils

IROs of the LRC act as chairpersons to a number of Joint Labour Committees (JLCs) and Joint Industrial Councils (JICs). They also chair joint meetings of unions and management in various employments.

JLCs are statutory bodies established under the Industrial Relations Acts 1946-2004 to provide mechanisms to regulate rates of pay and conditions of employment in particular industries and trades, particularly in situations where trade union organisation is weak. JLCs are composed of employers' and workers' representatives in a particular industrial sector, who meet regularly to discuss and agree terms and conditions to apply to specified workers in that sector. When a JLC agrees terms and conditions, it makes proposals to the Labour Court for approval.

The LRC has the task of reviewing the operation of JLCs to determine whether to establish new committees or abolish existing ones. The LRC's recommendations are sent to the Labour Court for assessment and to the Minister for Enterprise, Trade & Employment for final approval.

JICs are voluntary negotiating bodies, consisting of representatives of workers and employers in particular industries and trades. JICs can be registered with the Labour Court, subject to certain qualifying conditions. Agreements made through a JIC can also be registered and enforced in law.

THE RIGHTS COMMISSIONER SERVICE

The Rights Commissioner Service investigates cases under certain employment-related Acts, primarily in relation to individual cases rather than employee groups. Cases can be referred to a Rights Commissioner under the following statutes:

- Adoptive Leave Acts 1995 & 2005.
- Carer's Leave Act 2001.
- Competition Act 2002.
- European Communities (Protection of Employment) Regulations 2000.
- European Communities (Protection of Employees on Transfer of Undertakings) (Amendment) Regulations 2003.
- Industrial Relations Acts 1946-2004.
- Maternity Protection Acts 1994 & 2004.
- National Minimum Wage Act 2000.
- Organisation of Working Time Act 1997.
- Parental Leave Acts 1998 & 2006.
- Payment of Wages Act 1991.
- Protection of Employees (Fixed-Term Work) Act 2003.
- Protection of Employees (Part-Time Work) Act 2001.
- Protections for Persons Reporting Child Abuse Act 1998.
- Protection of Young Persons (Employment) Act 1996.
- Safety, Health & Welfare at Work Act 2005.
- Terms of Employment (Information) Acts 1994 & 2001.
- Unfair Dismissals Acts 1977-2001.

While the Rights Commissioner Service operates as a service of the LRC, Rights Commissioners are independent in their functions.

Positive intervention prior to Rights Commissioner involvement
Where the complaint or dispute simply concerns a legal entitlement, or a difference of opinion regarding the interpretation of a legal entitlement, every effort should be made by the employer to settle the matter locally without recourse to a Rights Commissioner.

Reviewing the issue, with the aid of any appropriate employment legislation, may assist you to identify the critical factor. This information can be presented and explained to the employee involved. If the employee is still unsure, check your understanding with your company's HR advisor. It might be necessary to explain in more detail with appropriate documentation to the employee. This proactive communications process is a good employee relations exercise and is less time-consuming than preparing and presenting a case to a Rights Commissioner.

The Rights Commissioner Process

Referring a case to the Rights Commissioner

Cases may be referred jointly or by either party, by completing the appropriate form available through the office of the Rights Commissioner service. These forms are issued to assist claimants in submitting complaints under the relevant employment legislation. They also help to focus the complainant's description of the key elements of the issue.

Objection to a Rights Commissioner investigation

A party to a dispute may object to a Rights Commissioner's investigation, where the case has been referred under the Industrial Relations Acts 1946-2004 or under the Unfair Dismissals Acts 1977-2001. Where such an objection is made, the Rights Commissioner cannot investigate the case. Instead, the original applicant can request the Labour Court or the Employment Appeals Tribunal, depending on which Act the case is being referred under, to hear the case.

A similar right of objection does not apply for referrals under certain employment-related Acts. A Rights Commissioner investigates such cases in the first instance and, if his/her recommendation or decision is not accepted by both parties, it then may be referred on appeal to the Labour Court or Employment Appeals Tribunal, as appropriate, for a recommendation.

Submissions to the Rights Commissioner

Rights Commissioner hearings are formal, but not adversarial. Each side is given the chance to present their case fully. The Rights Commissioner can ask for additional information or clarification on the submissions presented. Written submissions, while not compulsory, are helpful to the participants and the Rights Commissioners.

Define your views on the dispute in simple and brief language. Use bullet points to describe the issue and list these in chronological sequence. Remember the Rights Commissioner may know very little about your industry, even less about your company or your operating policies and procedures.

Your objective is to demonstrate that you have been fair and equitable in the issue. Ideally, you will be in a position to demonstrate clearly or prove what has taken place up to the date of the hearing. You can also express your views on the case in relation to company policy, practice and procedures, if this is applicable to the issue.

The Rights Commissioner will decide how to conduct the hearing.

The Rights Commissioner's function is to issue decisions or recommendations based on the facts and on any evidence presented at a hearing. Therefore, you must ensure that relevant information referred to in the written submission (such as witnesses' statements, payslips, correspondence or any other evidence) is available at the hearing, with copies attached to the main submission as appendices.

Rights Commissioners issue the findings of their investigations in the form of either non-binding recommendations or decisions, depending on the legislation under which a case is referred.

In many cases, it is possible, with the assistance of the Rights Commissioner, to settle disputes between the parties on the day of a hearing. Be prepared to listen carefully to the Rights Commissioner and to the employee's submission, which may be different to your understanding of the case and may therefore open up an immediate opportunity for a solution. If you identify such a position, share your views with the Rights Commissioner, who will be happy to tease out this observation to help you to arrive at an agreeable or amicable solution.

It may be prudent, where an issue does not have far-reaching consequences, to request the Rights Commissioner to seek agreement from the parties at the hearing, prior to the case being heard, to accept the eventual Rights Commissioner's recommendation or decision. This can save time and disruption and recognises the impartial nature of the Rights Commissioner process. It also removes the opportunity of the other party to appeal the recommendation or decision.

Alternatively where the issue has far-reaching consequences or could establish a costly precedent, it is obviously not a good idea to make advance agreements to accept a recommendation or decision, as you may wish to appeal this to the Employment Appeals Tribunal or Labour Court, particularly where the recommended solution could have serious cost implications.

Appeals
Either of the parties to a case may appeal the recommendations or decisions of a Rights Commissioner to either the Labour Court or to the Employment Appeals Tribunal, depending on the case.

THE EMPLOYMENT APPEALS TRIBUNAL

The Employment Appeals Tribunal (EAT) is an independent body set up to provide a prompt, fair, inexpensive and informal means for individual employees to seek remedies for alleged infringements of their statutory rights and to adjudicate on employment disputes under the following statutes:

- Adoptive Leave Acts 1995 & 2005.
- Carer's Leave Act 2001.
- Competition Act 2002.
- European Communities (Protection of Employment) Regulations 2000.
- European Communities (Protection of Employees on Transfer of Undertakings) Regulations 2003.
- Maternity Protection Acts 1994 & 2004.
- Minimum Notice & Terms of Employment Acts 1973-2001.
- Organisation of Working Time Act 1997.
- Parental Leave Acts 1998 & 2006.
- Payment of Wages Act 1991.
- Protections for Persons Reporting Child Abuse Act 1998.
- Protection of Employees (Employers' Insolvency) Acts 1984-2001.
- Protection of Young Persons (Employment) Act 1996.
- Redundancy Payments Acts 1967-2003.
- Terms of Employment (Information) Acts 1994 & 2001.
- Unfair Dismissals Acts 1977-2001.

The EAT is made up of three people who listen to submissions from claimants regarding issues and make a determination on each case. EAT hearings are formal and the business is conducted in a similar way to a court of law.

Employers are advised to take such cases seriously and to be well-prepared to defend their position with facts that can be substantiated. If the company adviser considers that, for procedural or other reasons, your case is weak, you should consider negotiating a settlement of the case, either directly with the individual concerned or through their representative, prior to the EAT hearing.

You should consider all the facts first. You may have been correct in your decisions, but may not have followed acceptable procedures, which could result in the loss of the case. This may be more costly than negotiating a settlement. It is important therefore, that you consider the advice of an experienced person to make a judgement, based on the critical facts of the case.

The Employment Appeals Tribunal Process

When an application is received, the EAT sends, by registered post, a copy of the claim form and a notice of appearance to the party against whom the claim is being made.

In an unfair dismissal case, the employee must apply to the EAT within six months of being dismissed.

When the case is allocated a hearing date, both parties will be advised of this in advance of the hearing. Note that it can take up to four or five months from the date of application for a case to be heard.

Companies or individuals appearing before the EAT are not required to have representation, legal or otherwise, although there is a provision for representation in the regulations. Companies or individuals appearing before the Tribunal without representation will not be placed at a disadvantage, as the three-person Tribunal will ensure fair process.

A party to an application should bring to the hearing any relevant documents or other evidence that he/she intends to rely upon in support of the case. Such documents may consist of evidence of unemployment or social welfare payments, payslips, conditions of employment, policy and procedure handbooks, income tax statements such as a P45 or P60. You should have a complete statement of the case, ensure witnesses are available and that you have any supporting documentation concerning actions and the rationale and history of any actions taken.

When the case is heard, the decision of the EAT is communicated to the parties as soon as possible after the hearing.

In the event that the EAT finds in favour of an employee, and the employer does not comply with the decision of the Tribunal, there are procedures for the employee to process a request for enforcement of the decision or determination.

THE LABOUR COURT

The Labour Court provides a free and comprehensive service for the resolution of industrial relations disputes and also deals with matters arising under employment equality, working time, national minimum wage, part-time work and fixed-term work legislation.

The Labour Court is not a court of law. It operates as an independent and impartial industrial relations tribunal, hearing both sides in trade disputes and then issuing recommendations, setting out its opinion on the dispute and the terms on which it should be settled. These recommendations are not binding on the parties concerned. Ultimately, the responsibility for the settlement of a dispute rests with the parties.

However, the Labour Court can make determinations that are legally binding on the parties, when dealing with cases involving breaches of registered employment agreements. Also, the Labour Court's determinations under the following Acts are legally binding:

- Employment Equality Acts 1998 & 2004.
- Industrial Relations Acts 1946-2004.
- National Minimum Wage Act 2000.
- Organisation of Working Time Act 1997.
- Pensions Acts 1990 & 2002.
- Protection of Employees (Fixed-Term Work) Act 2003.
- Protection of Employees (Part-Time Work) Act 2001.

Court of Last Resort

The role of the Labour Court in dispute resolution is to act as court of last resort. In other words, local dispute resolution arrangements in the company, and the other dispute resolution machinery of the State (such as the Labour Relations Commission or the Rights Commissioner service), should have been fully used before a case comes before the Labour Court.

The Labour Court Process

The Labour Court investigates disputes by requiring the parties to provide written submissions of their positions in relation to the dispute, and, subsequently, by holding hearings at which both parties attend. The hearings are usually held in private, unless one of the parties requests a public hearing.

Generally, the Labour Court deals with disputes referred to it by a Rights Commissioner or the LRC, when their efforts have failed to get the parties to agree on a solution or where a recommendation has been rejected.

The Labour Court deals with disputes in five stages.

Stage 1: Referral
Depending on the circumstances, the referral may come from a Rights Commissioner, the LRC or directly from a party to a case.

Stage 2: Agree date of hearing
A suitable date and venue for a hearing is provided to the parties as soon as possible after the date of referral. If it is difficult for either party to attend, another date may be agreed between the Labour Court and the parties.

Stage 3: Parties make written submissions
The parties supply the Court with written submissions, stating their positions in relation to the dispute. In industrial relations, working time, national minimum wage, part-time work and fixed-term work cases, six copies of the submission should be delivered to the Court, by post or by hand (but not by fax), no later than three working days prior to the date of the hearing.

These submissions form the basis of the Court's investigation of the dispute at the hearing, so it is important that they are clear and sufficiently detailed to convey the critical aspects of the issues involved.

In equality cases, separate procedures apply, and the Labour Court will advise the parties of these procedures at the time of referral.

Stage 4: Formal hearing
Both parties are present at the formal hearing and read their written submissions to the Court members. They answer questions from the Chairperson and the Court members and may challenge any of the facts presented by the other party. This is a formal Court environment and the parties must obey the Chairperson throughout the proceedings.

Stage 5: Issue of recommendation / determination / decision
The Labour Court will issue a written recommendation for the resolution of a dispute several weeks after the hearing. Where an appeal is made to the Labour Court against the decision of a Rights Commissioner or an Equality Officer, the Court will issue a determination, which can uphold the original decision of a Rights Commissioner or Equality Officer, vary it or overturn it.

CHAPTER 3
SAFETY, HEALTH & WELFARE

INTRODUCTION

In 2006, there were 50 work-related fatalities reported to the Health & Safety Authority, not to mention the thousands of serious and minor injuries and the hundreds of thousands of lost hours. For every one of these occurrences, there were probably 10 near misses. These are frightening figures, which alone should be sufficient motivation for employers to engage professionally with safety, health and welfare issues, needs and requirements throughout Irish businesses.

The most recent change to safety legislation was enacted in September 2005, when the Safety, Health & Welfare at Work Act 2005 was enacted, replacing the Safety, Health & Welfare at Work Act 1989. The new legislation has broadened the duties and responsibilities for employers, and introduced new control features and penalties for non-compliance and negligence, in the event of accidents. There are also additional statutory instruments to follow – for example, a code of practice for employers on testing for intoxicants.

The safety, health and welfare of people at work is the responsibility of every employer and manager. This is an obvious consideration for employers, who are very much aware of the risks to their business, resulting from major claims for compensation arising from injuries and even loss of life at work. Insurance companies may also have special compliance requirements, so apart from the legal and moral reasons for managing safety, health and welfare in a professional manner, there are also additional basic business reasons for doing so.

Within the new Act, managers, and not just the company, are clearly defined as being responsible. This is a significant responsibility – for example, if there is a serious accident, the manager responsible for the safety of the individual(s) concerned may be liable personally if he/she failed in any way in his/her duty of care to employees.

The responsibility of the employer, in simple terms, is to identify any particular hazard or risk of accident associated with the work in each and every occupation and area in the company and to engineer such hazards or risks out of existence. Where this is not completely possible, the employer must reduce the risks or hazards considerably through safe working practices and training. This approach, coupled with the provision of appropriate safety clothing and safety equipment, is intended to significantly reduce the exposure to hazards and prevent accidents. Of course, employee compliance with such initiatives is imperative and hence the need for a systematic approach to safety education, as well as specific on-the-job training.

The legislation also provides the employer with an approach to help achieve the desired safety, health and welfare standards. This is referred to as the safety statement. In fact, it is not just a statement, as the name implies, but a practical working brief to guide all employees (including managerial staff) through the process of identification of risks and the creation of safe working practices.

In addition to safety legislation, the employer also has a duty of care, under tort law, to safeguard the safety of employees. Six specific duties are identified under common law (some of these duties overlap with the safety legislation):

1. Employers must provide a safe system of work.
2. Employers must provide a safe place of work.
3. Employers must provide safe equipment, plant and machinery.
4. Employers will engage competent employees and a safe number thereof.
5. The employer must have in place rules of conduct and enforce them so that employees can work in a safe manner.
6. Employers should inform employees of any dangers that might reasonably be expected to be unknown to the employee.

This chapter deals with many of the procedural aspects of safety, health and welfare at work and should be considered in the light of the reader's understanding of their own company's products or services, the environment, employee knowledge and skill-sets, hazards or risks and procedures for eliminating or reducing such risk. Also, **Chapter 4** contains a *précis* of the statutory requirements of the 2005 Act.

Consultation

The Safety, Health & Welfare at Work Act 2005 requires that employers consult with their employees and make arrangements to help ensure co-operation between them to prevent accidents and ill-health in the workplace.

You must consult with employees and/or their safety representatives in advance so as to give employees as much time as possible to consider, discuss and give an opinion on the matters, before managerial decisions are made and procedures are applied. Consultation involves listening to employee opinions and taking their views into account as part of the decision-making process. Any information given must be sufficient to allow employees to participate fully and effectively in the consultation process.

By actively promoting and supporting employee participation in all aspects of workplace health and safety, you will help gain employee support and commitment. During the process, you will undoubtedly learn something about the work and the environment that could be extremely important in designing safety practices and procedures.

Safety Representatives

Employees have the right to select and appoint a safety representative to represent them in consultations with their employer on issues relating to health and safety in the workplace. It is recommended that the employer proactively encourages and supports safety representatives and, if necessary, takes the initiative to activate the process.

Safety Committees

A safety committee is a group of individuals, representative of the employer and employees, whose function is to consult on workplace health and safety matters. The Safety, Health & Welfare at Work Act 2005 sets out guidelines for the operation of safety committees (see **Chapter 4**). It is recommended that the employer proactively encourages and supports this process and, if necessary, takes the initiative to establish safety committees.

Employee Compliance & Co-operation

Every employee has an obligation in law to co-operate with the employer's instructions regarding safety policies, practices and procedures. In addition, each employee is also responsible for their own safety, and for the safety of colleagues who may be affected by their acts or omissions. These employee responsibilities must be conveyed to all employees as clearly as the company's standards and procedures.

Safety training requirements should be reviewed annually, like any other business function, to ensure that the knowledge and skill-set requirements are updated constantly to match the needs of the business.

You are more likely to get full co-operation on the development, installation and maintenance of safety practices, if those involved in the work are consulted and have participated in the overall safety process.

Contractors

You should establish and maintain procedures for controlling health and safety aspects of contractors' work. These should include:

- For short-term contracts, safety and health aspects should be suitably checked by questionnaire or review. Pre-planning is necessary for medium or long-term contracts. This will involve carrying out a full safety and health pre-qualification procedure.

- Ensuring that all contractors employed work in a safe manner at all times, adhere to the requirements of safety legislation and that appropriate precautions are taken to ensure the safety, health and welfare of employees, customers or members of the general public who may be affected by the work.

- Ensuring that the contractor has prepared an up-to-date safety statement for the project to be undertaken. This can be developed in conjunction with the client company.

- Defining responsibility for, and setting up communication links between, appropriate levels of the organisation and the contractor before work starts and throughout the contract.

- Providing relevant safety training and induction of contractor personnel, where necessary, before the contracted work begins.

- Monitoring safety and health aspects of contractor activities on site.

- Establishing procedures for communication of accidents and incidents involving the contracted employees.

Contractors must have multiple approaches to ensuring the safety of their employees. In the first instance, they have the responsibility to ensure their employees are aware of all the safety policies, practices and procedures applicable to them in a general sense and within the context of their particular occupational disciplines. In addition, they will have a generic overview of the need to integrate into a client company's procedures and the importance of maintaining an active awareness.

Safety Records

Safety records are a good source of information for safety assessment and are also a requirement, particularly in the event of an investigation process following an accident.

If you maintain statistics about all incidents and accidents in the company, it may provide valuable insights into trends and hazards from which you can prioritise your activities and focus on the most urgent safety matters arising from the historical data.

Depending on the nature of the work and the safety issues that seem to be occurring or which are inherent in certain jobs or areas, you may have to engage in sophisticated analysis and seek specialist help to develop safe working practices for all the company's activities.

Evaluating Safety Practices

Some companies may have quite simple work environments with minimum hazard exposure, others might have complex processes involving many different types of hazards, and there will be many somewhere in between.

Generally, manufacturing companies have a higher level of hazards and require a systematic approach both to the identification of the risks and the engineering-out of these through new methods. For such environments, it is important to use both internal and external safety specialists, managers, engineers and other technical specialists to carry out regular safety audits and assist with the creation of the safe practices methods and training.

Ensure that the employees' safety representative accompanies the safety auditor to highlight issues and answer queries.

This process will contribute greatly to the creation and maintenance of a safe workplace and will consequently reduce injuries to staff and the lost time due to absence arising from accidents at work.

First Aid

Apart from first aid stations, which should be regularly checked and supplied with relevant equipment for each section of the operation, it is necessary to have a person qualified to apply the necessary first aid for employees (a First Aid Officer).

Determining adequate and appropriate first aid equipment depends on several factors such as:

- The size of the workplace.
- The numbers employed.
- Dispersal of employees.
- Employees working away from their employer's premises.
- Workers in isolated locations.
- Any hazards arising.
- Access to medical services.

Safety regulations set out guidelines for such equipment and the minimum requirements for first aiders (or First Aid Officers).

Designate a suitable person or persons as a First Aid Officer, in relation to the complexity and diversity of the work and the numbers employed. Ensure that he/she is trained appropriately and passes any appropriate tests. Some employers may already be fortunate to have some employees who have qualified in this area with St. John's Ambulance Brigade or the Civil Defence and who are willing to take up the role.

First aid and safety training suppliers can be requested to help assess basic first aid equipment requirements, until an in-house person is sufficiently trained to determine the needs.

Hygiene

Sickness, infections, slips, trips and falls, which can result in lost time, can be avoided by regular cleaning of all the work areas, walkways and clearways.

It was obviously imperative that the pharmaceutical, chemical, food processing and healthcare manufacturing industries develop excellent hygiene procedures, so their stringent rules and regulations are a good model to consider when determining housekeeping standards. However, for a construction company or light engineering manufacturing company, these would be impractical and impossible to maintain. Each company will require different standards that reflect specific needs, and which addresses any manufacturing process where there is an associated risk and/or where hygiene procedures specifically contribute to the elimination or reduction of such risk.

Do a walkabout with an employee safety representative and check the environment. Set up a questionnaire to suit the walkabout sequence and have someone score the key features on a regular basis, such as once a week or once a month, as warranted by the particular environment. Take appropriate actions based on the results of this hygiene safety inspection.

Ergonomics

Ergonomics can be defined as the study of how working conditions, equipment and machinery can be arranged in order that people can work with them more effectively or efficiently, and which builds in safety protections and practices.

The Safety, Health & Welfare at Work (General Application) Regulations 1993 contain specific provisions for employees who work on workstations and visual display units. These 1993 Regulations are due to be updated in line with the 2005 Act (see **Chapter 4)**.

A badly arranged workstation can lead to a number of health problems, such as eyestrain, muscles and joints pain, swollen wrists, backache, fatigue and stress. As an employer, you are required to evaluate the health and safety of employees at their workstation, with particular reference to eyesight, physical difficulties and mental stress. Appropriate steps must be taken to control any identified risks to health and safety.

Use screen protectors for those who spend most of their time working on computers, ensure they take breaks away from the screen as often as possible and also consider the state of the equipment, the seating and posture in terms of the workstation layout.

In manufacturing companies, repetitive motions in continuous process production work can lead to health problems. Therefore, the design of the manufacturing workstation is important.

When such repetitious work was subject to incentive payment schemes, companies used Industrial Engineers (or Work Study Officers) to ensure the workstation was designed initially to ensure easy operation and thus maximise the output. Ergonomics were a necessary part of the training of the engineers. This 'built-in' examination is practically extinct, so some alternative assessment method needs to be considered.

Manual Handling

Injuries due to manual handling activity are the most common cause of workplace injury in Ireland, accounting for a third of all non-fatal injuries.

The Safety, Health & Welfare at Work (General Application) Regulations 1993 outline the requirements that must be adhered to in relation to the manual handling of loads. Although these regulations are still to be updated under the Safety, Health & Welfare at Work Act 2005, it is likely that the manual handling regulations will not be amended to a great degree.

Where the manual handling of a load may involve a risk of injury to an employee, particularly to his/her back, the employer must take measures to avoid the need for such manual handling, where possible. Such measures may require you to reorganise the work, the load sizes, etc or to use mechanical equipment or other means to eliminate manual handling.

Where organisational measures alone cannot eliminate manual handling, and where manual handling cannot be avoided, the work should be organised so that the risks of manual handling are reduced as far as possible.

Employees have different physical capacities based on body weight, physical fitness, abilities and disabilities, some of which are known and some unknown. Some objects are just too heavy to lift. Training therefore, where manual handling is unavoidable, is essential and must be related to maximum weights for various categories of people, load dimensions and also on lifting techniques. The Health & Safety Authority (HSA) has published guidelines on lifting activities that involves risk, taking into account weight, repetition, individual capacity and posture.

Noise Exposure

In addition to the Safety, Health & Welfare at Work Act 2005, there are a number of EU Directives and Regulations that specifically require certain measures to be taken to protect employees from the risks associated with noise. These regulations set out the recommended daily noise exposure levels.

Noise is any unwanted sound, which by its intensity, regularity and loudness, will cause psychological and physical problems. Exposure to noise may pose a variety of health and safety risks to employees, such as hearing loss, stress, increased risk of accidents and physiological effects.

If it is not possible to eliminate the risks resulting from exposure to noise in the workplace, you must reduce the risks to the lowest level reasonably practicable – for example, by using soundproofing material, relocating noisy machinery and providing appropriate ear protectors.

Fire & Other Emergencies

The first phase of planning emergency response procedures begins with an investigation into what could go wrong. Experienced employees are a great source of information but, depending on the nature of the environment, specialist assistance might be required.

Develop evacuation procedures, provide training and practise drills, install fire alarms, provide fire-fighting equipment, particularly appropriate fire extinguishers to match the environmental hazards.

Even the most sophisticated plans and systems can break down, therefore regular practise and upgrading is essential. It is also essential to have contingency plans in place.

Obviously, the size and complexity of the work premises is a guiding factor. A small company with few employees engaged in office work with immediate and easy ground-level access and egress would need very little by way of procedures and regular evacuation practise to satisfy safety needs. Alternatively, if the offices were situated in a high-rise building, evacuation procedures and regular practise might be extremely important.

In heavy industry or in large companies, fire fighting and evacuation procedures may be critical. Having a group of experienced and well-trained personnel is essential. In companies that have multiple risks of fires and explosions, it is essential to have company fire fighting units with professionally-equipped tenders and other support equipment in addition to a well-trained team. Such companies, when engaged in setting up a new facility, can use the local fire brigade services to help assess the new facility, recommend the most suitable services and train the fire-fighting crew recruited for the purpose. For a company with such a high level of fire, explosion or other serious risks, it is highly recommended that they seek professional assistance with the assessment, planning and implementation phases.

Working with Chemicals & Other Dangerous Substances

This section relates to chemicals and dangerous substances in various states such as solids, liquids, gases, dust, fibres, vapours, droplets, smoke, fumes and odours.

Many companies have a variety of chemicals that are used as part of the manufacturing process. Others may store a wide range of chemicals, some of which might be dangerous enough in their own right, but absolutely lethal if mixed with other stored chemicals through damaged containers or other accidental event.

It is necessary, therefore, for the employer to have full information on the risks associated with each chemical and the actions required if any person comes into contact with such chemicals.

It is important to ensure safe storage and movement procedures throughout the lifecycle of each chemical and to establish a safe reclaim or disposal procedures for used, or spent, chemicals.

Label all chemicals correctly and include a grading for easy identification as to the level of danger and the potential hazards involved. Highlight the dangers of any mixture of the various chemicals in storage and the procedures for safe storage, as well as the protective clothing to be worn, the handling procedures, the dispensing procedures, the training for handling and immediate actions to be taken by those involved in emergency situations. Provide systematic training and regular reinforcement of the risks associated with dangerous substances, not only for employees who work with the chemicals, but also those who are in the environment where the chemicals are used or transported.

Assess the short, medium and long-term exposure risks for employees and arrange for medical screening as recommended by a qualified medical practitioner. The specialist will consider the chemicals in relation to occupational exposure limit guidelines for each substance. Monitor the health of the employees involved within the recommended frequency and maintain the records for inspection and for consideration in the event of a medical condition developing.

Construction

This is a wide and varied industry with both large and small contractors involved in a wide range of building and maintenance activities on a scale from building a garden wall to constructing skyscrapers.

If one has the opportunity to look at a large scale building project on a busy day, the potential dangers seem immediately imminent and obvious. With gigantic cranes carrying heavy objects over the heads of construction workers, engineers and site managers alike, one would expect daily occurrences of fairly serious accidents. Surprisingly, this is not the case, although accidents do occasionally occur.

Perhaps the fact that the employees at all levels are fairly familiar with the building site environment means that they are more aware of the potential risks and react accordingly. This, coupled with fairly stringent rules and procedures, policed by engineers with clear responsibilities for safety, have helped to reduce the level of accidents on building sites.

Given the large numbers of foreign nationals currently employed in the construction industry, it is important to ensure that they understand inherent dangers if they do not have sufficient language abilities to appreciate the procedures and risks. This may mean translating safety procedures, training and signs into different languages.

There are specific statutory regulations – the Safety, Health & Welfare at Work (Construction) Regulations 2006 – that set out the minimum safety requirements required in the construction industry.

Safe Driving

Where employees drive company vehicles, or where part of an employee's job involves driving, you should incorporate a safe driving policy into the company's safety statement. You should consider the following:

- Choosing vehicles with advanced safety features.
- Regular maintenance of company vehicles.
- Providing training, information and clear policies and procedures to drivers regarding safe driving rules, speeding, the use of seat belts,

mobile phones, smoking, fatigue avoidance, driving under the influence of alcohol, drugs or medication.

Health & Safety Authority

The Health & Safety Authority (HSA) is the national body in Ireland responsible for securing health and safety at work. It was established under the Safety, Health & Welfare at Work Act 1989.

The main functions of the HSA are to:

- Promote the prevention of accidents, dangerous occurrences and personal injury at work, in accordance with the relevant statutory provisions, and to encourage and foster measures promoting the safety, health and welfare of persons at work.

- Promote and provide education and training in the safety, health and welfare of persons at work.

- Encourage co-operation with, and between, employee representatives and employers and any other bodies, as appropriate, with regard to the prevention of risks to safety, health and welfare at work in accordance with the relevant statutory provisions.

- Make any arrangements that it considers appropriate for providing information and advice on matters relating to safety, health and welfare at work.

- Make any arrangements that it considers appropriate to conduct, commission, promote, support and evaluate research, surveys and studies on matters relating to the functions of the HSA.

- Make adequate arrangements for the enforcement of the relevant statutory provisions.

- Monitor, evaluate and make recommendations to the Minister of Enterprise, Trade & Employment regarding implementation of, and compliance with, the relevant statutory provisions and best practice relating to safety, health and welfare at work, and the review and maintenance of relevant records by employers.

Personal Injuries Assessment Board (PIAB)

The Personal Injuries Assessment Board Act 2003 provided for the establishment of a statutory body (the PIAB) to offer independent assessment of personal injury compensation for victims of workplace, motor and public liability accidents.

The key objectives of PIAB are to:

- Reduce significantly the delivery cost of awarding compensation due to claimants, without altering the level of compensation.

- Implement a less adversarial, and faster, settlement process for personal injury claims, where claimants have an entitlement to compensation.

- Reduce the length of time it takes to finalise a compensation claim. Under the court system, it can take approximately three years to settle a claim. It generally takes nine months to settle a personal injury claim *via* PIAB.

The PIAB acts as a mediation process to assist parties to come to an early settlement, but only if the defendant has accepted that there is no dispute about liability. PIAB will only be involved where the question of fault is not at issue.

Based on written material supplied to it by both sides, and without holding any hearings (a paper-based system), the PIAB can provide the parties with a compensation figure that either side can accept or reject.

SAFETY STATEMENT

A safety statement is a comprehensive declaration of procedures designed to eliminate or minimise any risks or hazards to employees and others in the workplace.

A risk or hazard is anything in the workplace that could cause harm to an employee – for example, electrocution from exposed wiring, slips, trips or falls arising from an untidy environment, cuts or abrasions from sharp objects. There is a wide range of potential hazards in every workplace, to a greater or lesser degree, depending on the type of work involved.

The safety statement assists in maintaining a workplace that ensures the safety, health and welfare of all staff, customers, suppliers and other visitors to the company premises (or off-site, if the employee is required to work away from company premises).

The safety statement must be developed, systematically implemented and maintained. This is a management duty and responsibility.

Legal Obligations

The Safety, Health & Welfare at Work Act 2005 requires all employers, including self-employed persons, to produce a written safety statement. The Act, however, provides that small companies with up to three employees only have to apply a basic code of practice, which the Health & Safety Authority has committed to put in place.

The safety statement is a comprehensive and specific code of practice for an organisation, and even smaller companies are well-advised to familiarise themselves with the requirements of the safety statement and be as comprehensive as possible in their management of the safety function.

For companies with more than three employees, the safety statement continues to be an important requirement. If inspectors from the Health & Safety Authority find that a company does not have a safety statement, or that a company's safety statement is inadequate, they can instruct the company to immediately prepare and implement safety procedures or to revise the safety statement.

General Contents

- Identify potential hazards.

- Assess risk levels associated with those hazards.

- Detail arrangements and resources required to ensure the safety, health, and welfare of employees and risk reduction policies and procedures.

- List the names and job titles of the persons with responsibility for health and safety within the organisation and ensure all employees are aware of who has such responsibilities.

- Specify arrangements for consultation with employees with regard to health and safety in the workplace and for ensuring their co-operation in implementing the safety statement.

The identification of hazards/risks

At one end of the scale, there are jobs that, by their nature, are obviously hazardous – such as fire-fighters, people working with explosives in mining, deep sea divers, people working in a variety of jobs on oil rigs, etc. At the other end of the scale, there are office administrators or clerks, computer operators, shop assistants in fashion stores, receptionists, typists, etc, where the risks are negligible compared to the previous groups.

In all of these diverse occupations, the approach to protecting the individual is the same, although the level of detail and management response to hazards varies significantly. For example, a fire-fighter must take calculated risks within certain understood parameters when carrying out the job. Entering a blazing building would not be acceptable unless you were trained in fire-fighting techniques, had passed a variety of physical and psychological tests, were wearing safety clothing that was tested and rated to certain standards, carried breathing apparatus, had communications equipment, carried cutting tools and a variety of other conditions. On the other hand, a receptionist in a hotel may only have to be trained in the correct sitting posture, have the correct seating and have a computer screen filter to satisfy the basic occupational safety requirements for that occupation.

It is obvious, therefore, that each job must be assessed on its own merits to determine the particular hazards, no matter how trivial they may appear at a first glance, and something done to reduce or eliminate any form of risk. Such risks could be from fatigue, eye strain, back strain, pulled muscles, burns from welding equipment, explosions at kilns and numerous other sources and occupations. Back strain from lifting may be more prevalent and more obvious than back strain from sitting at a computer but both are legitimate hazards arising from different occupations and requiring employer intervention to mitigate the particular risk.

Employees are probably the best source of information concerning the key characteristics of the work and should be asked to help in the identification of hazards. However, remember that the incumbent may be overly familiar with the work and may find it difficult to articulate the hazards. So, make sure that several people, and ideally a safety specialist, checks out all jobs for hazards – particularly those jobs that clearly involve moving parts, sharp edges, excess weight, electrical equipment, etc, as they will undoubtedly contain more hazards than other jobs.

Once the risks or hazards have been identified, the job of eliminating or reducing the employee's exposure begins. The objective is to change the activity or task to make the work safer.

There may be none or very few hazards associated with a particular occupation but it is in the 'line of fire' of another operation, which could potentially put them at risk – for example, someone working on an assembly line with very little effort or fatigue elements but who sits too close to a moving part of another piece of equipment under someone else's control. So, extend the risk assessments to the locality in a logical way to seek out any second level risks.

Mental and physical demands

When going through the process of identifying risks or hazards consider both the mental and physical demands of each job in terms of the duties, responsibilities, targets, objectives, hours of work and the interactions with others.

Questions to ask experienced employees

- What are the hazards?

- Have injuries occurred in the past on this work and if so how and why?

- What work is being done and can it be done differently? Different methods, materials, etc.

- Why is something being done in a particular way? Can it be done differently? As part of another operation? Using new or modified equipment? Replacing the hands-on elements with automated or semi automated tools?

- Where something is being done. Can it be done elsewhere with less exposure to employees? Use a different internal or external location?

- When something is being done. Can it be done at a time when there are fewer people affected by the operation in question?

- How it is done. Could methods or procedural changes result in reducing or eliminating risk? Are there new methods, tools or equipment available in the market for doing the work? Could they be adopted or adapted by the company?

Promoting the Safety Statement

Communications is critical. The safety statement should be made available to all employees in the workplace, whether permanent, temporary or contracted – for example:

- Issued individually to each employee.

- Included as part of the company Human Resource manual/employee handbook.

- Retained at the company's reception desk.

- Displayed in the staff canteen or staff room.

- Copies available within employees' immediate work area through their immediate manager.

- Included at training sessions, with particular reference to their work.

New employees should be made aware of the safety statement when they are undergoing induction training.

Responsibility

Managers and supervisors have a responsibility to ensure that the safety statement is up-to-date and fully operational at all times, and that employees' practices in the workplace are in compliance with the safety statement practices and procedures.

The employer should advise employees that they are legally obliged to co-operate in maintaining a safe workplace and that failure to comply with safety procedures may result in disciplinary action up to, and including, dismissal. Employers can include non-compliance with safety procedures in the company's definitions of gross misconduct under the company's disciplinary procedures and, therefore, eligible for dismissal.

Updating

It is necessary that the safety statement is reviewed on a regular basis and is kept up-to-date.

Keep all employees informed of amendments to the safety statement and ensure that any changes are incorporated into all subsequent training programmes.

BULLYING & HARASSMENT

While bullying, harassment, sexual harassment, intimidation, abuse and belittling has been a part of working life for a considerable period of time, it is only in recent years that the extent of such behaviour and the damage it causes has become clear. Subsequently, protections and actions to eradicate it from Irish working life have been put in place through legislation and many companies now have stringent procedures in place to protect employees.

The onus of responsibility is on the employer to detect and resolve any form of bullying in the workplace. Bullying and harassment in the workplace can affect the health of employees and must be treated the same as any other risk that requires the employer to develop policies, practices and procedures to identify and resolve issues. Aside from a common law duty of care, employers are also obliged by the Safety, Health & Welfare at Work Act 2005 to:

> 'manage and conduct work activities in such a way as to prevent, so far as is reasonably practicable, any improper conduct or behaviour likely to put the safety, health and welfare at work of his or her employees at risk'

However, employees must also take some responsibility for their own behaviour at work and, if possible, to flag unacceptable behaviour in others to a manager. The Safety, Health & Welfare at Work Act 2005 requires employees to:

> '... not engage in improper conduct or behaviour that is likely to endanger his or her own safety, health and welfare at work or that of any other person.'

Definitions of Bullying & Harassment

It is not possible to have one comprehensive definition of what constitutes bullying and harassment, since such behaviour can take many different forms.

The *Report of the Task Force on the Prevention of Workplace Bullying* (2001) defines workplace bullying as:

> 'Workplace bullying is repeated inappropriate behaviour, direct or indirect, whether verbal, physical or otherwise, conducted by one or more persons against another or others, at the place of work and/or in the course of employment, which could be regarded as undermining the individual's right to dignity at work.

An isolated incident of the behaviour described in this definition may be an affront to dignity at work but as a once-off incident is not considered to be bullying.'

The Equality Act 2004 defines harassment as:

'... any form of unwanted conduct related to any of the discriminatory grounds (gender, marital status, family status, sexual orientation, religion, age, disability, race or membership of the travelling community), being conduct that has the purpose or effect of violating a person's dignity and creating an intimidating, hostile, degrading, humiliating or offensive environment for the person.'

The Equality Act 2004 also provides a definition for sexual harassment:

'... any form of unwanted verbal, non-verbal or physical conduct of a sexual nature, being conduct that has the purpose or effect of violating a person's dignity and creating an intimidating, hostile, degrading, humiliating or offensive environment for the person.'

Bullying and harassment can take the form of verbal (words), physical (gestures) or visual nature (production, display or circulation of material). Such unreasonable behaviour can include one or more of the following:

- Humiliation.
- Victimisation.
- Intimidation and threats, whether explicit or implicit.
- Verbal abuse or insults.
- Aggression and physical abuse.
- Intrusion such as stalking, pestering or spying.
- Being treated less favourably than other employees.
- Exclusion.
- Undermining.
- Excessive monitoring of work.
- Withholding of work-related information.
- Unwarranted and undue blame for circumstances beyond victim's control.
- Regularly manipulating an employee's job content and targets.

Such actions are sometimes cited in cases of constructive dismissal. If proven, they could result in significant costs for the company.

Dealing with Bullying & Harassment

Some employees are sufficiently assertive to resolve the issue themselves directly with the offender and may not report the matter formally to their manager as per the stated procedures. However, if a manager hears of such a case, he/she is obliged to investigate as the behaviour is out of line with company policy and also because the individual might be engaged in similar behaviour with another employee who is incapable of dealing with the issue.

Generally bullies target people when they think they will be able to get away with the act. These are people who may be so intimidated and frightened that they will be submissive to the bully, which satisfies the bully's need for power and control of another person. In fact, the bully is generally a coward and needs to be dealt with quickly and without any ambiguity. Often, the bully has a psychological problem and needs counselling and monitoring. However, they may not be able to fit back into a company, once discovered, and can resign or, alternatively, if the behaviour is particularly pronounced, and is also detailed as gross misconduct in the company's disciplinary procedures, be dismissed from the employment.

Managers or executives must be careful to ensure the protection of all types of employees but those who are more prone to bullying require particular monitoring when a bully has been identified. The company must ensure that any employee may make a complaint without fear or risk of reprisals.

In extreme cases, the employee being bullied may decide to leave the company because he/she is unable to cope or deal with the bullying. Later, he/she may decide to take a case against the company for constructive dismissal based on the bullying. If their claim is proven, it can prove costly for the company, as it has a duty of care to protect all employees in their employment.

Recommended procedures

You should develop an anti-bullying, anti-harassment and anti-sexual harassment policy and procedure, including reporting and investigation processes. Ensure that all employees are informed of the company policy and the procedures that will be applied, either when an employee reports bullying/harassment or when the company discovers such incidents and takes the initiative to investigate and resolve the issue. The definitions should be included in the company's definitions of gross misconduct.

Include the policy in the company's safety statement and Human Resource manual or employee handbook. The policy should be included in the induction training process and you may wish to consider specific training on the prevention and resolution of workplace bullying and harassment, particularly for management.

The policy should include an informal and a formal process for dealing with incidents of bullying and harassment. You may wish to designate one or more managers or other competent employees as a contact person, who can listen and advise about complaints of bullying and harassment at work and is able to explain the procedures in place to resolve it. Obviously, it is important that the contact person receives the appropriate training. In smaller companies, if the complaint is made by, or against, a senior manager, it may be necessary to use the expertise of an external HR specialist to help resolve the issue.

Both the informal and formal processes should include the following steps:

- The employee reports bullying (in whatever form) to the manager as per the stated procedures.

- The manager records the details.

- The employee (if possible) is advised to inform the alleged offender that their behaviour is unacceptable. The employee should state that, if the bullying happens again, he/she will be obliged to make a formal complaint and confirms this to his/her manager.

- If the employee is unable to directly deal with the alleged offender, the person's manager must advise the alleged offender that his/her behaviour is not acceptable to the employee concerned. The manager must pursue the matter directly with the alleged offender.

- The matter then becomes a formal complaint. The employee making the complaint becomes the complainant and the alleged offender is referred to as the respondent. Just like the process set out in the disciplinary procedures, the alleged offender is innocent until proven guilty.

The objective of the informal process is to resolve the issue with the minimum of conflict and stress for the individuals concerned. A problem-solving approach is used to ensure that the inappropriate behaviour complained of is eliminated and that good working relationships are maintained. This might be achieved by way of an apology, an agreement that the conduct will not be repeated or an explanation about what occurred so that both parties understand the other's point of view.

However, an employee has the right to bypass the informal process and, instead, to access the formal process. The formal process may also need to be invoked, if the alleged behaviour is of a serious nature.

Investigative procedures must be fair and equitable. Remember that an accusation needs some form of solid evidence. The respondent is innocent, until proven guilty. Review the investigative procedures for industrial relations in **Chapter 2**, for further information on the steps involved in conducting an investigation.

STRESS

Stress can be injurious to health and welfare and, as such, must be eliminated from the workplace, where possible. Some stress may be an inevitable aspect of certain occupations, such as air traffic controllers (at the top end of the scale), and employers need to be particularly careful in planning the work patterns, breaks and support for such jobs.

Stress is now a commonplace word that we sometimes use rather casually to describe how pressured we are. Pressure, however, is not stress, although it can lead to stress. The dictionary describes stress as 'putting under strain'. In a work context, this can mean physical, mental or emotional stress – for example, arising from anxiety or overwork.

Stress testing (in the context of physical objects) generally means subjecting a product or material to different types of forces, until the product or material breaks down to a state where it is no longer viable or capable of operating as it was intended. If you apply this to the human condition, the potential damage that this can, and does, cause is immense.

Stress can arise from a wide range of forces, both internal and external in nature, and from both imagined and real sources.

Causes of Stress

According to the Irish Congress of Trade Unions (ICTU), the most commonly reported causes of occupational stress include:

- Inadequate time to complete the job properly.
- No clear job description or chain of command.
- No recognition or reward for doing well.
- No way to voice complaints.
- Too much responsibility, with too little authority.
- Unco-operative fellow workers.
- Job insecurity.
- Prejudice in the workplace.
- Unpleasant or hazardous working conditions.

Incorrect job design can also lead to regular pressure to achieve unreasonable targets, which can eventually lead to stress. Many jobs are, in fact, not designed at all; they just evolve, as activities are expanded.

Within the work environment, stress can be attributable to internal and external forces. An employee's own personality or behavioural traits or understanding of what is required of them, their perception of themselves, their shortfalls in abilities and a host of other reasons can bring about an unhealthy stress level.

Undue pressures from a manager, or even a broader organisational culture, can also have the same unhealthy impact. Such pressure can arise from bad management and, sometimes, can be malicious in nature, where a manager uses this approach to intimidate so as to get commitments or results over and above the norm. However, they break the organisational and legal guidelines in doing so, and any extra performance achieved is mitigated by poor relationships and a breakdown in trust. Such performance is unsustainable.

The impact of stress on our behaviour can be devastating, creating irrationality in our thinking and actions. Examples of ill-health arising from stress can include heart problems, ulcers, migraine, eating disorders, sleep deprivation, fatigue, increased alcohol consumption, loss of concentration, mental breakdown, etc, all of which can contribute to a wide range of further reactions, including loss of capacity to work, earn a living and interact with others, to name but a few.

Signs of Stress

These include:

- Absenteeism.
- Labour turnover.
- Doctors' medical certificates (specific in some cases, vague in others).
- Aspects of the environment (internal politics).
- Employees appearing to be fearful (possibly of their immediate manager).
- Low productivity and poor performance.
- Tiredness and irritability.
- Indecisiveness.
- Poor timekeeping.
- Physical illnesses such as headaches.
- Increased alcohol consumption.

Stress Prevention & Management

- Understand the nature of stress.

- Ensure stress is engineered out of jobs, where possible.

- Ensure stress arising from bullying and harassment by colleagues or managers is monitored and eliminated. Develop policies and procedures to monitor and control such behaviour and ensure employees are aware of what is acceptable and unacceptable behaviour.

- Introduce stress prevention policies and programmes.

- Carry out regular checks.

- From time to time, get professional advice and improve stress management techniques.

SMOKE-FREE WORKPLACES

The introduction of the workplace anti-smoking laws in Ireland, rather surprisingly, has been a huge success. This is particularly so within the licensed premises where most problems were anticipated. However, the change for non-smokers is a vast improvement from the previous levels of passive smoke exposure. Despite this general success, it is important to understand and maintain the legislative requirements.

A person who smokes in a workplace is in contravention of the Public Health (Tobacco) Acts 2002 & 2004, and is guilty of an offence. In addition, the occupier, manager or any other person deemed to be in charge of the workplace where the contravention occurs is also guilty of an offence.

The legislation does not prevent people from smoking but restricts where people may smoke.

You may find it useful to share the following information with staff:

- Smoking is dangerous for humans.

- Smokers who are also exposed to other people's smoke have an increased exposure to this danger.

- Environmental tobacco smoke (ETS) is made up of thousands of chemicals as gases and particles, many of which are known to cause cancer.

- Smoke, which is not inhaled, represents approximately 85% of that released. This smoke can be even more harmful.

- Passive smoking affects the eyes and nose, throat and lungs.

- Tobacco is virtually the only source of nicotine-related carcinogens. Experiments have confirmed that the non-smoker, including children and babies, absorbs these carcinogens from passive smoking.

- Discarded cigarettes and matches are a fire hazard.

Workplace Exemptions

There are exemptions from this prohibition on smoking in the workplace for:

- Prisons and Garda station detention areas.
- Psychiatric hospitals.
- St. Patrick's Institution.
- Nursing homes and maternity homes.

- Hospices.
- Religious order homes.
- Central Mental Hospital.
- Residential areas within third level education institutions.
- Hotel, guesthouse and B&B bedrooms.

However, employers may decide, even within the designated exemptions, not to allow smoking. Even in such exempt environments, as much precaution must be taken as necessary to protect any non-smokers from the passive inhalation of tobacco smoke.

Employer Responsibilities

- Ensure that the workplace is smoke-free.
- Ideally, a total smoking ban without any designated areas should be pursued, but this may not be practicable.
- Define, if feasible, any outside uncovered location where employees may smoke and provide suitable fireproof containers.
- Display notices and signs to remind employees, customers and members of the public of the workplace smoking ban and directing smokers to the designated outdoor facility. The sign should also state to which manager an employee may make a complaint, regarding breaches in the smoking policies, practices and procedures.
- Company transport is also an enclosed workplace and, therefore, must be smoke-free.
- Communicate and consult with all employees with regard to the development of appropriate policies, practices and procedures regarding the smoking ban, in line with legislative requirements.
- Train designated employees to deal professionally with any person, customers, or otherwise, who are in breach of the smoking ban.
- Enforce the agreed policies, practices and procedures.
- Apply disciplinary procedures regarding any employee's non-compliance within the legislative provisions and within the company's internal disciplinary procedures. Consider including non-compliance as a gross misconduct offence.
- Be quite specific on the smoking ban requirements and also the duty of care under safety, health and welfare legislation.

FIGURE 24: SAFETY, HEALTH & WELFARE AT WORK CHART

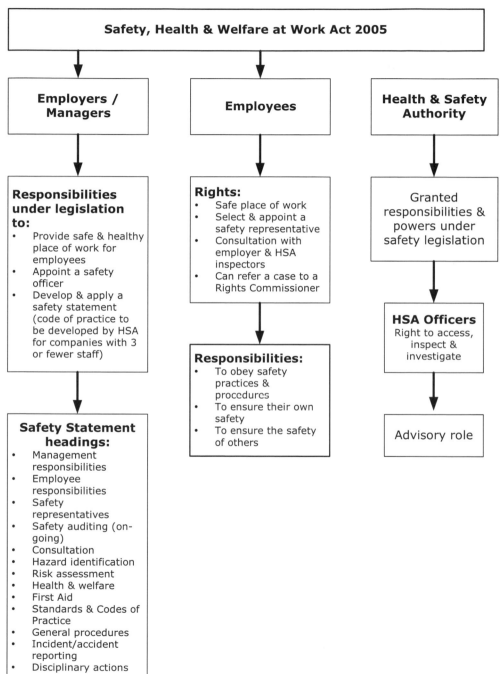

Safety, Health & Welfare at Work Act 2005

Employers / Managers

Employees

Health & Safety Authority

Responsibilities under legislation to:
- Provide safe & healthy place of work for employees
- Appoint a safety officer
- Develop & apply a safety statement (code of practice to be developed by HSA for companies with 3 or fewer staff)

Rights:
- Safe place of work
- Select & appoint a safety representative
- Consultation with employer & HSA inspectors
- Can refer a case to a Rights Commissioner

Granted responsibilities & powers under safety legislation

Responsibilities:
- To obey safety practices & procedures
- To ensure their own safety
- To ensure the safety of others

HSA Officers
Right to access, inspect & investigate

Advisory role

Safety Statement headings:
- Management responsibilities
- Employee responsibilities
- Safety representatives
- Safety auditing (on-going)
- Consultation
- Hazard identification
- Risk assessment
- Health & welfare
- First Aid
- Standards & Codes of Practice
- General procedures
- Incident/accident reporting
- Disciplinary actions
- Training

CHAPTER 4

EMPLOYMENT
LEGISLATION

INTRODUCTION

Employment law in Ireland provides regulations for employers and employees with regard to the management and protection of people at work.

The legislation offers guidance, consistency, fairness and protection for employees. It also provides a process to allow employees to pursue claims against an offending employer.

Employers have a multitude of responsibilities to their employees under Irish employment legislation and it is certain that these laws will continue to develop and expand each year, placing more and more pressures and responsibilities on the employer.

Although the regulations are predominantly targeted at employers, there are many features that apply to employees. Employers are entitled to expect that their staff will comply with such requirements. Employees may be subject to disciplinary action, if they are non-compliant.

So, the legislation equally supports the employer and the employee, within the provisions and procedures of the various Acts, through arbitration, investigation and the development of recommendations or determinations, to resolve employment-related issues. The legislation also provides appeals mechanisms, up to and including the High Court.

While compliance might be a basic aspiration for some employers, many go beyond basic statutory requirements as a company policy. This approach is generally found in companies that have a positive or proactive employee relations culture and where performance and flexibility through positive motivation are high on the management agenda.

In this chapter, each of the main pieces of employment legislation have been reviewed and compressed into their key requirements, so as to help the reader with minimal experience in this area to understand the purposes and requirements of each Act or regulation. The chapter provides an outline of the legislation for the reader and is neither a comprehensive reflection of all employment-related Acts nor a comprehensive statement or a legal interpretation of the contents of each of the Acts covered. In addition, pending legislation or case law may change the summaries provided.

Employers with particular issues should review the relevant section. When developing policies, practices and procedures to implement statutory provisions, you may find it difficult to reconcile the necessary changes with your current business status. If in doubt, it is advisable to seek assistance.

Employment Law/Industrial Relations Process

Overview

The main intention of this chapter is to provide a quick reference to key employer obligations and employee rights.

Employers are obliged to familiarise themselves with the provisions of all legal requirements and to ensure that these are properly applied within their business.

Note that each Act may have been amended several times since its introduction and, while the first Act is often still referred to as the primary Act, there may be more updated legislative requirements contained in the subsequent amendments and/or Statutory Instruments (SIs), which are issued from time to time to provide further direction or provisions. These multiple Acts may have three or four editions; however, they are described by date – for example, the date of the first edition and date of the last edition – thus, the Industrial Relations Acts 1946-2004.

It is important for an employer to ensure that he/she is applying the most up-to-date requirements.

Industrial Relations Processes

The dispute, complaints, claims, appeals, penalties and fines processes are summarised below. These change slightly from one Act to another. Therefore, employers must familiarise themselves with the appropriate process in relation to any dispute, the Act under which it is to be processed, the appropriate industrial relations route for the issue, the appeals processes in case of necessity and any fines or penalties that might arise for non-compliance.

In general, claims by individuals can be referred to a Rights Commissioner, the Labour Relations Commission, the Equality Tribunal, the Labour Court or the Employment Appeals Tribunal. These are the industrial relations investigative and decision-making bodies established to assist companies and employees to resolve issues within the context of the employment legislation.

Appeals may be processed through the same bodies, but may change in sequence, depending on the appropriate starting point for a particular issue.

When the industrial relations processes are exhausted without a resolution, the issue may be appealed to the Circuit Court or High Court. Again, this depends on the issue, the industrial relations process and the appeals mechanism. Normally, issues may only be referred for interpretation to the High Court on a point of law or where the actual process is being challenged.

Example – an Unfair Dismissal Case

If an employee considers that he/she has been unfairly dismissed, he/she may submit a claim for redress under the Unfair Dismissals Acts 1977-2001 to a Rights Commissioner or directly to the Employment Appeals Tribunal. If a claim is made directly to the Tribunal, one of the parties must notify the Tribunal that he/she objects to the claim being heard by a Rights Commissioner.

A written notice of the claim, which must contain certain prescribed particulars, must be submitted by the employee (preferably by registered post) either to the Rights Commissioner Service or the Employment Appeals Tribunal.

The time limit for submitting a claim for redress for unfair dismissal is six months. However, this may be extended to 12 months, in cases where exceptional circumstances have prevented the lodgement of the claim within the normal timeframe.

A Rights Commissioner, on receipt of a claim from an employee, will send a copy of the claim to the employer. The Rights Commissioner will then give the parties an opportunity to be heard and to present any evidence relevant to the claim.

It is not compulsory for the employer to attend a hearing. However, it is recommended that the employer take the initiative to resolve the issues immediately (and ideally, amicably) with the employee concerned.

The Rights Commissioner may explore opportunities to resolve the issue at a hearing through discussion, negotiation and subsequently joint agreement. However, failing that, the Rights Commissioner hears and reviews the parties' written submissions and will issue a written recommendation to the parties for the resolution of the dispute, specifying one of the remedies below.

Either party may appeal the recommendation to the Employment Appeals Tribunal. This appeal must be made within six weeks of the date on which the Rights Commissioner communicated the recommendation to the parties. The Employment Appeals Tribunal will copy the appeal notice to the other party.

The Tribunal will give the parties an opportunity to be heard and to present any evidence relevant to the appeal. The Tribunal then will issue a written determination in relation to the appeal, specifying, as in the case of a Rights Commissioner, one of the remedies listed below.

There is a right of appeal by either party to the Circuit Court from a determination of the Tribunal. This appeal must be made within six weeks of the date on which the Employment Appeals Tribunal communicated its determination to the parties.

Remedies

Where an employee has been unfairly dismissed, under the Unfair Dismissals Acts 1977-2001, depending on the merits of the case, he/she can be awarded:

- Re-instatement in his/her old job, thereby entitling the employee to benefit from any improvement in terms and conditions of employment that may occur between the date of dismissal and the date of re-instatement.

- Re-engagement in his/her old job, or in a suitable alternative job, on conditions that the adjudicating body considers reasonable.

- Where financial loss has been sustained by the employee, financial compensation in respect of such loss, subject to a maximum of two years' remuneration. The precise amount of compensation can depend on such matters as where the responsibility for the dismissal lay, the measures taken to reduce financial loss by the claimant or the extent to which negotiated dismissal procedures were followed, if these existed.

- Where no financial loss has been sustained by the employee, financial compensation may be awarded subject to a maximum award of four weeks' remuneration.

- Where ownership of the business in which the dismissal occurred has been transferred to a new owner, an award of compensation may be made to the employee against the new owner, who is required to take on liability for any claim for unfair dismissal against the former employer. This responsibility arises for employers under transfer of ownership of an enterprise – see later in this chapter.)

In calculating financial loss (for the purpose of compensation), payments to an employee under the social welfare and income tax codes will be disregarded.

Non-compliance of employer

Where an employer has neither implemented nor appealed a Rights Commissioner's recommendation, an employee may submit a claim (in writing of the claim on an appropriate claim form) to the Employment Appeals Tribunal, seeking implementation of the recommendation.

In such cases, the Employment Appeals Tribunal is empowered to issue a determination without rehearing the case and, if it upholds the claim, to confirm the recommendation of the Rights Commissioner in his/her determination.

Failure to appear before the Employment Appeals Tribunal where a subpoena is served, and/or failure to produce documentation, is an offence liable, on summary conviction, to a monetary fine.

Employee claims routes

In addition to the Rights Commissioner/Employment Appeals Tribunal/Labour Court route, an employee may take a case for wrongful dismissal to:

- The civil courts.
- The Director of the Equality Tribunal.

In the civil courts, damages for wrongful dismissal (breach of contract) are not restricted to the upper limitation in unfair dismissal cases of two years' remuneration.

However, the employee must choose between a common law action and a claim under the Unfair Dismissals Acts 1977-2001 (the route described above). He/she cannot pursue both concurrently.

Nonetheless, the employee may change a claim between redress in common law and unfair dismissals legislation, subject to the following:

- The employee retains the right to damages at common law for wrongful dismissal, up to the time that either a Rights Commissioner makes a recommendation in the case or a hearing by the Employment Appeals Tribunal has commenced.
- An employee retains his/her right to redress under the unfair dismissals legislation, up to the time that his/her claim for damages for wrongful dismissal in the civil courts has commenced.

If an employee who has been dismissed has referred the dismissal case to the Director of the Equality Tribunal, under the Employment Equality Acts 1998 & 2004 and, either a settlement has been reached by mediation or the Tribunal has begun an investigation, the employee is not entitled to seek redress under the Unfair Dismissals Acts 1977-2001 in respect of the dismissal, unless the Director of the Equality Tribunal, having completed his/her investigation, directs otherwise.

Conclusion

Since there are different submission routes, processing and appeals procedures for each Act, an employer who is not familiar with these processes is advised to seek professional assistance.

ADOPTIVE LEAVE ACTS 1995 & 2005

Purpose

The Adoptive Leave Acts 1995 & 2005 provide entitlements for employees to take **unpaid** leave from work in relation to the adoption of children under certain conditions and to take **paid** time off to attend certain pre-adoption classes and meetings that he/she is obliged to attend within the State (such as with social workers or health service officials).

Provisions & Procedures

Eligibility

* Male and female employees who adopt children.

* An employed sole male adopter.

* An employed adopting father, where the adopting mother has died.

All employees who adopt are entitled to adoptive leave, regardless of length of service.

Adoptive leave

* The adoptive leave entitlement is a minimum period of 26 consecutive weeks' **unpaid** leave (for leave commencing on or after 1 March 2007; otherwise, 20 weeks).

* The employee is required to provide the employer with four weeks' written notice of a request for adoptive leave.

* The written notice should contain the expected date of placement and the proposed date for commencing the adoptive leave.

* The employee must provide formal evidence of adoption placement as soon as is reasonably practicable. For Irish adoptions, this must be no later than four weeks after the day of placement. For foreign adoptions, the employee must present a copy of the declaration of eligibility and suitability (issued under the Adoption Act 1991 by the Adoption Board/Authority) before the commencement of adoptive leave (or additional adoptive leave – see below – whichever is the earlier).

* Details of the placement must be provided to the employer as soon as practicable thereafter.

- The employee must provide return-to-work written notification to the employer four weeks before the end of the leave period.

Additional adoptive leave

- An employee who has taken adoptive leave may apply for a maximum of 16 weeks' additional *unpaid* adoptive leave (for leave commencing on or after 1 March 2007; otherwise, 12 weeks).
- This extra leave must commence immediately after the scheduled adoptive leave.
- The employee must notify the employer in writing of his/her intention to take additional adoptive leave, either when first requesting adoptive leave or at least four weeks before his/her original scheduled date of return to work.
- An employee who has already scheduled additional adoptive leave may cancel this leave four weeks in advance of such leave commencing by observing the same four weeks' written notification requirements.
- In the case of foreign adoptions, some or all of the additional adoptive leave may be taken immediately before the placement date.
- The employee must provide return-to-work written notification to the employer, four weeks before the end of the leave period.

Postponing or terminating adoptive leave

- An employee may cancel or postpone a notification for adoptive leave by providing written notification to the employer. This will not affect his/her overall adoptive leave entitlements.
- In the event of the child (for whom adoptive leave was taken) being hospitalised, an employee can apply to his/her employer to postpone all or part of the adoptive leave or additional adoptive leave period.

Pre-adoption classes and meetings

- An employee is entitled to *paid* time off to attend certain pre-adoption classes and meetings that he/she is obliged to attend within the State (such as with social workers or health service officials).
- The employee must provide written notification of the date(s)/time(s) of the class(es) or meeting(s), at least two weeks before the date of the first class to be attended or the class or meeting concerned, as appropriate.
- If the employee is unable to provide advance notification of pre-adoption classes or meetings, for reasonable reasons, he/she may provide written

evidence of having attended the class or meeting, within one week of the class or meeting taking place, and an explanation as to why she/he was unable to supply the necessary written notice.

Protection of employment rights

- Annual leave entitlements that accrue to an employee during adoptive leave will be granted in accordance with the terms of the Organisation of Working Time Act 1997.

- Employees retain their rights to public holidays that occur during adoptive leave, and such days are given as days off in lieu at the end of the leave.

- Service continuity and the rights of an employee with regard to employment are maintained while on adoptive leave, other than the rights to remuneration. Remuneration has a wide definition and not only includes salary, but also benefits such as health insurance, pension contributions, etc.

- The employee has the right to return to the same or equivalent and suitable work, including location and pay, on terms that are not substantially less favourable.

- Training, probation or apprenticeship, interrupted by adoptive leave, is temporarily suspended until after the leave period.

CARER'S LEAVE ACT 2001

Purpose

The Carer's Leave Act 2001 provides entitlements for employees to take *unpaid* leave to provide full-time care for a person in need.

Provisions and Procedures

Eligibility

- An employee must have one year's continuous service with the same employer.
- The person being cared for must satisfy the eligibility requirements of the Department of Social & Family Affairs (DSFA).

Carer's leave

- The carer's leave entitlement is a minimum of 13 weeks' *unpaid* leave, up to a maximum of 104 weeks.
- Carer's leave may be taken in one block, or in several separate blocks, of time, subject to the minimum/maximum criteria above.
- The employee is required to provide the employer with six weeks' notice of application for carer's leave.
- The employee must provide the employer with a copy of the approval decision of a DSFA officer.
- The employer and the employee must jointly sign a carer's leave agreement two weeks before such leave begins.
- If any changes in the leave terms of the agreement are required, both parties must jointly agree to the modifications in writing.
- Only one person may be on carer's leave at any one time in respect of the same person.
- An employee may not be on carer's leave in respect of two or more persons at any one time, except when two such persons reside together. This exception may only be used once.
- If an employee takes carer's leave in number of blocks, a period of six weeks must elapse before they may take a further period of carer's leave in respect of the same person.

- Subject to certain exceptions, carer's leave ceases when the employee ceases to provide personally the full-time care for the approved person.

- Employees may work or participate in training or education courses for up to 15 hours in a week, while on carer's leave.

- Employees on carer's leave must give at least four weeks' written notice of their intended date of return to work.

Protection of employment rights

- Annual leave and public holiday entitlements accrue only in respect of the first 13 weeks of carer's leave for each of the persons approved.

- Service continuity and the rights of an employee with regard to employment are maintained while on carer's leave, other than the rights to remuneration. Remuneration has a wide definition and not only includes salary, but also benefits such as health insurance, pension contributions, etc.

- The employee has the right to return to the same or equivalent and suitable work, including location and pay, on terms that are not substantially less favourable.

- Training, probation or apprenticeship, interrupted by carer's leave, is temporarily suspended until after the leave period.

EMPLOYEES (PROVISION OF INFORMATION & CONSULTATION) ACT 2006

Purpose

The main objective of the legislation is to provide for the establishment of a general framework allowing employees the right to important information regarding their employment in relation to the state of the business and to allow for constructive consultation between the employer and the employees regarding such information.

Provisions & Procedures

The information and consultation rights of employees are protected in specific situations – for example, collective redundancies and transfers of undertakings – under the Protection of Employment Act 1977 (as amended), the European Communities (Protection of Employees on Transfer of Undertakings) Regulations 2003 and the Transnational Information & Consultation of Employees Act 1996. The new Act is without prejudice to these existing rights to information and consultation.

Definitions

- An **undertaking** is defined as a public or private undertaking carrying out an economic activity, whether or not operating for gain, including private businesses, semi-state companies and several public sector bodies.
- **Information** means the supply of information from the employer to the employee representatives in order to enable them to acquaint themselves with the subject matter and to examine it.
- **Consultation** is the exchange of views and establishment of dialogue between the employee representatives and the employer.
- A **negotiated agreement** is an agreement negotiated by the employer and the employees (or their representatives) that establishes one or more information and consultation arrangements.
- An **employee representative** is an employee who is elected or appointed to represent the workforce in information and consultation arrangements with the employer.

Employee rights

An employee employed in an undertaking with 50 or more employees has a right to information and consultation. However, the legislation is being introduced on a phased basis:

- From 4 September 2006, it applies to undertakings with 150+ employees.

- From 23 March 2007, it applies to undertakings with 100+ employees.

- From 23 March 2008, it applies to undertakings with 50+ employees.

Establishing information and consultation arrangements

An employer may initiate the process to negotiate an information and consultation arrangement with employees and/or their representatives.

Alternatively, a minimum of 10% of the workforce may request, in writing, that the employer enter into negotiations. The employer is then required to enter such negotiations. The parties must establish an information and consultation agreement within six months of commencing negotiations. This period may be extended by agreement of the parties.

Arrangements for information and consultation should be formalised in a negotiated agreement and by defining the standard rules of operation.

Negotiated agreement

A negotiated agreement should be recorded in writing, dated, signed by the employer, approved and countersigned by the employees concerned and maintained and readily available for inspection by the parties.

A negotiated agreement should state:

- The duration of the agreement and any procedures for its re-negotiation.

- The subjects for information and consultation.

- The method and timeframe by which information is to be provided – for example, directly to employees or their representatives.

- The method and timeframe by which consultation is to be conducted – for example, directly with employees or their representatives.

- The procedure for dealing with confidential information.

Employee approval may be given by a majority of employees voting or where a majority of employee elected representatives approve the agreement in writing. The employer must ensure that any voting procedure is fair, confidential, is capable of independent verification and that all employees have the opportunity to vote.

At any time before a negotiated agreement expires, or within six months after its expiry, the parties involved in the agreement may renew it for any further period they think fit. A renewed negotiated agreement continues from the date it would have expired. To avoid any ambiguity, the agreed date of the renewal agreement and its termination date should be stated in the document.

Pre-existing agreements

Pre-existing written agreements for information and consultation that embody the principles of the Act and satisfy certain minimum requirements will be adequate if they are already in place.

A pre-existing agreement should be similar to the negotiated agreement, in that it should be in writing, dated, signed by the employer, approved by the employees, applicable to all employees to whom the agreement relates and available for inspection by the parties.

Standard Rules

Schedule 1 of the Act sets out Standard Rules for information and consultation arrangements, including:

- An Information & Consultation Forum must be established, composed of employee representatives who are employed by the undertaking.

- The Information & Consultation Forum should have a minimum of three members, but not more than 30, and may agree its own internal structures.

- Employee representatives to the Forum should be elected in accordance with Schedule 2 of the Act (see below for election procedures) and the employer should facilitate this.

- In the absence of elections, the employees can appoint representatives. The method for this should be agreed with the employer, stated clearly in writing and maintained for review in the event of a dispute.

- Arrangements for meetings of the Forum should be agreed between the employer in consultation with the employees and/or their representatives. The employer may not unreasonably withhold consent to any proposals made by employees or their representatives.

- The employer should meet with the Forum at least twice a year. Where there are exceptional circumstances, the Forum has the right to request a meeting with the employer. The employer should not unreasonably withhold consent to this meeting.

- Minutes of meetings between the employer and the Forum should be jointly approved.

- Before any meeting with the employer, the Forum is entitled to meet without the employer being present.

- Members of the Forum may inform employees of the content and outcome of its meetings.

The Standard Rules detailed in Schedule 1 of the Act will apply and an Information & Consultation Forum will be established, where:

- The parties agree to adopt the Standard Rules and the procedures for electing employee representatives (Schedule 2 of the Act); or
- The employer refuses to enter into negotiations within three months of receiving a written request from employees; or
- Where the parties involved in negotiations cannot agree to an information and consultation arrangement within the time limits.

Where the Standard Rules apply to an undertaking, as soon as practicable, but not later than six months after they first become applicable, the employer must comply with their requirements.

After a minimum initial period of two years from the establishment of the Information & Consultation Forum, and thereafter on a basis agreed by both parties, the application of the Standard Rules to an undertaking may be reviewed by the Forum and the employer, and both parties may enter into negotiations for the purpose of changing the rules or procedures.

If the terms of a negotiated agreement are not approved by both parties, the Standard Rules shall apply until two years have passed. If, during this period of two years, the parties re-enter negotiations and approve a negotiated agreement, then the Standard Rules will not apply.

Practical arrangements for information and consultation

The employer must cover any expenses that arise due to the operation of the Information & Consultation Forum and should provide the members with any financial resources necessary and reasonable to enable them to perform their duties in an appropriate manner.

Employees' representatives

The employer must make arrangements for the election and appointment of one or more employee representatives to the Information & Consultation Forum.

Alternatively, where it is the practice of the employer to conduct collective bargaining negotiations with a trade union or any other excepted body that represents at least 10% of the workforce, the members of such trade unions or other bodies are entitled to elect and appoint one or more employee representatives from amongst their members.

Schedule 2 of the Act sets out procedures for the election of employee representatives to the Forum:

- The employer, in consultation with existing employees, must appoint a returning officer, whose duties include the organisation and conduct of nominations and elections. The returning officer may authorise other persons to assist in the performance of the duties of returning officer.

- The returning officer must perform his/her duties in a fair and reasonable manner and in the interests of an orderly and proper conduct of nomination and election procedures.

- In order to participate in an election, the voter must be employed in the undertaking.

- Employees who put themselves forward as candidates must have more than one year's continuous service with the employer.

- Candidates must be nominated by at least two employees, or by a trade union or other excepted body with whom it is the practice of the employer to conduct collective bargaining negotiations.

- If the number of candidates exceeds the number of members to be elected to the Forum, the returning officer will arrange for a poll to be taken.

- Voting in the poll must take place by secret ballot on a day or days to be decided by the returning officer and according to the principle of proportional representation.

- The employer is responsible for any costs arising out of the nomination and election procedure.

An employee representative to the Forum must be afforded any reasonable facilities, including *paid* time off (providing that it does not impair the efficient operation of the undertaking), to enable him/her to perform his/her functions as an employee representative promptly and efficiently.

An employee representative must not be penalised by an employer for performing his/her functions in accordance with this Act.

Information and consultation

The employer should provide information in such a way to allow the Information & Consultation Forum to conduct an adequate study and in good time so it can prepare for consultation.

The Act defines the type of information the employer must share:

1. Information on the recent and probable development of the undertaking's activities and economic situation.

2. Information and consultation on the situation, structure and probable development of employment within the undertaking and on any

anticipatory measures envisaged, particularly where there may be a threat to employment.

3. Information and consultation on decisions likely to lead to substantial changes in work organisation or in contractual relations, including those covered by the Protection of Employment Act 1977 (as amended) and the Transfer of Undertakings Regulations 2003.

Consultation should take place:

* Ensuring that the method, content and timeframe thereof are appropriate.

* At the relevant level of management and representation, depending on the subject under discussion.

* On the basis of information supplied by the employer and of the opinion which the employees representatives are entitled to formulate.

* So as to enable the Forum to meet the employer and obtain a response, and the reasons for that response, to any opinion they might form.

* With a view to reaching an agreement on decisions referred to in 3 above that are within the scope of the employer's powers.

Confidentiality

Any individual who, at any time, is or was involved in any information and consultation discussions must not disclose to employees or to third parties any information that, in the legitimate interest of the undertaking, has been expressly provided in confidence.

This duty of confidentiality continues to apply after the cessation of the individual's employment or the expiry of his/her term of office.

However, the individual may disclose information, which has been expressly provided to him/her in confidence, to employees and to third parties when they are also subject to a duty of confidentiality under this Act.

Employers may withhold information or not undertake consultation if they believe that disclosure and/or consultation could:

* Seriously harm the functioning of the undertaking; or

* Be prejudicial to the business; or

* Is prohibited by any enactment.

Co-operation

When defining or implementing practical arrangements for information and consultation, the employer and employees and/or their representatives should work in a spirit of co-operation, having due regard to their reciprocal rights, duties and the interests both of the undertaking and of the employees.

EMPLOYMENT EQUALITY ACTS 1998 & 2004

Purpose

To promote equality and prohibit discrimination in employment.

Provisions & Procedures

Definitions

- **Direct discrimination** occurs when one employee is treated less favourably than another, due to his/her membership of one or more of the nine groups listed as discriminatory grounds (see below).

- **Indirect discrimination:** The 1998 Act contains two definitions:

  1. **Gender discrimination** occurs when an employer operates discriminatory practices favouring one gender that cannot be justified by objective factors. For example, if male employees were the only ones entitled to work overtime or if an employer specified a female-only category for a receptionist position.

  2. **Non-gender discrimination** occurs when an employer operates discriminatory practices affecting persons belonging to one of the remaining eight groups and which cannot be justified as being reasonable in all the circumstances concerning the issue.

- **Harassment** is any form of unwanted conduct related to any of the discriminatory grounds, being conduct that has the purpose or effect of violating a person's dignity and creating an intimidating, hostile, degrading, humiliating or offensive environment for the person.

- **Sexual harassment** is any form of unwanted verbal, non-verbal or physical conduct of a sexual nature, being conduct that has the purpose or effect of violating a person's dignity and creating an intimidating, hostile, degrading, humiliating or offensive environment for the person.

Discriminatory grounds

The 1998 Act specifies that direct and indirect discrimination (and victimisation) is taken to occur when one person is, has been, or would be treated less favourably than another person for any of the following reasons: gender; marital status; family status; sexual orientation; religion; age; disability; race; or membership of the traveller community.

Recruitment and selection

Throughout the recruitment and selection process (see **Chapter 1**), employers must avoid bias and not discriminate on any of the nine categories above against those seeking access to employment. This applies to:

- Job advertisements.
- Job application forms.
- Short listing.
- Selection tests.
- Interviews.

Remuneration

Employees are entitled to the same rate of remuneration as another employee who, at that or any other relevant time (three years before or after), is carrying out like work or similar work for the same employer or an associated employer. In certain circumstances, special provisions apply in relation to a person with a disability.

Under the terms of the legislation, agency workers can be paid more or less than other employees. They can only claim for unequal remuneration comparable to remuneration with another agency worker who is carrying out like or similar work for the same employer or an associated employer.

Conditions of employment

All employees (carrying out like or similar work) are entitled to the same terms of employment. The legislation prohibits discrimination with regard to:

- Access to overtime, shift work, training, work experience or opportunities for promotion.
- Disciplinary measures.
- Transfers to other work.
- Redundancies and dismissals.
- Lay-off and short-term working.

Vicarious liability

Under this Act, employers are responsible for an employee's actions during the course of his/her employment, whether or not it was carried out with the employer's knowledge. A suitable defence for an employer is to prove that they took reasonable and practical steps to prevent such discriminatory activities from occurring – for example, sound policies, practices and procedures, communications and training.

EMPLOYMENT PERMITS ACTS 2003 & 2006

Purpose

To provide rules and procedures for persons seeking employment permits to work in Ireland, to regulate the number of such permits and to provide certain protections for foreign nationals in employment.

Provisions & Procedures

Definitions

*   The term **foreign national** refers to a person who is not a citizen of the Irish State. In the 2003 Act, the term used was **non-national**. This term was changed as non-national suggests that the person has no nationality!

Eligibility

All foreign nationals (except those defined below) who wish to work in Ireland must apply for an employment permit based on a specific job offer and in advance of taking up any employment.

A work permit is not required for:

*   A citizen of a member state of the European Economic Area (EEA) and their spouse or children who are under 21 years or are dependent on the working parent. The countries in the EEA are: Austria; Belgium; Cyprus; Czech Republic; Denmark; Estonia; Finland; France; Germany; Greece; Hungary; Iceland; Ireland; Italy; Latvia; Liechtenstein; Lithuania; Luxembourg; Malta; Netherlands; Norway; Poland; Portugal; Slovakia; Slovenia; Spain; Sweden; and the United Kingdom.

*   Swiss nationals are not required to have work permits in Ireland, under a special agreement.

*   Persons granted refugee status and family members of such persons.

*   Persons who have temporary leave to remain in Ireland on humanitarian grounds and who have been in the asylum process.

*   Persons permitted to remain in the State by the Minister for Justice, Equality & Law Reform and who have permission to work without an employment permit.

*   Persons on work authorisation/working visas.

- Post-graduate students, where the work is an integral part of their course and where the college has provided suitable evidence of this.

- A person who holds a work permit from a member state and is required to work in Ireland as part of that contract. The duration is related to the person's contract of employment.

- Persons with permission to remain as a parent of an Irish citizen.

The Minister may, to protect employment in Ireland, place restrictions on additional accession states to the European Union in the future.

For example, nationals of the Republic of Bulgaria and Romania, which became full members of the European Union in January 2007, do not have an automatic right to work in Ireland. Workers from these two countries must apply for work permits. However, the Minister for Enterprise, Trade & Employment has said that they would be given preference over nationals from outside the European Economic Area (EEA) in work permit applications. This decision will be kept under review and examined again in 2008.

Application for employment permits

Either a foreign national or an employer may apply for a work permit to work in Ireland through the Department of Enterprise, Trade & Employment using the appropriate application forms. The application must be made prior to the person taking up the appointment.

A foreign national may not make an application, unless an offer of employment has been made in writing to him/her.

If an employer is making the application, the employer must have taken all possible steps to offer the employment to a citizen of:

- One or more Member States of the EEA; or

- The Swiss Confederation; or

- A combination of any of the two areas above.

The prescribed fee must accompany a new or renewal application for an employment permit.

Certain job categories and employment sectors can be eligible or ineligible for employment permits. As these can change from time to time, it is advisable to check with FÁS before taking the time to make a formal application. When determining the eligible and ineligible employment categories, the following are taken into consideration:

- The shortage of qualifications or skills required for economic and social development and competitiveness.

- The economic sector or sectors that will be involved in the achievement of such economic and social development and competitiveness.

The 2006 Act specifies the grounds under which the Minister for Enterprise, Trade & Employment has the power to refuse to grant an employment permit.

Where the Minister refuses to grant an employment permit, the applicant will receive written notification of the decision and the reasons for it. The Act also provides the applicant with an opportunity to appeal that decision.

The Minister has the power to revoke an employment permit under certain conditions and must notify the permit holder and his/her employer in writing of the decision to revoke and the reasons for it. The revocation decision can be appealed.

The holder of an employment permit or the relevant employer can apply to renew an employment permit. This should be done before the permit is due to expire.

The Minister for Enterprise, Trade & Employment may make regulations at any time specifying:

- The duration of permits.
- The maximum number of permits that may be granted during a period.
- The maximum number of permits in respect of a specified economic sector.
- Categories of employment eligible or otherwise for employment permits.
- The minimum remuneration applicable and related to the qualifications or skills that a foreign national is required to possess.

The terms of reference of an employment permit

The foreign national may only work within the specified employment category stated on the permit.

The holder of an employment permit is entitled to work for different employers within the designated sector specified and within the other stated terms in the employment permit. He/she does not have to reapply for a new permit.

The holder of an employment permit is not allowed to:

- Transfer the permit to another foreign national.
- Allow another foreign national to use the permit to enter into the service of an employer in the State or be in employment in the State.

An employer cannot:

- Transfer the employment permit to another person.

- Use the permit to employ a foreign national other than the foreign national to whom it has been granted.
- Use the employment permit for employment other than that stated in the permit.

An employment permit must specify the period for which the foreign national concerned may be employed in the State. This period should not exceed two years beginning on the date the permit is granted. However, a longer period may be requested and granted by regulations issued by the Minister for Enterprise, Trade & Employment, if there are reasonable grounds for the application.

If a foreign national applies for an employment permit, it must include a description of the economic sector in which he/she is permitted to be employed.

Where an employer makes an application for a permit, it must include a description of the employment in respect of which the permit has been granted and a statement of the remuneration and any deductions, where agreed, for board and/or accommodation

An employment permit may also contain:

- A statement of the requirement under the National Minimum Wage Act 2000 that the foreign national concerned will not be paid less than the national minimum hourly rate of pay by his/her employer and a greater amount having regard to equality and anti-discrimination requirements.
- A statement that a new application for the granting of an employment permit may be made in respect of the foreign national concerned.
- A summary of the principal employment rights of the employee.

The original of an employment permit will be issued to the foreign national concerned and a copy of the permit will be issued to the person who will employ the foreign national.

Employer responsibilities

An employer must not employ a foreign national within the State, if the person is not automatically entitled to work in the country (such as citizens of the European Union or European Economic Area) or does not possess a valid employment permit. Failure to comply with this provision, or the obstruction of any person investigating under the Acts, can result in a fine and/or imprisonment.

It is an offence for an employer to seek to recover, or to make any deductions, from an employee who holds a work permit relating to any charge, fee or expense arising out of:

- The permit application or its renewal.
- The recruitment of the permit holder for the employment in respect of which the application was made.
- Any amount previously paid to the permit holder in respect of travelling expenses incurred by him/her in connection with taking up the employment in the State.

Employers are prohibited from retaining personal documents belonging to the holder of an employment permit, such as:

- Passport.
- Driving licence
- Identity card.
- Documents relating to any account held with a financial institution.
- Any documents relating to the skills, qualifications or experience of the foreign national.
- Travel or other personal documents.

An employer must not penalise an employee or threaten penalisation against an employee for exercising their rights or for giving evidence in any proceedings under this legislation.

The employer is required to keep records of all information related to the employment of foreign nationals to whom an employment permit has been granted.

Employment Permit Schemes

New employment permit arrangements for workers from outside the European Economic Area (EEA) were introduced from 1 February, 2007.

Green Card Scheme

The Green Card Scheme replaces the previous Work Visa/Work Authorisation scheme, which has been discontinued. This new scheme is for professional and associate professional occupations where there are skill shortages, such as in the information and communications technology, healthcare, construction, engineering, financial services and research sectors. The list of occupations (available on the Department of Trade, Enterprise & Employment's website, http://www.entemp.ie) has been identified after taking advice from the Expert Group on Future Skills Needs and will be reviewed on a regular basis.

Green Cards will be issued for two years initially, and normally will lead to the granting of permanent or long-term residence after that. Green Card holders will also be permitted to bring their spouses and families to join them immediately.

No labour market needs test is required for the Green Card applications, so advertising with FÁS, EURES (European Employment Services) or newspapers is not necessary.

Work Permits

The revised Work Permit Scheme is mainly for non-Green Card occupations in the €30,000 to €60,000 annual salary range. Work permits will be granted only in exceptional circumstances for occupations with salaries below €30,000.

Work permits will be granted initially for a period of two years, and then for a further period of up to three years.

Vacancies that are the subject of Work Permit applications will be the subject of a rigorous labour market needs test, to establish that they cannot be filled by nationals within the EEA. This test will include both advertising with FÁS and EURES and in local and national newspapers.

There are a number of categories of employment for which Work Permits applications will not be considered, because it is clear that vacancies can be filled from within the EEA. These occupations also will be detailed on the Department's website, http://www.entemp.ie.

Intra-Company Transfer Permits

A new Intra-Company transfer scheme for trans-national senior management, key personnel and trainees is also being introduced. The purpose is to allow multi-national companies to transfer these staff between branches in different countries, or to transfer staff with particular skills, knowledge and expertise on a temporary basis in a start-up situation.

These permits will only be available for those with annual salaries above €40,000, who can clearly show that they fit into one of these three categories (senior management, key personnel or trainees) and who have been with the sending company for one year.

These permits will be for a period of two years initially, with the possibility of an extension for up to a further three years.

No labour market needs test will be required in respect of Intra-Company Transfer Permits.

Spousal/Dependant Permits

These permits will allow the spouses and dependants of employment permit holders, who are entitled to reside here, to apply for work permits and to help support their families.

These applications will not require a labour market needs test and may be in respect of any occupation in the labour market.

European Communities (Protection of Employees on Transfer of Undertakings) Regulations 2003

Purpose

To safeguard the rights of employees in the event of a transfer of an undertaking, a business or part of a business from one employer to another, as a result of a legal transfer, merger or take-over of a lease. The Regulations do not apply to sea-going vessels.

Provisions & Procedures

Definitions

- *A transfer* means the transfer of an economic entity that retains its identity.
- An *economic entity* is an organised combination of resources, which has the purpose of engaging in an economic activity, whether for profit or not, or whether it is central or subsidiary to another economic or administrative entity.
- With regard to an *undertaking*, in Ireland, the term 'enterprise' is normally used.
- The *transferor* is the former employer, whether an individual or a company, who, by reason of a transfer, ceases to be the employer.
- The *transferee* is the new employer, whether an individual or a company, who, by reason of a transfer, becomes the employer.

Eligibility

The Regulations apply to any person:

- Working under a contract of employment.
- Employed through an employment agency.
- In the service of, or holding office under, the State, including civil servants, officers of the Health Service Executive, VECs or harbour authorities and members of the defence forces or An Garda Síochána.

Terms and conditions of employment

Any rights and obligations on the former employer, arising from a contract of employment that exists on the date of a transfer, must be maintained by the new employer.

The new employer must preserve the terms and conditions of any collective agreements that existed before the transfer until the expiry of the collective agreement or the application of a new collective agreement.

Dismissals and termination of employment

The transfer of an undertaking, business or part of an undertaking or business does not form grounds for dismissal of an employee, by either the former employer or the new employer.

A dismissal based wholly on the grounds of a transfer, and not on economic, technical or organisational reasons that entail changes in the workforce, may constitute an unfair dismissal under the Unfair Dismissals Acts 1977-2001.

Bankruptcy or insolvency

The Regulations do not apply where the former employer is the subject of bankruptcy or insolvency proceedings.

However, if the sole or main reason for bankruptcy or insolvency proceedings is to avoid legal obligations within the regulations under this Act, the Regulations will apply to a transfer effected by the former employer.

Information and consultation

In a transfer situation, both the former employer and the new employer must inform the representatives (see below) of the employees affected by the transfer of:

- The date or proposed date of the transfer.
- The reasons for the transfer.
- The legal implications of the transfer for the employees and a summary of any relevant economic and social implications of the transfer for them.
- Any measures envisaged in relation to the employees – for example, where employees are reassigned to another department.

The former employer should provide this information to the employee representatives, as soon as possible but no later than 30 days before the transfer occurs.

If the former employer or the new employer foresee any potential changes in relation to employees, he/she must consult with the employee representatives as soon as reasonably practicable, not later than 30 days before the transfer is carried out, in relation to any such measures, with a view to reaching an agreement.

Representation of employees

If there are no trade unions or staff associations, the employer is required to facilitate arrangements for employees to choose representatives, such as by means of an election. The employer must put in place a procedure, whereby the employees may elect through fair process an employee to represent them for the purpose of the information and consultation provisions.

Whether or not an undertaking, or part of an undertaking, preserves its autonomy after a transfer, the status of the employee representatives either remains in force or fair election procedures are activated to allow the employees to elect new representatives.

INDUSTRIAL RELATIONS ACTS 1946 - 2004

Purpose

To establish the institutional bodies and procedures for the resolution of employee/employer industrial relations disputes in Ireland. The Act regulates the right to take industrial action, and the manner in which such action may be taken.

The industrial relations institutions are:

- The Labour Relations Commission.
- The Rights Commissioner Service.
- The Labour Court.

The main committees under the statutory provisions of these Acts that support the voluntary nature of the industrial relations process are:

- Joint Labour Committees.
- Joint Industrial Councils.
- Registered employment agreements.

There is no charge to employer or employee for the services of the LRC, the Labour Court or the Rights Commissioner services.

The industrial relations officers are practical and experienced specialists and are there to help with practical advice.

Both the LRC and the Labour Court are as anxious as the parties involved to achieve an amicable solution if possible and, failing that, to make a recommendation, which is as fair and equitable as possible to all concerned, while having regard to statutory requirements and local custom and practice.

Provisions & Procedures

Definitions

- A **trade dispute** means any dispute between employers and employees connected with the employment, or non-employment, or the terms or conditions of, or affecting, the employment of any individual.
- **Industrial action** means any action which affects (or is likely to affect) the terms or conditions of a contract, whether express or implied, and which is taken by any number or body of employees in order to compel their

employer, or to aid other workers in compelling their employer, to accept or not to accept terms or conditions of employment.

- A *strike* is a cessation of work by any number or body of employees acting together, or a refusal to continue to work, in order to compel their employer, or to aid other workers in compelling their employer, to accept or not to accept terms or conditions of employment.

Eligibility

The Acts protect any individual who is or was employed, whether or not in the employment of the employer with whom a trade dispute arises. This definition does not include:

- A member of the defence forces or of An Garda Síochána.
- A person who is employed by, or under, the State.
- National and secondary teachers.
- Officer of an educational committee.
- An officer of a local authority, vocational education committee or school attendance committee.

Labour Relations Commission

The Labour Relations Commission (LRC) was established under the Industrial Relations Act 1990. It is responsible for the promotion of good industrial relations through a range of services, primarily to prevent and/or resolve disputes:

- An advisory service on general industrial relations matters.
- A conciliation service.
- Preparation of codes of practice related to industrial relations, after consultation with unions and employer organisations. The LRC also offers guidance on codes of practice and help in resolving disputes concerning their implementation. Such codes of practice are admissible as evidence in cases referred to the Rights Commissioner, LRC, Labour Court, Employment Appeals Tribunal or in proceedings before a court.
- Monitoring of industrial relations activities, conducting and/or commissioning research in industrial relations matters.
- Responsibility for the Rights Commissioner Service.
- Assisting Joint Labour Committees and Joint Industrial Councils in the exercise of their functions.

At the request of one or more of the parties to a trade dispute, or on its own initiative, the LRC may offer its services with a view to resolving the dispute.

Trade disputes should be referred in the first instance to the LRC, unless there is specific provision for direct referral to the Labour Court.

Rights Commissioner

The LRC has responsibility for the Rights Commissioner Service under the Industrial Relations Act 1990.

An individual employee may refer a dispute to a Rights Commissioner under the following statutes:

- Adoptive Leave Acts 1995 & 2005.
- Carer's Leave Act 2001.
- Competition Act 2002.
- European Communities (Protection of Employees on Transfer of Undertakings) (Amendment) Regulations 2003.
- European Communities (Protection of Employment) Regulations 2000.
- Industrial Relations Acts 1946-2004.
- Maternity Protection Acts 1994 & 2004.
- National Minimum Wage Act 2000.
- Organisation of Working Time Act 1997.
- Parental Leave Acts 1998 & 2006.
- Payment of Wages Act 1991.
- Protection of Employees (Fixed-Term Work) Act 2003.
- Protection of Employees (Part-Time Work) Act 2001.
- Protection of Young Persons (Employment) Act 1996.
- Protections for Persons Reporting Child Abuse Act 1998.
- Safety, Health & Welfare at Work Act 2005.
- Terms of Employment (Information) Acts 1994 & 2001.
- Unfair Dismissals Acts 1977-2001.

Investigations under these statutes, except for the Payment of Wages Act 1991, are heard in private.

The Rights Commissioner's recommendations and *legally binding* determinations may be appealed to the Employment Appeals Tribunal, with the exception of claims under the Organisation of Working Time Act 1997, which must be appealed to the Labour Court. A determination of an appeal by the Employment Appeals Tribunal is *legally binding*.

Labour Court

The Labour Court was established by the Industrial Relations Act 1946, to provide a process for investigating and resolving industrial disputes. Its main functions are:

- The establishment and servicing of Joint Labour Committees and the ratification of minimum wages and conditions of employment proposed by these committees.

- The registration and variation of certain employment agreements relating to pay or conditions of employment.

- The registration and servicing of Joint Industrial Councils.

- The investigation of disputes and making recommendations and/or determinations on appeals against the recommendations of a Rights Commissioner.

The Labour Court may make ***non-legally binding*** recommendations in disputes. The parties to the dispute have the final responsibility to consider the recommendations and to resolve the dispute. However, the Labour Court may make a decision that is ***legally binding*** in cases that have been appealed against a Rights Commissioner's recommendation.

Joint Labour Committees

These committees are responsible for establishing statutory minimum rates and working conditions in specific industries. The committees are equally made up of members representing employer and employee groups. Joint Labour Committees are generally established for industries where there is poor collective bargaining and/or where the rates of pay tend to be low.

When rates and conditions are developed by the Joint Labour Committees, they are submitted to the Labour Court for approval. Once approved under a regulation order, employers are legally bound to apply terms that are not less favourable than the Joint Labour Committee's minimum rates.

Joint Industrial Councils

Joint Industrial Councils are voluntary negotiating bodies for particular industries and are made up of representatives from employers and trade unions in Ireland.

The rules of such Joint Industrial Councils include procedures for industrial dispute resolution before industrial action.

Industrial relations officers of the LRC act as chairpersons to the Joint Industrial Councils.

Registered Employment Agreements

These are collective agreements between either:

- A trade union or trade unions and an employer or employer organisation.
- A Joint Industrial Council.

Such agreements contain:

- Rates of pay.
- Conditions of employment.
- Disputes procedures.

Trade disputes

Strikes and other forms of industrial action have the potential to involve a number of unlawful acts (such as interfering with trade or business, conspiracy, trespass, nuisance and inducing breaches of contract). However, industrial relations legislation gives trade unions (including officials and members) a number of immunities that protect them against civil and criminal proceedings in relation to those potentially unlawful actions, where they have complied with the provisions of the legislation and are acting in contemplation or furtherance of a trade dispute.

The main precondition to lawful industrial action is that there must be a trade dispute in existence. If such a trade dispute exists, the trade union, its officials and members have immunities from potential tort actions by the employer. These immunities are restricted to trade unions that hold a negotiation licence from the Minister for Enterprise, Trade & Employment.

Where agreed procedures (either by way of custom and practice or provided for in collective agreements) exist for the resolution of individual grievances, these immunities will only apply to disputes concerning individual workers, and only when the procedures have been resorted to and exhausted. The agreed procedures can include the referral of the issue to external third parties such as a Rights Commissioner, the LRC, the Labour Court or the Employment Appeals Tribunal.

MATERNITY PROTECTION ACTS 1994 & 2004

Purpose

To provide leave entitlements and procedures for employees relating to maternity.

Provisions & Procedures

Eligibility

- Full-time permanent and regular part-time employees.
- There is no service-related restriction.
- Employees on a fixed-term contract have maternity entitlements, up until the date the contract is due to expire.

Maternity leave

- The maternity leave entitlement is a minimum period of 26 weeks' *unpaid* maternity leave (for leave commencing on or after 1 March 2007; otherwise, 22 weeks).
- The employee must advise her employer, in writing, of her intention to take maternity leave as soon as is reasonably practicable, but no later than four weeks before the commencement date.
- The employee must produce a medical certificate, confirming her pregnancy and specifying the date of the expected week of confinement.
- Maternity leave should commence no later than two weeks before the end of the expected week of confinement, as defined in a medical certificate. The requirement for two weeks' leave to be taken before the birth may be varied on medical advice.
- Maternity leave should finish no earlier than four weeks after the end of the expected week of confinement.
- The employee must provide the employer with at least four weeks' written notice of her intention to return to work following maternity leave, and must confirm this again in writing two weeks before her scheduled date of return.
- Employees on maternity leave, if eligible, may claim social welfare maternity benefits.

Additional maternity leave

- An employee who has taken maternity leave may apply for a maximum of 16 weeks' additional maternity leave if required (for leave commencing on or after 1 March 2007; otherwise, 12 weeks), commencing immediately after the scheduled maternity leave.

- The employee must notify the employer in writing of her intention to take additional maternity leave, either when first requesting maternity leave or at least four weeks before her original scheduled date of return.

- An employee who has already scheduled additional maternity leave may cancel this leave four weeks in advance of such leave commencing, by observing the same four weeks' written notification requirements.

- The employee must provide the employer with at least four weeks' written notice of her intention to return to work from her additional maternity leave. She is also required to confirm this again in writing two weeks before her scheduled date of return.

- If an employee falls ill during the last four weeks of her maternity leave (and intends taking additional maternity leave, having submitted the correct notification to her employer), or becomes sick during her additional maternity leave, she may submit a written request to her employer to terminate the additional maternity leave. If her employer agrees to the termination of additional maternity leave, the date of termination should be jointly agreed between the employee and the employer. The employer should give written notification of a decision to the employee as soon as is reasonably practicable. This absence from work will then be treated as a normal absence due to illness. The employee is not entitled to resume the terminated leave.

- Additional maternity leave does not qualify for social welfare maternity benefit payments.

Postponement of maternity leave or additional maternity leave

- In the event that the child for whom maternity leave is being taken is hospitalised, the employee may submit a written request to her employer to postpone part of the maternity leave and/or additional maternity leave.

- An employer may request written evidence, in the form of a letter or other appropriate document from the hospital, confirming that the child has been hospitalised.

- The employer should notify the employee in writing of his/her decision regarding postponement as soon as possible after receiving a request.

- If the employer agrees to postpone the leave, the employee will return to work on a mutually agreed date. This should be before the maternity leave or additional maternity leave is due to end.

- The maximum period of postponement of maternity leave or additional maternity leave is six months.

- Within seven days of the child concerned being discharged from hospital, the employee is entitled to resume her postponed leave.

- An employee must provide written notification to her employer of her intention to resume maternity or additional maternity leave. This should be supplied as soon as reasonably practicable but no later than the day on which the employee resumes such leave.

Ante-natal classes

- An expectant employee is entitled to *paid* time off work to attend one set of ante-natal classes (other than the last 3 classes in such a set).

- An expectant father has a once-off right to *paid* time off to attend the last two ante-natal classes in a set attended by the expectant mother.

- Paid time off to attend ante-natal classes is subject to at least two weeks' advance written notification to the employer of the dates and times of the class or classes. However, if the employee is unable to provide this notification, through no fault of his/her own, within one week of the class concerned the employee should provide the employer with evidence of him/her having attended the class and indicate the circumstances that caused him/her not to be able to comply with the requisite notification.

Ante-natal care and post-natal care

- An employee is entitled to *paid* time off for ante-natal and post-natal (up to 14 weeks immediately following the birth) care appointments. Employees are entitled to as much time off as necessary to attend such appointments, including travel time.

- The employee should give as much notice as possible to her employer.

- The employee must give the employer at least two weeks' notice of such appointments. However, if the employee has to attend an unscheduled ante-natal or post-natal appointment, within one week of the appointment the employee should provide evidence to her employer of having kept the appointment and indicate the circumstances that caused her not to be able to comply with the requisite notification.

Breastfeeding

Mothers may take breastfeeding breaks or adjusted working hours for up to six months after the birth, as either:

- Time off work, without loss of pay, to facilitate breastfeeding when facilities are provided in the workplace; or

- A reduction in her working hours, without loss of pay, to facilitate breastfeeding when facilities are not provided in the workplace.

Arrangements should be agreed and documented in advance. They may comprise:

- One break of 60 minutes; or

- Two 30-minute breaks; or

- Three 20-minute breaks; or

- Any number and duration of breaks as may be agreed between the employee and her employer.

Special Leave

In the event of the death of the mother after the birth of the child, the father is entitled to special leave.

The procedures are as follows:

- If the mother's death occurs within 16 weeks of the birth, the father is entitled to take *unpaid* leave up to the end of the 16th week.

- If the mother's death occurs after the end of the 16th week after the birth, but before the end of the 24th week, the father is entitled to take *unpaid* leave up to the end of the 24th week.

- Any leave to which the father is entitled must commence within seven days of the mother's death.

- The father must request such leave from his employer in writing no later than the day the leave is due to commence and should state the length of leave he intends to take.

A father on special leave may postpone the leave in the event of his child (for whom leave was taken) being hospitalised. Procedures for postponing such leave are:

- The employee must submit a written request to his employer to postpone leave (whether part of the main leave period, the main leave period and the additional leave period, or the additional leave period or part of it).

- The employer should notify the employee of his/her decision in writing as soon as possible after receiving such a request.
- The maximum period of postponement of leave or additional leave is six months.
- Within seven days of the child being discharged from hospital, the employee is entitled to resume his postponed leave.

Health and safety leave

This applies to employees who:

- Are pregnant.
- Have recently given birth, not more than 14 weeks previously.
- Are breast-feeding, having given birth no more than 26 weeks previously.

Employers are required to carry out a risk assessment to determine whether there are any risks for an employee inherent in the job. The employer must eliminate such risks, if possible, or provide alternative suitable work where there are no such risks and, ideally, should ensure that this work is agreeable to the employee. Otherwise, the employee is entitled to health and safety leave.

Health and safety leave entitlements and procedures are as follows:

- An employee on health and safety leave is entitled to be paid her usual wage/salary by the employer for the first 21 days of her leave.
- Following this period, if her PRSI contributions are sufficient, she may claim social welfare payments from the Department of Social & Family Affairs.
- The employer must provide a certificate of health and safety leave for the employee, if requested, and must provide the employee and/or the safety representative with the results of the risk assessment and actions.
- Health and safety leave ends when the employer can provide suitable work without risk.
- Health and safety leave ends when maternity leave commences, when the employee stops breastfeeding or, if the employee has not stopped breastfeeding, then 26 weeks after the birth.
- If the employee becomes aware that her condition is no longer such that she is vulnerable to the risk(s), she should provide written notification of this to her employer as soon as possible. When an employer receives such a notification, and has no reason to believe that the employee would be vulnerable, health and safety leave ends and she must return to work.

Protection of employment rights

- While an employee is absent from work on maternity leave, additional maternity leave, leave or additional leave for the father in the event of the death of the mother after the birth, health and safety leave, or if part of such leave is postponed in the event of hospitalisation of a child or during a period of natal care absence, the employee is deemed to have been in the employment of the employer throughout the leave period.

- Such absence will not affect any right (other than the employee's right to remuneration during such absence), whether conferred by statute, contract or otherwise, related to the employee's employment. Remuneration has a wide definition and not only includes salary, but also benefits such as health insurance, pension contributions, etc.

- An employee returning from leave has the right to return to the same *or* equivalent and suitable work and location and pay. This must incorporate any improvement to the terms and conditions of employment to which the employee would have been entitled had she/he not been absent.

- Training, probation or apprenticeship periods, interrupted by maternity leave are temporarily suspended until after the leave period.

MINIMUM NOTICE & TERMS OF EMPLOYMENT ACTS 1973 - 2001

Purpose

To protect the employee's rights to notice when they are been terminated from employment.

Provisions & Procedures

Eligibility

The Act applies to employees with at least 13 weeks' continuous service.

Exemptions

The Act does not apply to the following:

- Immediate family of the employer, provided that they live with him/her and are employed in the same private house or farm.
- Established civil servants.
- Member of the permanent defence forces (except temporary staff in the army nursing service).
- Members of An Garda Síochána.
- Seamen signing on under the Merchant Shipping Act 1894.

Notice Period

Length of Service	Minimum Notice Period
13 weeks to 2 years	1 week
2 years to 5 years	2 weeks
5 years to 10 years	4 weeks
10 years to 15 years	6 weeks
More than 15 years	8 weeks

Misconduct

The Act does not affect the right of the employer to dismiss an employee outside these notice periods, for reasons of gross misconduct. It is important, however, that the employer follows fair procedures, before deciding to dismiss – including clear definitions of gross misconduct.

Employer's right to notice

The employer has a right to receive a minimum of one week's notice from an employee, who has at least 13 weeks' continuous service with the employer and intends to leave his/her employment.

Waiving rights to notice or accepting pay in lieu of notice

An employee or an employer may waive right to notice. The employer may decide to make a payment in lieu of notice, based on what the person would have earned if they worked out their notice.

The date of termination shall be the date on which notice, if given, would have expired.

NATIONAL MINIMUM WAGE ACT 2000

Purpose

The National Minimum Wage Act 2000 provides that an experienced adult worker must be paid an average hourly rate of pay that is not less than the national minimum wage, which is adjusted from time to time.

Provisions and Procedures

Eligibility

- Employees aged 18 years or over are entitled to receive pay not less than the national minimum hourly rate, calculated on an average rate of pay.

- Employees aged under 18 years are entitled to receive pay not less than 70% of the national minimum hourly rate, calculated on an average rate of pay.

- An employee aged 18 years or over, who has entered employment for the first time, is entitled to an hourly rate of pay not less than 80% of the national minimum hourly rate of pay during their first year of employment and a rate of not less than 90% of the national minimum hourly rate of pay in their second year of employment.

- A trainee aged 18 years or over, who undergoes a course of study or training authorised by their employer during normal work hours. Such courses are prescribed in regulations made by the Minister for Trade, Enterprise & Employment.

Exemptions

This Act does not apply to the remuneration of a person who is the spouse, father, mother, grandfather, grandmother, stepfather, stepmother, grandson, grand-daughter, brother, sister, half-brother or half-sister of an employer, and who is employed by the employer, or an apprentice as defined in the Industrial Training Act 1997 or the Labour Services Act 1987.

Reckonable and non-reckonable pay

Reckonable pay relates to payments or benefits-in-kind that are allowable in calculating an employee's average hourly rate of pay, to determine whether they are being paid their minimum entitlement under this Act. Reckonable components include:

- Basic salary.
- Shift premium.
- Productivity-related payments such as piece and incentive rates, commission and bonuses.
- Monetary equivalent of board and lodgings (subject to limits as prescribed by the Minister for Enterprise, Trade & Employment).
- Any service charge distributed through payroll.
- Any payments in a casual work contract, where there is a protection provision related to zero hours.
- Any reckonable pay earned in a pay reference period that is paid in the previous or following pay reference period

Non-reckonable components include:
- Overtime premium.
- Call-out premium, on-call or stand by allowance.
- Premium for unsocial hours.
- Premium for public holidays, Saturdays and Sundays (where worked).
- Service pay.
- Allowances for special or additional duties, including those of a post of responsibility.
- Tips or gratuities paid into a central fund managed by the employer and paid through payroll.
- Payments in relation to periods absent from work due to annual leave, sick leave, adoptive leave, parental leave, protective, lay off, on strike or time for which an employee is paid in lieu of notice.
- Payments for expenses incurred by an employee in carrying out his/her employment, such as allowances for travel, subsistence, tools and clothes.
- Benefits-in-kind, except those relating to board and lodgings.
- Pension contributions paid by the employer.
- Payments (allowance, gratuity or compensation for loss of office) made to an employee on their retirement, resignation or redundancy.
- Compensation payments, such as for an injury or loss of equipment or tools.
- Payments other than those related to his/her capacity as an employee.
- Monetary awards under a staff suggestion scheme.
- Loans from the employer.

Method of calculating average hourly rates of pay

For calculation purposes, a pay reference period is a period not exceeding one month.

Working hours includes overtime, time spent travelling on official business and on training or study authorised by the employer during normal hours.

The employee's average hourly rate of pay is his/her gross remuneration (pay before tax or PRSI are deducted) earned in a pay reference period, divided by his/her working hours in that pay reference period. This must not be less than the minimum hourly rate of pay specified by law.

Minimum wage entitlement

An experienced adult worker must be paid an average hourly rate of pay not less than €8.30 per hour (from 1 January 2007, increasing to €8.65 from 1 July 2007).

Changes in these rates are at the discretion of the Minister for Enterprise, Trade & Employment and made from time to time.

ORGANISATION OF WORKING TIME ACT 1997

Purpose

To establish statutory rights for employees with regard to entitlements to working time. rest periods, and holidays.

Provisions & Procedures

Defining the average working week

- The maximum average working week is 48 hours. Averages may be balanced out over a reference period of four, six or 12 month periods.

- A reference period is a consecutive period of time, excluding any period of statutory annual leave, sick leave, leave related to maternity, adoptive, parental or carer's leave legislation.

Break entitlements

- Employees are entitled to a 15-minute rest break after 4.5 consecutive hours of work.

- After six consecutive hours of work, the total minimum rest break entitlement is 30 minutes.

- Shop employees who work more than 6 consecutive hours, and whose hours of work include the hours 11.30 am to 2.30 pm, must be allowed a break of one hour, which must commence between 11.30 am and 2.30 pm.

- Employers must not request, or allow, employees to take their break period at the end of their working day.

Rest entitlements

- Employees are entitled to a minimum of 11 consecutive hours' rest in each 24-hour period.

- Employees engaged in work involving special hazards or heavy physical or mental strain (referred to as special category employees) may only work an absolute maximum of eight hours in any 24-hour period.

- Employees are also entitled to a minimum of 24 hours' continuous rest period in each seven-day period.

- If the rest day is preceded by a working day, a 35-hour break period is required. For technical or necessary organisational reasons, this may be difficult and the employer may make alternative arrangements in consultation with the employee. Employers should be prepared to demonstrate the legitimacy of such requirements.

- Unless defined otherwise in a contract of employment or within a collective agreement, an employee is entitled to have Sunday off as the weekly rest period. Where the weekly rest period is averaged over two weeks, at least one of the rest days over the two weeks must be a Sunday.

- Employees have statutory rights under this Act with regard to Sunday working. If an allowance is not already included in the rate of pay, they are entitled to supplementary/premium pay for Sunday working.

Night work

- A night worker may only work an average of eight hours per 24-hour period, calculated over a reference period of two months.

- A special category night worker (who may be engaged in work involving special hazards or heavy physical or mental strain) may work no more than eight hours in each 24-hour period as an absolute limit. No averaging/ reference period is allowed.

Restrictions

In cases where an employee also works for another organisation, his/her joint working hours must not exceed those allowed under this Act. Employers must ensure that this does not happen; it may be difficult to control but employers should ask the question and also ensure this restriction is clearly stated in the contract of employment.

Statement of terms and conditions of employment

Under the Terms of Employment (Information) Acts 1994 & 2001, employees are entitled to a written statement (for example, a contract of employment) concerning their terms and conditions of employment. This statement must include terms and conditions relating to daily and weekly rest periods, including the times and duration.

Notification of working time

Employers are required to provide notification of hours of work to employees. Where such information is not stated in the employee's contract, or in any other document, the employer is required to inform the employee of the working time requirements.

Where working times requirements vary, the employer must provide as much notice as possible to the employee regarding working time changes, while having regard to the provisions in this legislation on rest. This notification may be by way of regular notices placed at pre-defined locations.

Having inconsistencies in working times and breaks can lead to fatigue, which can cause performance and safety issues. It makes more sense to plan working times and breaks carefully to maximise rest opportunities and improve performance accordingly.

Annual leave entitlements

Holiday pay is earned in relation to the time worked by each employee. All employees are eligible to accrue holiday entitlements, calculated as:

- Four working weeks in a leave year in which the employee works 1,365 hours (unless the employee changes employment); or

- One-third of a working week per calendar month in which the employee works 117 hours; or

- 8% of the hours worked in a leave year, subject to a maximum of four working weeks.

If more than one of these calculation methods can be applied, and the leave entitlements are different under the different calculation methods, the calculation to be used is the one that gives the greater holiday entitlement.

A working week is defined as the hours the person usually works in a week. The leave year commences on 1 April and finishes on 31 March the following year. However, an employer may decide to operate a different leave year (for example, 1 January to 31 December), provided the employee's entitlements are not diminished by the change.

Eight months' service qualifies the employee for an unbroken annual leave period of two consecutive weeks (unless otherwise agreed or governed by collective agreements or employment regulation orders). These two weeks can include any public holidays or periods of certified illness.

The legislation does not prevent the employer and the employee entering into arrangements more favourable than the statutory minimum provisions.

Employees are entitled to be paid before the annual leave commences. Pay for annual leave must be at the normal weekly rate or in proportion to the normal weekly rate. Where board and lodging is included as part of the remuneration package, an amount must be paid as compensation for the annual leave period calculated at the prescribed rate for such board and/or lodgings.

Any annual leave taken is included as hours worked for the purpose of calculating leave entitlements as these are hours the employee would have worked had they been at work on the day(s).

Annual leave is scheduled at the employer's discretion, while having consideration for the employee's needs, such as holiday time with his/her family and the opportunity for rest and recreation.

The employer must consult with the employee at least one month prior to such leave being taken. Generally, such consultation takes place well in advance of this, to allow employees to plan and book holidays and in the interests of creating and maintaining good employee relations.

Although an employee is entitled to take all of his/her statutory minimum annual leave within the leave year, he/she may take or agree to carry over annual leave but only within the first six months of the new leave year.

An employer must not implement, or agree to, payments in lieu of annual leave. The one exception to this is where the employment is being terminated by either party, in which case the employee must receive pay for any outstanding annual leave entitlements.

Employees who fall ill during a holiday may reschedule an annual leave day by agreement with their employer, if a medical certificate covering the illness period is provided to the employer.

Public holidays and entitlements

There are nine public holidays each year as follows:

1. New Year's Day (1 January).
2. St. Patrick's Day (17 March).
3. Easter Monday.
4. First Monday in May.
5. First Monday in June.
6. First Monday in August.
7. Last Monday in October.
8. Christmas Day (25 December).
9. St. Stephen's Day (26 December).

The term "Bank Holiday" is often used to describe these nine public holidays, as well as other days, such as Good Friday (the Friday before Easter Sunday). However, only these nine days have legal standing – employees have no entitlement in law to other days off.

The employee is entitled, as the employer determines and having regard to the needs of the business, to:

- A **paid** day off on the scheduled public holiday, or within a month after that day; or
- An extra day's pay; or

- An extra day's annual leave.

Employees may request their employer, at least 21 days before a public holiday, to determine which of the three approaches is to be applied. The employer is required to provide at least 14 days' notification to the employee stating which approach is to be applied. Ideally, the notice should be longer and, if possible, the whole year should be scheduled in advance to integrate the annual and public holiday scheduling for all employees. This allows for practical planning for both the company and each employee.

Where an employee ceases to be employed during the week ending on the day before the public holiday, and the employee has worked for that employer for the four weeks preceding that week, the employee is entitled to receive a normal day's pay.

Part-time or casual employees must have worked 40 hours in the 5 weeks ending on the day before the public holiday to avail of the public holiday entitlement.

Holiday records

Employers are required to maintain records for each employee of all annual leave and public holidays taken and the arrangements they applied. They must ensure that these accurately reflect the entitlements for each employee. These records may later be required by the employer to defend any case taken by an employee.

Unforeseeable or emergency circumstances

An employer is not obliged to comply with the daily rest, rest breaks, weekly rest or night work provisions, where unforeseen circumstances or an emergency occurs that could not have been avoided even with the employer's due care or which were beyond the employer's control. However, proper communication is important and records should be maintained.

PARENTAL LEAVE ACTS 1998 & 2006

Purpose

Provides entitlements for employees who are parents to take **unpaid** leave from work under certain parental-related conditions. The Acts also contains a provision for special **paid** leave, defined as *force majeure* leave.

Provisions & Procedures

Eligibility

- Male and female employees who are the natural, or adoptive, parent of a child or acting *in loco parentis*.

- The employee must have one year's continuous service with the employer concerned. However, employees with three months' continuous service on the last day for commencing such leave may have one week's parental leave for each month of continuous employment up to the commencement of such leave.

- Parental leave must be taken before the child reaches eight years of age, or in the case of a disabled child, before the child reaches 16 years of age.

Parental leave

- The parental leave entitlement is a minimum period of 14 consecutive weeks' **unpaid** leave.

- Leave may be taken as a continuous block, or in separate periods, by agreement with the employer.

- There is an equivalent leave entitlement for each child – however, the total leave may not exceed 14 weeks in any 12-month period, unless specifically agreed with the employer.

- Parents may not combine their parental leave entitlements and parental leave entitlements are not transferable from parent to parent, except where both parents of a child are employed by the same employer.

- The employee should provide as much notice as possible of his/her intention to avail of parental leave, in writing to the employer, but not later than six weeks before the commencement of the leave.

- If the employer agrees to the parental leave request, a confirmation document should be drafted at least four weeks before the commencement of the leave. This should state the agreed dates, the manner in which the leave is to be taken and should be signed by both the employer and the employee. A copy should be issued to the employee.

Postponing or terminating parental leave

- If an employer believes that a request for parental leave at a specific time would have a substantial adverse effect on the business, the employer can postpone the leave for a period up to six months from the original requested leave period. However, there must be genuine business reasons for postponing the request for parental leave – for example, the unavailability of a suitable replacement, seasonal variations in the volume of work or the number of employees already on parental leave. The employer must consult with the employee about the proposed postponement and should then notify the employee in writing, explaining the circumstances.

- After a confirmation document has been drafted and signed, the employer and the employee may jointly agree to postpone and amend the parental leave times and dates. The confirmation document should be revised accordingly.

- An employer can terminate parental leave, if he/she believes that the employee is using the leave for a purpose other than taking care of the child concerned. Obviously, the employer should be aware of the need for satisfactory evidence, before making such a decision.

Force majeure leave

The Parental Leave Acts provide for special leave, known as *force majeure*, for employees in circumstances where the presence of the employee is indispensable. This category of leave is **paid** and is separate to parental leave.

Force majeure leave is for situations where, for urgent family reasons, owing to illness or injury of a person specified in the categories below, the immediate presence of the employee is indispensable:

- A child or an adopted child of the employee.
- The husband/wife/partner of the employee.
- The parent or grandparent of the employee.
- The brother or sister of the employee.
- A person for whom the employee has a duty of care.
- A person other than specified above, who resides with the employee in a relationship of domestic dependency if, in the event of injury or illness,

one reasonably relies on the other to make arrangements for the provision of care (including same-sex partners).

The *force majeure* leave entitlement is three days' **paid** leave in a 12-month period or five days' in any 36-month period. A part-day is considered to be one full day. Any additional leave required by the employee may be requested from the employer but, if approved, it is **unpaid**.

The employee must provide written notice to the employer as soon as is reasonably practicable.

Protection of employment rights

- Annual leave entitlements that accrue to an employee during parental leave will be granted in accordance with the terms of the Organisation of Working Time Act 1997.

- Employees retain rights to public holidays that occur during parental leave. Such days are given as days off in lieu at the end of the leave.

- Service continuity and the rights of an employee with regard to employment are maintained while on parental leave, other than the rights to remuneration. Remuneration has a wide definition and not only includes salary, but also benefits such as health insurance, pension contributions, etc.

- The employee has the right to return to the same or equivalent and suitable work, including location and pay, on terms not substantially less favourable.

- Training, probation or apprenticeship, interrupted by parental leave, is temporarily suspended until after the leave period.

PAYMENT OF WAGES ACT 1991

Purpose
To provide protection for employees in relation to the payment of wages.

Provisions & Procedures

Eligibility
Applies to employees who have entered into a contract of employment, express or implied, whether it is written or expressed orally.

Methods of payment of wages
Wages must be paid by one or more of the following methods:

- Cheque, draft or other bill of exchange.
- Postal, money or paying order.
- Credit transfer.
- Cash (in legal tender).
- A document of a Central Bank, a trustee savings bank (or other financial institution listed in the Central Bank Act 1971) account holder that is intended to enable payment for the sum specified in the document.
- Draft payable on demand.
- Any other modes of payment specified by regulations made by the Minister of Enterprise, Trade & Employment, in consultation with the Minister for Finance.

Statement of wages
Employers are obliged to supply each employee with a written statement setting out his/her gross wages and specific details of any deductions made from that amount. This statement must be issued once payment is made to the employee. The employer must ensure that these details remain confidential.

Deductions from wages
An employer is not entitled to make deductions from an employee's wages unless:

- Required by law – for example, income tax (PAYE) and pay related social insurance (PRSI).

- Provided for in the employee's contract of employment, such as a provision for breakages or till shortages.
- Agreed in writing with the employee – for example, health insurance or trade union subscriptions.

However, there are restrictions in relation to deductions or payments received:

- If they arise from any act or omission of the employee (including suspension without pay, fines for damage to company property, etc).
- If they are in respect of the supply to the employee by the employer of goods or services that are necessary to their employment (for example, tools and equipment).

To avoid ambiguity and disputes, details of any such arrangements need to be in writing and the deduction(s) should be clearly authorised by the employee.

If a deduction is made in relation to an act or omission of the employee, where the employee is liable within the terms of the contract, at least one week prior to the deduction the employee must be given precise details of the reason for, and amount of, the deduction in writing and with reference to the particular clause involved.

If challenged, the details of the clause and the amount deducted will be judged by any external third party on the basis of the contract, fair process, and fair and reasonable application.

PROTECTION OF EMPLOYEES (FIXED-TERM WORK) ACT 2003

Purpose

To provide protection for employees employed under fixed-term contracts.

Provisions & Procedures

Definitions

- ***Fixed-term contracts*** are sometimes referred to as specified purpose contracts. A fixed-term contract can refer either to a specified period of time or to the completion of objectives or a project.

Conditions of employment

- Fixed-term employees must not be treated less favourably than full-time employees, in terms of their pay and conditions, solely because they are fixed-term employees.

- Exceptions to this central requirement of the Act are where the conditions of employment of a permanent employee relate to a pension scheme or where the fixed-term employee's hours of work are less than 20% of the permanent employee's hours. Then, an employer may treat a fixed-term employee less favourably, if he/she can provide an objective and justifiable reason. If challenged, this reason will be subject to examination by a Rights Commissioner or the Labour Court, so the reason needs to be logical and legitimate. If in doubt, it is advisable to get advice.

- Employers must ensure that fixed-term employees have the same opportunity as other employees to apply for any permanent positions and that such information is readily available, at least by way of a prominent notice in the workplace. Likewise, the employer should facilitate access for training to enhance the fixed-term employee's skills and employment opportunities.

- Comparison claims by a fixed-term employee are restricted to a *pro rata* comparison based on the hours of work ratio between the permanent employee and fixed-term employee.

- Fixed-term employees must receive annual leave and public holiday entitlements on the same basis as permanent employees.

Selecting a comparable permanent employee for comparison

If a fixed-term employee requests the company to review his/her terms and conditions and/or pay under this Act, because of perceived or alleged discrimination, there are clear terms against which the comparison is measured. For the fixed-term employee's claim to succeed, it must satisfy at least one of the following criteria:

- The fixed-term employee must be doing the same, or similar, work as a permanent employee or be interchangeable in their work.

- The work of the fixed-term employee is of a similar nature, or with minimal differences, to that of a permanent employee.

- The work of the fixed-term employee is of comparable value to that of a permanent employee.

- The selection of a comparable employee can also apply where an employee works for an associated employer. The employee can select a comparable employee in another company if both companies are subject to the terms and conditions of a collective agreement, which has been approved by the Labour Court.

- Where there is no immediate in-company comparable employee or specific collective agreement, the Act allows for external comparisons, within the same industry or industrial sector. The criteria for judging the case remains as above.

Written statement

The employer must provide the fixed-term employee with a written statement, as soon as practicable, which establishes the end of the contract or relationship and the objective reason for it – for example:

- Achievement of a specific date – the end of a three-month period.

- Completing a specific task, objectives or project.

- The occurrence of a specific event – the end of another employee's maternity cover.

Where the employer proposes to renew a fixed-term contract, he/she must provide the fixed-term employee with a written statement outlining the objective grounds for the renewal and why an indefinite contract is not possible. Such written statements are admissible as evidence in any proceedings under this Act. Employers must ensure that the objective reason provided is honest, justifiable, reasonable and fair.

Successive fixed-term contracts

Where a fixed-term employee completes, or has completed, a third year of continuous employment with same employer or associated employer, his/her contract may be renewed only once more for an additional fixed-term of not longer than one year.

Where a fixed-term employee completes two or more continuous fixed-term contracts, the aggregate of the contracts must not exceed four years.

Claims for unfair dismissal may be allowed where there is alleged abuse or attempts at avoiding the provisions of the Act. In determining qualifying service within the terms of the unfair dismissal legislation, the duration of the fixed-term contracts are added together.

PROTECTION OF EMPLOYEES (PART-TIME WORK) ACT 2001

Purpose

To provide protection for employees employed on a part-time basis.

Provisions & Procedures

Definitions

- A **part-time worker** is an employee whose hours of work are less than the normal hours of work of any other comparable full-time worker in the company in which they work.

- A **comparable employee** means any other employee who, for the purpose of assessing fair and equitable treatment, would be considered a fair comparison. For example, an employee who is employed by the same employer, by an associated employer or by an employer who is in the same industrial sector and where such work would be of the same or similar nature, or where the differences are negligible, or where they would be considered to be interchangeable in terms of the work, or where the work performed by the part-time employee is of equal or greater value to the other employee.

- A **casual worker** means a person working for a period of less than 13 weeks for the employer or where such service, in conjunction with any other service periods, could not be regarded as regular or seasonal work. On objective grounds, or within the terms of a Labour Court-approved collective agreement, a casual worker may be treated less favourably than a comparable full-time employee with regard to a particular condition of employment.

- An **agency worker** is an employee engaged by a person or agency to work for a third party. Agency workers may only be compared with other agency workers.

Eligibility

Any part-time employee who is:

- Working under a contract of employment.
- An apprentice.

- Employed through an employment agency.
- In State-related employment.

Conditions of employment for part-time workers

A part-time worker may not be treated less favourably (on a *pro rata* basis) than any other part-time or full-time worker, except on objective and reasonable grounds.

A part-time worker must work at least 20% of the standard full-time worker hours to be considered for any pension scheme eligibility under the Act.

Employer responsibilities

The onus of responsibility for part-time employees under this Act rests with whomever the contract of employment is with and whoever pays the wages.

In the case of agency workers, normally the contract of employment is with the agency and the agency pays the wages. Thus, the agency is responsible for ensuring that the part-time employee is not treated less favourably than other agency workers who work full-time.

On the other hand, responsibilities under other Acts, such as the Safety, Health & Welfare at Work Act 2005, still rests (predominantly) with the employer to whom the person is contracted.

Holiday entitlements for part-time employees

Part-time employees are entitled to receive 8% of their hours worked in a leave year as holidays, subject to a maximum of four working weeks' paid annual leave.

Full-time workers requesting part-time work and *vice versa*

There is no obligation on employers, within this Act, to agree to such changes in conditions. However, the Labour Relations Commission has developed a Code of Practice relating to access to part-time working, the purpose of which is to promote the development of policies and procedures governing access to part-time working and to stimulate wider access to part-time working options.

PROTECTION OF YOUNG PERSONS IN EMPLOYMENT

Purpose
To protect the health of young people at work and to ensure that any work carried out during the school year does not put a young person's education at risk.

Provisions & Procedures

Legislation
- Protection of Young Persons (Employment) Act 1996.
- Protection of Young Persons Act 1996 (Employment in Licensed Premises) Regulations 2001 (SI No.350 of 2001).
- Protection of Young Persons Act 1996 (Bar Apprentices) Regulations 2001 (SI No.351 of 2001).

Definitions
- A *child* is a person under 16 years of age or under the school-leaving age, whichever is the higher.
- A *young person* is a person who has reached 16 years of age or the school-leaving age (whichever is higher), but is less than 18 years of age.
- *Light work* is work, which is not industrial in nature, and which is not likely to be harmful to the safety, health or development of children or to their attendance at school or their participation in vocational guidance or training programmes.

Eligibility
The legislation applies to young persons under 18 years of age.

Employer responsibilities
- Employers must not employ persons under 16 years of age in a regular full-time job.
- Employers may hire persons aged 14 and 15 years on light work during school holidays, or part-time during the school term, or as part of an approved work experience or educational programme (approved by the

Department of Enterprise, Trade & Employment), provided that the work is not harmful to their safety, health, or development.

- Employers are required to check the date of birth of the young person or child, to maintain records of such information and to ensure that they obtain the permission of the parent or guardian if employing a person under 16 years of age.

- Employers are required to provide young workers with a copy of the *Official Summary of the Protection of Young Persons (Employment) Act 1996* (available from the Department of Enterprise, Trade & Employment), together with their terms and conditions of employment within one month of commencing employment. A copy of the Act must also be posted in an easily accessible place.

Light work

An employer may employ a child, who is over the age of 14 years, to do light work, during any period outside the school term, provided that:

- The hours of work do not exceed seven hours in any day or 35 hours in any week.

- The work is not harmful to the safety, health and development of the child.

- During the period of the summer holidays, the child does not do any work for a period of at least 21 days.

An employer may employ a child, who is over the age of 15 years, to do light work, during school term time, provided that the hours of work do not exceed eight hours in any week.

Rest periods

A child under the age of 16 must have:

- A half-hour rest break after 4 hours work. The child is not entitled to be paid in respect of this break.

- A daily rest break of 14 consecutive hours' off work.

- A weekly rest break of two days off, which should be consecutive, where possible.

The minimum period of rest each week may be interrupted (on activities that do not extend beyond two hours in each day or are separated, exclusive of breaks) provided that, in each period of seven days, the cumulative rest period is two days.

Night and early morning work
Young persons (16- and 17-year olds) are only permitted to work between 6am and 10pm.

Exceptions to this rule must be provided for in Regulations – for example, The Protection of Young Persons Act 1996 (Employment in Licensed Premises) Regulations 2001 (SI No.350 of 2001) permits young people employed on general duties in a licensed premises to be required to work up to 11pm on a day that does not immediately precede a school day during a school term where the young person is attending school. Otherwise, 16- and 17-year olds can work until 10 pm, but must not work the following day until after 6am; alternatively, they can work until 11pm, but must not work until after 7am the following day.

Work at sea
Compensatory rest breaks can be given in place of the rest breaks specified in the Act for young workers employed in fishing or shipping, provided it is reasonable to do so and that the person has a representative (such as a trade union official), who is consulted on the arrangements.

The defence forces
Rules concerning hours of work, night work and rest breaks do not apply to young persons engaged in active or operational service duties or on training in the defence forces. However, compensatory breaks must be provided within three weeks of completion of such duties.

Close relatives and farming
Rules concerning hours of work, night work and rest breaks do not apply to young persons engaged in work in family business or farms, provided that the conditions of employment satisfy health and safety requirements and that the development of the young person is not put at risk.

More than one job
The combined hours of work of a young person with more than one job must not exceed the maximum working hours allowed above. It is advisable for employers to include a statement to that effect in the contract of employment.

Work experience or training
Employers may employ persons of 15 years of age as part of a training programme recognised by FÁS or by the Minister for Enterprise, Trade & Employment. Similarly, employers may employ 14/15 year olds who are full-time second-level students as part of a work experience or educational

programme, provided such programmes are restricted to an eight-hour day or a 40-hour week.

Employment of young persons in licensed premises

- Before employing a young person, the employer must obtain the written permission of the parent or guardian of the young person.

- A code of practice has been developed by the Department of Enterprise, Trade & Employment that sets out the duties and responsibilities in relation to the employment of young persons on general duties in licensed premises. It covers 16- and 17-year olds, including all second level students (excluding bar apprentices in the licensed trade), who are employed at any time in licensed premises. Employers should review the code of practice and ensure that it is signed by all relevant parties and that a copy is retained in the young person's file.

- An employer may employ a young person to carry out general duties in a licensed premises and may require the young person to work up to 11 pm on any one day, providing the following day is not a school day for the young person or, alternatively, where the young person is not permitted to commence work until 7 am or later on the following day.

- An employer who employs a young person in a full-time capacity as an apprentice in a licensed premises may require the young person to work up to midnight on any one day, where the young person will not be required or permitted to commence work until 8 am or later on the following day and is supervised by an adult.

REDUNDANCY PAYMENTS ACTS 1967 - 2003

Purpose

To place statutory obligations on employers regarding the termination of employment for reasons of redundancy and to define minimum redundancy entitlements for employees, based on length of service and remuneration.

Provisions & Procedures

Definitions

- A *redundancy* is when an employee is terminated from employment (other than a dismissal for reasons of performance or behaviour issues) and is not replaced.
- *Reckonable service* means the amount of service allowed for the purposes of calculating the redundancy lump sum.
- *Lay-off* is when the employer has no work for an employee or group of employees. It can be for a fixed term or can be from week to week, having regard to the changing circumstances of work. It is generally seen as a temporary solution to a downturn in business, where it is likely that the circumstances will improve in the short term. The employee receives no pay during a lay-off and may be entitled to social welfare payments.
- *Short-time working* is where the employer has less work than usual in the company and puts employees on a reduced working week.

Eligibility

- Employees between 16 and 66 years of age.
- Employees must have 104 weeks' continuous service with the same employer.
- Where an employee is employed under a "fixed purpose" contract, and the exact duration of the contract was incapable of being determined at inception, if the contract is not renewed following the fulfilment of the purpose, a redundancy can arise.

Reckonable Service

Leave of absence for any of the following is allowable as reckonable service:

- Adoptive leave.

- Maternity-related leave.
- Parental leave.
- *Force majeure* leave.
- Carer's leave.
- Any other absence allowed by the employer.

In addition, the employee's continuity of service is not broken for:

- Sickness (with exceptions).
- Lay-off.
- Annual leave.
- Service in the defence forces.
- Any other absence authorised by the employer (other than voluntary resignation).
- Absence due to a lock-out.

Non-reckonable service

During (and only during) the three years ending on the date of termination of employment, the following absences are defined as non-reckonable service:

- Absences in excess of 52 weeks for occupational accident or disease.
- Absences in excess of 26 weeks other than for occupational accident or disease.
- Absence by reason of lay-off by the employer.
- Absence due to a strike.

Employee's right to redundancy for lay-off or short-time working

An employee is not entitled to redundancy payment by reason of lay-off or short-time working, unless the lay-off is for four or more consecutive weeks or the lay-off or short-time working is within a period of 13 weeks, for a series of six or more weeks of which not more than three were consecutive.

The employee is required to provide notice in writing of his/her intention to claim a redundancy payment not later than four weeks after the cessation of the lay-off or short-time. If, after the expiry of the relevant period, and not later than four weeks after the cessation of the lay-off or short time, an employee, in lieu of giving to his employer a notice of intention to claim, terminates his contract of employment and provides one week's notice in writing, the notice shall be deemed to be a notice of intention to claim.

Legitimate reasons for redundancy

- Where the business has ceased, or is due to cease or diminish.

- Where the employer has decided to carry on the business with fewer or no employees, whether by requiring the work to be done by other employees or otherwise.

- Where the employer has decided that the work for which the employee had been employed should be done in a different manner, for which the employee is not sufficiently qualified or trained.

- Where the employer has decided that the work for which the employee was employed should be done by a person, who is also capable of doing other work, for which the employee is not sufficiently qualified or trained.

Selection of employee for redundancy

The selection process is generally on a 'last in, first out' basis where possible – except where the company cannot select on that basis because those employees remaining would not have the necessary abilities to do the remaining work to an acceptable level of performance and where training the remaining employees would not be a viable solution for reasons of cost or other valid reasons.

Employers should ensure that the records relied upon for selecting employees on a last-in first-out basis are available and accurate. The selection process, if not on the basis of last in, first out, should be fair, equitable, and objective. The employer will be required to demonstrate the reasoning.

Employer responsibilities

- Provide a minimum period of notice of redundancy to each employee who is to be made redundant, depending on their length of service, as set out in the Minimum Notice & Terms of Employment Acts 1973-2001.

- Ensure a fair and equitable selection process for redundancy.

- Pay the employee a service-related lump sum on termination.

- Complete the redundancy payment form, RP50, and submit the appropriate documentation to the Department of Enterprise, Trade & Employment in order to claim a rebate

Calculating minimum redundancy entitlements

- When calculating the lump sum, the annual salary to be used for calculation is based on an employee's rate when the employer declares the redundancy and is subject to a maximum amount of €600 per week.

- The employee's entitlement, when calculating the amount of the lump sum, is two weeks' pay per year of reckonable service plus one additional week's gross pay.

- Where the reckonable service period is not an exact number of years, the 'excess' days are credited as a proportion of a year and are included in the redundancy entitlement calculation.

- To calculate reckonable service, see the sections on reckonable and non-reckonable provisions above.

Additional redundancy payments

In many cases, redundancy payments in excess of those required by the redundancy legislation are negotiated – like many other aspects of our industrial relations practices and procedures in Ireland, moving ahead of legislation on a voluntary basis.

While there is no obligation on employers to negotiate additional terms, any employers who have unionised representation generally will be involved in negotiating additional redundancy pay and the employer should be aware and prepared for such representations. The employees'/unions' rationale may be based on custom and practice in the company or locally.

Collective redundancies

Where there are to be multiple or collective redundancies, the employer must inform the Department of Enterprise, Trade & Employment and consult with the representatives of the employees at least 30 days before the intended redundancies. The objective of the consultation process is to allow the employees to voice their views and, if possible, to avoid or reduce the effect of the redundancies. The discussion can also include the selection process and the timing of the redundancies.

Collective redundancies are defined as:

- Five redundancies in a company employing 20 to 50 employees.
- Ten redundancies in a company employing 50 to 100 employees.
- 10% redundancies in a company employing 100 to 300 employees.
- Thirty redundancies in a company employing more than 300 employees.

Time off to seek employment

During the two weeks prior to the redundancy, the employee must be allowed reasonable **paid** time off to look for new employment or to make arrangements for training for future employment. The employer is entitled to ask the employee to furnish evidence of such arrangements.

SAFETY, HEALTH & WELFARE AT WORK ACT 2005

Purpose

Every employer is required to ensure, so far as is reasonably practicable, the safety, health and welfare of all employees at work.

Provisions & Procedures

Duties & responsibilities of employers

- Manage safety, health and welfare in the workplace, to ensure the safety of employees and visitors. Employers sharing a place of work must co-operate to develop effective safety procedures.

- Appoint someone to manage the safety function. In large organisations, it may be appropriate to have a full-time Safety Manager.

- Provide the names of all those involved in safety activities within the company, including the safety representative, to all employees and to all contractors or visitors to the workplace location(s).

- Assess risks or hazards and develop and implement practices and procedures that will eradicate or reduce hazards at work – including hazards arising from noise, heat, cold, radiation or any other harmful physical sources or from unacceptable behaviour by managers or employees.

- Investigation of hazards and risks should be sufficiently regular to ensure that any changes in work practices are immediately assessed, hazards/risks identified and preventative practices implemented, employees and others trained and the safety statement is adjusted accordingly.

- Provide safety clothing and equipment and related training.

- Provide instruction and training to suit employees' training needs (ensuring that training is understandable) in all work-related activities, including safety requirements.

- Take each employee's specific capabilities into account in relation to safety, health and welfare and their related training requirements.

- Design safe means of entry and exit from work premises.

- Design plant, machinery and equipment, which is safe and with minimum risk to operators and employees, and ensure that all are properly and regularly inspected, serviced and maintained to ensure safe operations.

- Establish reporting procedures for accidents and dangerous occurrences and report such incidents to the Health & Safety Authority. Review such reports and modify practices and procedures, as necessary, to reduce risks further.

- Use only competent persons for the development and maintenance and training of safety practices.

- Ensure all safety practices, procedures and training apply equitably to all categories of employees, including part-time, contract, casual and people with different language/understanding requirements.

- Ensure employees do not bear the financial costs of any measures taken relating to their safety, health and welfare at work.

Safety statement

Employers are required to develop a safety statement, as a practical process for the identification of risks and hazards and for their elimination or reduction.

The safety statement should be easily accessible to all employees and updated on a regular basis to take account of any changes in the workplace, technology, equipment, work processes, etc. This requirement does not apply to companies with three employees or fewer. A Code of Practice is to be developed for such companies by the Health & Safety Authority.

Liability

Management has a responsibility for safety, health and welfare, including a legal exposure for managers making them personally liable in certain circumstances where it is found that, through negligence or contrivance, they failed in their duty of care for employees' safety. This applies to directors or managers, particularly where decision-making responsibility impacts on the safety, health and welfare of others.

Reasonably practicable

There is a requirement for employers to be 'reasonably practicable' when assessing work, identifying risks to safety, health and welfare and developing professional solutions to eliminate or reduce such risks to employees and others. It is always difficult to be definitive about what is or is not reasonable or practicable, because of the multitude of variations and circumstances in work and in workplaces. Nonetheless, each employer must determine this for their own particular company, environments and occupations and be prepared to stand over and demonstrate, in the event of an investigation, that their policies, practices and procedures were sufficient and that they were applied correctly. The onus of responsibility is on the manager responsible for such decisions and applications and, subsequently, the Chief Executive.

The following points are important when considering this requirement and any investigation or judgment regarding an employer's behaviour and liability will consider whether the employer:

- Carried out an analysis of safety, health and welfare.

- Put in place policies, practices, procedures, equipment, etc to eliminate or reduce any risks identified.

- Trained the people involved.

- Monitored any changes and modified the procedures to cater for any additional or different risks.

In the event of an accident, the employer may have to demonstrate that the circumstances were exceptional and unforeseen or that any additional procedural changes or other preventative measures would be impractical.

The employer will have to carry out accident and incident investigations to determine circumstance and fault. The results of this may partially mitigate the responsibility for the accident or reduce the liability in some cases. However, the onus is on the employer to prove the circumstances and to demonstrate that reasonable and practicable actions were taken to avoid such an occurrence and that, therefore, they have satisfied statutory requirements.

Duties and responsibilities of employees

- To co-operate with their employer on all safety, health and welfare matters.

- To attend work-related and safety, health and welfare training and to co-operate with associated assessments to ensure understanding and compliance as required – including the use of safety clothing and equipment and any other related procedures.

- To report on safety, health and welfare issues, including defective clothing and equipment.

- Not to be under the influence of any intoxicants (alcohol, drugs, any combination of drugs or of drugs and alcohol) while at work.

- Submit to any appropriate, reasonable and proportionate tests for intoxicants by (or under the supervision of) a registered medical practitioner.

- Not to engage in improper conduct or behaviour that could impact negatively on the safety, health or welfare of themselves or others.

- To comply with all safety provisions, to take care of their own safety, health and welfare and that of others who may be affected by their actions or omissions.

- When entering into a contract of employment, not to misrepresent himself/ herself to an employer with regard to the level of training or expertise allegedly acquired prior to commencement of employment. Such misrepresentations could result in risks to safety, health and welfare of themselves or others.

Safety consultation

Employers are required to consult with employees to develop effective safety, health and welfare practices and procedures for the company, including the sharing of information considered necessary or important.

The employer must consider any safety representations and proposals from employees and, as a consequence, to develop and integrate changes where these are found to be legitimate in supporting safety, health and welfare. This consultation process may be facilitated by the operation of a safety committee (see below).

Where arrangements for joint decision-making, involving the employer and employees, are already in existence, these arrangements shall include consultation in accordance with this provision.

The employer must give employees involved a reasonable amount of *paid* time off from work to enable them to acquire the knowledge and training necessary to discharge their functions in the consultation process.

Safety representative

Employees are entitled to select and appoint a safety representative at their workplace (or, in agreement with their employer, more than one safety representative) to represent them in consultations with their employer on safety, health and welfare matters.

A safety representative must be allowed to:

- Make representations to the employer on any matter relating to safety, health and welfare in the workplace.

- Make verbal or written representations to inspectors from the Health & Safety Authority on matters relating to safety, health and welfare in the workplace, including the investigation of accidents or dangerous occurrences.

- Receive advice and information from inspectors on matters relating to safety, health and welfare at the place of work.

- Consult and liaise on matters relating to safety, health and welfare at work with any other safety representatives who may be appointed in the same company, whether or not those safety representatives work in the same place of work, in different places of work under the control of the employer or at different times at the place of work.

- Inspect the whole workplace (or any part), after giving reasonable notice to the employer or immediately following an accident, dangerous occurrence or imminent danger or risk to the safety, health and welfare of any person.

- Investigate complaints relating to safety, health and welfare at work made by any employee, after giving the employer reasonable notice.

- Investigate accidents and dangerous occurrences, provided that he/she does not interfere with or obstruct the performance of any statutory obligation required to be performed by any person under provisions in safety legislation.

- Accompany an inspector from the Health & Safety Authority, who is carrying out a general inspection or investigating an accident or dangerous occurrence.

- Where an employee is interviewed by an inspector from the Health & Safety Authority with respect to an accident or dangerous occurrence, attend the interview, if the employee so requests and at the discretion of the inspector.

The employer and the safety representative should jointly agree the frequency of inspections, depending on the nature and extent of hazards in the workplace.

The employer must consider any representations on safety, health and welfare made by the safety representative and, so far as is reasonably practicable, take any action that he/she considers necessary or appropriate with regard to those representations.

The employer must give the safety representative a reasonable amount of time off from work (without loss of remuneration) to enable him/her to acquire, the knowledge and training necessary to do the job.

Employers should ensure that safety representatives are not victimised or penalised in any way for performing their functions as a safety representative.

In the event of an inspector from the Health & Safety Authority conducting an inspection in the workplace, the employer must inform the safety representative that this is taking place.

Safety committees

The main purpose of the safety committee is to assist the employer and employees concerned to comply with the relevant statutory provisions in relation to safety legislation.

Employees may select and appoint from amongst their numbers a safety committee to perform the functions assigned to safety committees under this Act. The number of members on a safety committee should not be less than three nor exceed one for every 20 persons employed in a workplace at the time the committee is appointed.

Where a safety representative (or representatives) has been appointed, then at least one safety representative should be selected and appointed by the employees to be a member of the committee.

The basic guidelines for the safety committee are as follows:

- Quorum not less than three persons.
- Membership should be made up of current employees and employer representatives.
- An employer representative must attend the first meeting of the committee to present all safety practices and the safety statement, if completed.
- The members of the safety committee must consider any representations on safety matters proposed by the employee and employer members.
- The committee must discuss and agree on schedules for committee meetings, facilities, etc with the employer.

Safety training

Employees are entitled to receive safety training without loss of remuneration.

New employees must be informed of the hazards and related safety requirements prior to commencement of work.

An employer should provide formal work and safety training:

- On the first day of employment, and when an employee is transferred to a different job within the company.
- When duties, responsibilities, equipment or methods are changed.
- When new work equipment or systems of work are introduced.
- On the introduction of new technology.
- When other employees are to carry out other work in their immediate vicinity.
- When contractors are to work in their immediate vicinity.

Emergency procedures

Depending on the nature of the work and/or the environment, it may also be necessary for the employer to make special provisions in the event of an emergency or a serious and imminent danger. Such procedures should be included in the safety statement and in employee training programmes.

Employers must:

- Provide the necessary measures to be taken for first aid, fire fighting and the evacuation of employees and any other individuals present in the workplace at the time.

- Arrange any necessary contacts with the appropriate emergency services, particularly with regard to first aid, emergency medical care, fire fighting and rescue work.

- Designate employees who have responsibility to implement such plans, procedures and measures and ensure that the number of designated employees, their training and the equipment available to them is adequate and relevant.

Assessing medical fitness to work

- Employees must co-operate with an employer's request to undergo a medical assessment to determine his/her fitness to perform work activities where such work includes risks to safety, health and welfare.

- Such medical assessments must be carried out by a registered medical practitioner.

- If the medical practitioner is of the opinion that the employee is unfit to perform work activities, the medical practitioner must notify the employer of that opinion and the likelihood of early resumption of work for rehabilitative purposes. The medical practitioner must also inform the employee accordingly, giving the reasons for that opinion.

- If an employee becomes aware that he/she is suffering from any disease or physical or mental impairment that would be likely to cause him/her to expose himself/herself or another person to danger or risk of danger, he/she is required to immediately notify the employer or the company medical practitioner, who shall in turn notify the employer.

- These requirements should be explained to the employee before employment commences, stated in any contract of employment and reiterated before any medical assessment.

Responsibilities of other persons

A person who designs, manufactures, imports or supplies any article for use at work must:

- Ensure (so far as is reasonably practicable) that the article is designed and constructed so that it may be used safely and without risk to health when used properly by a person in a workplace.

- Ensure that the article has undergone appropriate levels of testing and examination to ensure it is safe.

- Provide adequate information about the article to the persons to whom it is supplied, to ensure it is used safely.

- In the event of modifications, provide any revisions of the information and training for safe operation.

- Where the article is rented or leased, and where the person has a responsibility to do so, maintain the article in a safe condition and in compliance with the relevant legislation and supply safe operating instructions.

A person who erects, assembles or installs any article for use at a place of work, where that article is to be used by persons at work, must ensure that nothing in the manner in which it is erected, assembled or installed makes the article unsafe or a risk to health (so far as is reasonably practicable) when used at the place of work.

A person who manufactures, imports or supplies any substance for use at work must:

- Ensure (so far as is reasonably practicable) that the substance is safe and has undergone appropriate levels of testing and examination to ensure it is safe and is without risk to the user's health.

- Provide adequate information about the substance to the persons to whom it is supplied to ensure it is used safely. Substances made outside Ireland must be fully assessed and verified as being safe within Irish safety requirements.

TERMS OF EMPLOYMENT (INFORMATION) ACTS 1994 & 2001

Purpose

To define employer responsibilities for providing an employee with a written statement of their terms of employment within two months of the commencement of employment.

Provisions & Procedures

Definitions

- A ***contract of employment*** is an agreement between an employer or person and another person to do work for reward. The contract of employment does not have to be in writing to exist. If one person is working for another, the contract is implied.

Eligibility

Any person, regardless of full-time, part-time or hours of work status, working under a contract of employment or apprenticeship or employed through an employment agency or who is in the service of the State, is entitled to a written statement of their terms and conditions of employment.

Terms of employment

The terms of employment are the specific details of the relationship between the employer and the employee. The legislation sets out the minimum standards for such information. However, an employer may wish to increase the information and add other factors.

The statutory requirements for terms of employment are as follows:

- The name and address of the employer.
- The name of the employee.
- Place of work or places of work.
- Hours of work, including overtime requirements.
- The rate of pay, method of calculation and the interval between payments, and including overtime rates.
- Information regarding the pay review date applicable in the company, and as related to any national agreements or, in their absence, to whatever

review date is applicable (this is also required under the National Minimum Wage Act 2000. Also the employer must inform employees of their entitlement to seek a statement of their average hourly rate over the previous 12-month period).

- The job title and the nature of the work.
- Date of commencement of the employment and the expiry date, if temporary.
- If the contract is for a fixed period, the start date and the date on which the contract expires.
- Statutory and/or company rest and break periods.
- Paid leave entitlements.
- Information on the terms or conditions relating to incapacity for work due to sickness or injury, including, if applicable, payment during such leave.
- Pensions or pension schemes.
- Mutual notice entitlements, or the method of determining such notice.
- Information on collective agreements, if in force, and details of the parties involved.

The employer is required to issue this information, even to an employee who leaves the employment during the initial two-month period.

It is important to note that the employer is responsible for informing the employee of any changes that will affect the stated terms of employment.

Terms for young employees

Regulations under this Act require the employer to provide to persons under 18 years of age, in addition to the statement of the terms of employment, a copy of the *Official Summary of the Protection of Young Persons (Employment) Act 1996*, within one month of commencing employment.

Employment outside Ireland

Employers are required to issue additional information to employees who are required to work outside Ireland (temporarily or otherwise). The additional terms must clarify:

- The period of time working outside Ireland.
- The currency in which the person is to be paid.
- Any additional benefits that will apply during the period.
- Any terms relating to repatriation, following the period abroad.

UNFAIR DISMISSALS ACTS 1977 - 2001

Purpose

Provides protection for employees from dismissals based on unfair policies, practices and procedures and other actions.

Provisions & Procedures

Eligibility

- One year's continuous service.

- All employees, including part-time employees, apprentices and agency workers, are protected by this legislation and are entitled to make claims against their employer if they believe they were dismissed unfairly.

- The one year service requirement does not apply if the dismissal was as a result of trade union activity or any matter related to an employee's rights under maternity protection, adoptive, carer's leave, parental leave and minimum wage legislation.

- Continuous service is determined by rules set out in the Minimum Notice & Terms of Employment Acts 1973-2001. Separate periods of employment may be added together to determine eligibility. An investigating third party may consider whether a number of contracts of employment, between which there was no more than 26 weeks of a break, were in any way connected with the avoidance of liability by the employer.

The Acts do not apply to:

- Employees under 16 years.
- Employees who have reached normal retiring age.
- Persons working for a close relative in a private house or farm, where both live in the same house or farm.
- Members of the Defence Forces and An Garda Síochána.
- Persons undergoing full-time training or apprenticeship in FÁS.
- State employees, other than certain industrial categories.
- Officers of the Health Service Executive (other than temporary officers) and vocational educational committees.

The exclusions from the Acts of persons working for close relatives, and persons undergoing full-time training or apprenticeship in FÁS, do not apply where the dismissal results from the individual pursuing their entitlements under maternity protection, adoptive, carer's leave, parental leave and minimum wage legislation.

Fixed term/specified purpose contracts

Where the duration of a contract cannot be ascertained at the time the contract was made, a dismissal arising only due to the expiry of the fixed term or the completion of the specified purpose is not covered by the Acts, provided that the contract is in writing, is signed by both parties and contains a clause that the Acts shall not apply to such dismissal.

Where a further fixed term or specified purpose contract occurs, and there was no more than a three-month break, the employee may refer a case to a third party to determine whether the fixed nature or fixed purpose of the contract was wholly or partly connected with the avoidance of liability under the Acts.

Dismissals during probation or training

The Acts do not apply to the dismissal of an employee during a probationary period or while undergoing training, provided that the contract of employment is in writing and the duration of probation or training is one year or less and is specified in the contract.

The Acts also do not apply in relation to the dismissal of an employee who is on probation or undergoing training for the purpose of becoming qualified or registered, as the case may be, as a nurse, pharmacist, health inspector, medical laboratory technician, occupational therapist, physiotherapist, speech therapist, radiographer or social worker. However, this restriction does not apply where the dismissal is related to any maternity matter or where employees are attempting to pursue their rights under adoptive leave, parental leave, *force majeure* leave or carer's leave legislation.

The Acts do not apply in relation to the dismissal of a person who is or was under a statutory apprenticeship during the six months after the commencement of the apprenticeship and in a period of one month following the completion of the apprenticeship, provided the employee is not absent from work on leave which is protected. A statutory apprenticeship is an apprenticeship in an industrial activity designated by FÁS.

Lock-outs and strikes

The lock-out of an employee is regarded as a dismissal and will be deemed to be an unfair dismissal if, after a lock-out, that employee is not reinstated or re-engaged and one or more other employees are.

The dismissal of an employee for taking part in any industrial action is regarded as unfair, if one or more employees of the same employer who took part in the same industrial action were not dismissed or were subsequently re-instated or re-engaged and the claimant was not.

Employee's rights regarding practices and procedures

Employees are entitled to know the procedures that will be observed in the event of disciplinary actions by the employer, which could lead to their dismissal. They are entitled to receive this information within 28 days of commencing employment. Any changes to the procedure must be notified to the employee within 28 days of the change being made. If dismissed, the employee is entitled to receive a written copy of the reason for the dismissal.

Reasons for dismissals that are considered unfair

A dismissal is considered unfair, if related to:

- Membership of, or activities associated with, trade unions.
- Religious or political opinions; race, colour or sexual orientation; age; or membership of the travelling community.
- Legal proceedings against an employer, where an employee is a party or a witness.
- Unfair selection for redundancy.
- Unfair procedures relating to disciplinary matters.
- Maternity.
- The lock-out of an employee, if the employee is not re-instated or re-engaged and others employees are.

Reasons for dismissals that are considered fair

- The capability, competence or qualifications of the employee for performing his/her work.
- The conduct of the employee.
- The redundancy of the employee's job.
- The employee being unable to work, or to continue to work, in the position.

Burden of proof

Under this legislation, the onus of responsibility rests with the employer to prove that a dismissal was fair. It is obviously important that the process of decision-making and the records concerning such decisions are maintained by the employer to be able to defend any subsequent claims.

The employer, in all cases of dismissal, must apply fair policy, practice and procedures, which includes the individual's right to make representations to their employer regarding their case.

Disciplinary procedures

The employer must carry out a fair and unbiased investigation of all the facts of each case prior to any decision to dismiss an employee. Any person, for whatever reason, who could be construed as being biased against the employee concerned, should remove themselves, or be removed, from the investigative process and should have no input to the decision-making process.

In cases referred to a third party, the procedural test to establish fair or unfair practices or procedures is based on the employer's application of the laws of natural justice in dealing with dismissals arising from disciplinary issues. This includes an examination of the company practices and procedures and their actual application. The employee must have the right to:

- Be considered innocent of an offence, until proven guilty.
- Hear/receive the details of any complaint or allegations against them.
- Reply to any complaint or allegations and to have such replies considered.
- Have representation by an individual of their choice at any investigations, interviews, meetings or hearings about such complaints or allegations.
- Appeal to the employer concerning a decision.

Constructive dismissal

A constructive dismissal claim is where an employee's conditions of work are made so difficult that he/she feels obliged to leave. Constructive dismissal therefore infers that the employer (including managers, supervisors, etc) deliberately made life so difficult for them that they had no option but to leave. The individual must be in a position to present evidence that this was so.

Wrongful Dismissal

Persons who have not the required length of service may take a case under common law against an employer related to a dismissal on grounds other than fairness – for example, breach of contract. Redress for such claims is in the form of damages, rather than reinstatement or re-engagement.

PENDING LEGISLATION

Employment Rights Compliance

The Employment Rights Compliance Bill is currently being prepared and the Minister for Trade, Enterprise & Employment has stated that he is committed to publishing the Bill in 2007.

The new legislation arises out of a commitment made in the social partnership agreement, *Towards 2016*, to ensure better compliance with legal requirements and to support same through greater enforcement.

This is to be achieved by:

- Establishing the National Employment Rights Authority (NERA), dedicated to ensuring employment rights compliance. NERA will operate on an interim basis until the legislation is passed.

- Expanding the Labour Inspectorate, by trebling the number of inspectors to 90 by the end of 2007 and opening regional offices to ensure the rights of workers are protected in every region.

- Requiring improved record-keeping by employers, in order to protect workers' employment rights.

- Strengthening penalties for non-compliance and redress in all areas of employment law.

Unfair Dismissals

An amendment is expected to be made to Section 5 of the Unfair Dismissals Acts 1977-2001, regarding dismissals in industrial disputes and the need to protect against the potential misuse of collective dismissals.

Protection of Employment (Exceptional Collective Redundancies)

The Protection of Employment (Exceptional Collective Redundancies) Bill is at an advanced stage of drafting. It will address cases of collective redundancies where specific situations apply and will provide for the extension of unfair dismissals protection in situations where all employees are dismissed, following a strike.

The legislation will also provide for the establishment of a Redundancy Panel, drawn from the social partners, which can request the Minister for Enterprise, Trade & Employment to refer dismissal cases to the Labour Court for an opinion as to whether they are genuine redundancies. Based on that opinion, the Minister may refuse to pay a redundancy rebate.

Other expected provisions in the Bill include abolishing the upper age limit of 66 for qualifying for statutory redundancy.

Regulation of Employment Agencies & Agency Workers

New legislation is to be published that will reinforce the existing system of regulation of employment agencies, by requiring all employment agencies established and/or operating in Ireland to hold a licence. It also will put in place a statutory Code of Practice, covering standards of behaviour for employment agencies.

Code of Practice - Rights of Persons Working in Other People's Homes

The Labour Relations Commission (LRC) is preparing a Code of Practice that will set out the current employment rights and protections for those working in other people's homes. Once the draft is finalised, the LRC will submit it to the Minister for Enterprise, Trade & Employment for approval.

Joint Labour Committees

Another proposal in *Towards 2016* was to modernise the Joint Labour Committee system (JLC). The Labour Court is engaging with the social partners to determine how best to give effect to this proposal.

Safety, Health & Welfare

The Safety, Health & Welfare at Work (General Application) Regulations 1993 are due to be updated under the Safety, Health & Welfare at Work Act 2005, which replaced the Safety, Health & Welfare at Work Act 1989.

Sections of the 1993 Regulations already have been revoked by the Safety Health & Welfare at Work (General Application) (Revocation) Regulations 2005, although their provisions, for the most part, are included in the 2005 Act. The sections that have not been updated include:

- Use of Work Equipment.
- Personal Protective Equipment.
- Manual Handling.
- Display Screen Equipment.

- Electricity.
- First Aid.
- Notification of Accidents and Dangerous Occurrences.

INDEX

ABOUT THE AUTHOR

Pat Sheridan, Managing Director of 1 Stop HR Limited, has spent the last 30 years as a Human Resource Manager with American, French and Japanese multinational companies in the healthcare, food processing, mechanical and electrical engineering industries. He has also worked with the Irish Business & Employers Confederation (IBEC) as an Industrial Relations Consultant, servicing approximately 300 companies (manufacturing/service), providing Human Resource and Industrial Relations advice, direct negotiations with trade unions, assistance with HR strategic planning, preparation of a wide variety of cases for client companies and representing the companies before the Labour Court, Rights Commissioner and Labour Relations Commission. He has also prepared detailed briefing documents for solicitors and barristers on employment law issues that were referred to the High Court.

Pat has lectured in Human Resource Management in UCC and regularly writes for RecruitIreland.com, as well as contributing articles to a number of other publications.

Since 1993, Pat has operated a management consultancy company. Typical assignments include:

- Industrial relations problem resolution.
- Investigation and resolution of bullying and harassment cases and the preparation of investigative and resolution procedures for these issues.
- Investigation and resolution of various management issues.
- Major recruitment and executive sourcing assignments in Ireland and abroad.

- Employee-to-employee problem resolution, as a facilitator and management coach.
- Facilitating groups to investigate and to bring about productive change.
- Development of HR-related policies, practices and procedures for client companies.
- Preparation and presentation of training programmes for managers and supervisors.
- Outplacement development programme for managers.

Over the past number of years, he has developed, in conjunction with the 1 Stop HR team, a new Human Resource support service model to provide a more cost-effective and comprehensive service for companies, especially SMEs that have no in-house Human Resource Management.

1 STOP HR

1 Stop HR Limited is a HR service company, established to help managers to address Human Resource issues, through a range of tried and proven policies, practices and procedures, to customise these for different types of employment and to provide direct guidance for managers when dealing with Human Resource and Industrial Relations matters.

The company's objective is to develop relevant, structured and cost effective solutions.

Further information about 1 Stop HR's services is available at **www.1stophr.ie**.